Cook Descendants:

Inlaws and Outlaws

~

A Genealogy of the Descendants of Elias Cook

by
Patricia Lumsden

March, 2012

ISBN 978-1-105-50177-7

Introduction

Doing genealogy is not a cold gathering of facts but, instead, breathing life into all who have gone before. We are the storytellers of the tribe. All tribes have one. We have been called, as it were, by our genes. Those who have gone before cry out to us, "Tell our story! So, we do.

It goes beyond just documenting facts. We do not judge our ancestors as we did not walk in their shoes. We are here to report facts and that is all. It goes to who am I and why do I do the things I do. It goes to seeing a cemetery about to be lost forever to weeds and indifference and saying, "I can't let this happen." The bones here are bones of my bone and flesh of my flesh. It goes to doing something about it. It goes to pride in what our ancestors were able to accomplish, how they contributed to what we are today. It goes to respecting their hardships and losses, their never giving in or giving up, their resoluteness to go on and build a life for their family.

I tell the story of my family. It is up to that one called in the next generation to answer the call and take my place in the long line of family storytellers.

That is why I do my family genealogy, and that is what calls those young and old to step up and restore the memory or greet those whom we had never known before. (CR000)

This book contains the genealogical data I have compiled on the descendants of Elias Cook. I love family history, and for the most part, I enjoyed researching the Cook family. There were times when I was ready to give up in frustration, especially when wading through overgrown cemeteries and inhaling mosquitoes, or burning my eyes out over poor microfilm records. The thrill of connecting the various pieces of the Cook family puzzle, when they fit together, kept me going and made me hungry for more.

Many people helped me with this book, freely sharing their particular branch's information, pictures and stories. I give much thanks to those Cook(e) extended relatives and others, including Chris Cook, Carole Perkons, Iris Martin, Hal Lumsden, Jean (Robertson) Lundy, Betty Tambeau, Harvey Bishop, Lynda M. Cunningham, Bob Dunphy, Norma Cooke, Elizabeth Walker, Nancy McCullough, Eileen Cooke, the late Frances Peart, Joan MacKay, Ileen Hudson, Craig Avery, Wayne Cooke, Debbie Kellner, Kami Cooke, and my late uncle, Findlay Cooke, whose rough notes formed the starting point for this entire work.

With very few exceptions, all the Cooks in the County of Guysborough, N.S., are related. Most of the older family names of the Guysborough area will also have Cook family connections.

3

Most of the Cookes with roots in the Isaac's Harbour/Stormont area spell the name with the added "e". Sometimes, on very old documents in the U.S., the name was also spelled with the added "e"; however, the name is most commonly found spelled Cook.

One problem encountered was discrepancies in dates from one source to another. Sometimes the dates inscribed on cemetery headstones will differ from the church birth or death record. I also found a great difference in the census records from one ten year period to another. I have used whatever date I felt to be most logical in those cases.

In 2010, I began work on this revised edition. With the explosion of information available through online sources, much new material is now available in the genealogical realm. I purchased memberships in the New England Historic Genealogical Society, and Ancestry.com and was able to continue many of the early lines, especially those stemming from the daughters of early Cooks.

Please update and add to this work where you can. Any errors are unintentional on my part, but I am sure there must be some. If mistakes are found, please let me know, so that I can correct the information in my files.

Many we loved have passed away too soon...
We remember them often, in a thousand different ways....
In the morning....In the night.....When we look at the stars.....
A date....A song....A place....A smell.....

This book is dedicated to the memory of all those who have left us too soon.

Patsy Lumsden
2012
email: patricial__@hotmail.com

The Cook DNA Project

A Surname Project traces members of a family that share a common surname. Since surnames are passed down from father to son like the Y-chromosome, this test is for males taking a Y-DNA test. Females do not carry their father's Y-DNA and acquire a new surname by way of marriage, so the tested individual **must** be a male that wants to check his direct paternal line (father's father's father's...) with a Y-DNA12, Y-DNA37, or Y-DNA67 marker test. Females who would like to check their direct paternal line can have a male relative with this surname order a Y-DNA test. Females can also order an mtDNA test for themselves such as the mtDNA or the mtDNAPlus test and participate in an mtDNA project.

A **Cook/Cooke/Koch DNA Project** was begun through FamilyDNA.com. *Please visit the website for detailed information.* It's objectives are: To determine where individual families would fit within various Cook/Cooke/Koch genetic lines, to compare the various documented lines, and find possible placement for undocumented participants, to separate German, Irish, English, Scottish, etc., Cook/Cooke/Koch lines.

Since we are all related to one another if we go back far enough in time, it is important to only consider very close matches when we use DNA to resolve genealogical questions.

Two of my Cook(e) cousins were DNA tested:

Christopher Cook – a very distant cousin, a descendant of Elias Cook (1st), through his g-g-g-g-g grandfather Elias Cook (2nd), g-g-g-g grandfather Elias Cook (3rd), g-g-g grandfather Benjamin Cook, g-g grandfather William Cameron Cook, great-grandfather John Henry Cook, grandfather Albert Cook, father Murray Cook.

Kevin Cooke – my first cousin, a descendant of Elias Cook (1st), through his g-g-g-g-g-g-g grandfather Elias Cook (2nd), g-g-g-g-g-g grandfather Elias Cook (3rd), g-g-g-g-g grandfather Elias Cook (4th), g-g-g-g grandfather Wintrop Cook, g-g-g grandfather Edmund Cooke, g-g grandfather Charles Cooke, great-grandfather Marcus Cooke, grandfather Harold Cooke, Sr., father Harold Cooke (Junior).

The results of the 12 marker testing were **IDENTICAL**, proving that both are descendants of Elias Cook, as we have documented.

What is very surprising, is that the testing shows our Cook line is part of **Haplogroup G**, and not connected genealogically to ANY of the already established Cook lines in North America!

G is a very rare Haplogroup, representing only 3% of the world's population. Haplogroup G has an overall low frequency in most populations but is widely distributed within the Old World in Europe, Western Asia, northeastern Africa, Central Asia, South Asia, and Southeast Asia (including parts of China and the Malay Archipelago). It is most frequent in the Caucasus (found at over 60% in ethnic **North Ossetian** males and 30% in Georgian males). In Europe, haplogroup G is found at 5% in central and southern sections of the continent. It has relatively high concentrations in northern Sardinia (over 25%) and the Tyrol region of Austria (about 15%). In the British Isles, Scandinavia, and the Baltic countries it is uncommon; Britain and Norway for example at 1–2%. See [CR-DNA] for more details.

To put this whole issue in it's proper perspective: We are going back **HUNDREDS** of generations! We can only trace our Cooks back approximately 350 years with written records - DNA takes us back 3000 years!

The Early Years

Early legal documents from Massachusetts place our Cook forefathers around the Marblehead, Gloucester, Beverly, and Salem areas. It is probable that our Cook lineage stems from England. Many hundreds of Cooks migrated from various parts of England to the colonies of North America. Our earliest known ancestor was Elias Cook, and he lived in the Massachusetts area of New England in the late 1600's. [CR001]

Elias Cook (1st) was born around the year 1675. His marriage to Joanna Pederick on March 27/1698 took place at Marblehead, Mass. Joanna was the daughter of John and Miriam Pederick[CR002c]. The name is sometimes found spelled Petherick. In the book New England Marriages Prior to 1700, it is written that Joannah Pederick married Caleb Cook, on March 27, 1698. This is an error in transcribing from the original records. A search done by the New England Historic Genealogical Society has determined through checking the original records that it was Elias Cook, not Caleb, who married Joanna Pederick at Marblehead, on March 27, 1698. There are records of the births of three children. Their first son was Elias Cook (2nd), born April 30/1699. Miriam Cook, born 1701, and Elizabeth Cook, born 1703, are the two other children recorded as born to Elias and Joanna. Miriam married William Tucker on June 4/1722, and Elizabeth married Richard Blanch.

There is also record of a deed from Elias Cooke, fisherman of Marblehead, to grantee Joseph Adams, fisherman of Marblehead, property in Marblehead [CR002d].

It is believed that Elias married again, Intentions were recorded at Lynn., Mass. of Elias Cook of Beverly and Abigail Dillaway, of Lynn, in 1710. There were more children: Joanna Cook (bapt. June 22, 1712) and Benjamin Cook (bapt. Sept. 30, 1716).

Elias Cook (2nd) married Sarah Haynes on Feb. 24/1726, at Marblehead, Mass. Their oldest and three youngest sons were born at Marblehead. The five middle children were born at Gloucester, Mass. In 1738, Elias (2nd) lived in Sandy Bay [CR002], near Gloucester. He died at Marblehead in 1753. There are records available of the lives of some of the children, who probably stayed in the Massachusetts area. The son Elias (3rd) was our forefather who brought the line of Cooks to Nova Scotia.

Elias Cook (3rd) was the first child born to Elias (2nd) and Sarah Cook, on June 11/1726. At the age of 21, he married Lydia Searle, a daughter of John Searle, Jr., and Abigail (Dod) Searle.

Many of our Cook ancestors followed the sea. New England fishermen worked the Nova Scotian fishing grounds on a seasonal basis, catching, curing or drying their fish there, and returning with their goods ready for sale, to their New England homes for the winter months. By the terms of the Treaty of Paris, U.S. fishermen were permitted to dry their catch on "any of the unsettled bays, harbors and creeks of N.S., Magdalen Islands and Labrador." No doubt Elias (3rd) was familiar with the rich fishing grounds offered by the Chedabucto Bay area, which, in the early years, was as fine and as productive as any in the world. From the trade base at Canso, fresh and dried fish were shipped to New England and European ports.

In a document registered at Halifax on April 20/1761, approval was given for "Elias Cooke, John Heines, Isiah Nicklesons and Francis Grant", fishermen, for a grant of Tangier Island (off present Halifax County on the Eastern Shore), consisting of 40 acres[CR002b]. "They proposed immediately to settle a fishery. The Council did advise, that the said Island should be given to them upon conditions that they should constantly improve the same in the fishery and that they should not carry on any Trade with the Indians".

There is evidence that Elias (3rd) spent some time at Halifax. The baptism of Benjamin Cook is recorded at St. Paul's Church, Halifax, on March 6/1766. (From the record of Benjamin's birth, his parents were listed as Elias and Sarah Cook. Perhaps this is an error in the mother's name, for Lydia was still living in the early 1800's. Also, The 1817 census shows a Benjamin as having been born in the U.S.) In February, 1770, a Sherrif's Deed was executed against Elias Cook, fisherman, to settle an account of John Kerby, merchant. The deed was for a "lott of land with all the Buildings and Improvements thereon situate in the north part of the Town of Halifax in Argyle Street near the Court House".

By 1768, Elias (3rd) and his family had migrated to lands at the head of Chedabucto Bay, where, with a handful of other settlers, a small community was started and thrived. For at least fifteen years prior to the influx of persons arriving at the end of the Revolutionary War as Loyalists, the small settlement around "Chedabuctou" contained the only English site of habitation all along the shores of Chedabucto Bay from Canso to Louisbourg.

Cook's Cove, Guysboro, N. S.

X

Taken near the original Cook homestead.
The "X" is over the house my grandparents bought,
and where I grew up.

Elias (3rd) chose for himself and his family a homestead site that is surely one of the most picturesque in Nova Scotia. On the hillside overlooking the cove and Chedabucto Bay, the view today, as it was back then, is unsurpassed. The land is presently owned by Murray Cook, who is the sixth generation of Cooks (Murray/ Albert/ John Henry/ William Cameron/ Benjamin/ Elias) to be raised on the original homestead lot. Although there is no house there today, there were two houses built on the property over the years.

The original house was 28' x 24', built nearly at the top of the hill. Today, Murray has a cabin on the site, on top of the old cellar hole. According to family tradition, the first house caught fire one night. There were three black brothers who lived nearby, and saw the unfamiliar brightness in the sky. They quickly ran across the hill and put the fire out with some buckets of pig slop that were outside the house. The family, asleep inside, were saved by the fast action of the neighbours.

The second house was built when the public road shifted from the hilltop to nearer the water, where a wharf was later built. The second house was built by William Cameron Cook in 1846, using some of the boards from the old house. Over time, a large barn and several smaller outbuildings were built. That house lasted 147 years, and was demolished in 1993. (While

9

helping tear apart the interior of the house, Chris Cook saw the singed boards that had come from the old house, and saved several of them.)

When the U.S. Revolutionary War ended, hundreds of Loyalists were transported to Chedabucto in 1783, and grants of land given to them. The old settlers also applied for legal title to the lands they claimed as their own. In a memorial dated 1787, of Elias Cook and others, it states, "Had been settled - most of them since 1768 - on land formerly granted to Rev. Mr. Byron at Chedabucto, by leave and desire of Mr. Jonathan Binney.* They had built houses and made considerable improvements on the same. They ask for grants......The land has been assigned to the 60th Regiment, but these people should be provided for: Charles Morris, surveyor." (*Jonathan Binney was the Superintendant of the Fishery at Canso from 1764 until his house and property were destroyed by New England privateers in 1772. He was granted 1000 acres at the head of Chedabucto Bay, and he settled fishermen and their families on some of it.) [CR006]

A total of 1807 acres at the head of Chedabucto Bay was surveyed and laid off for the old settlers, with Elias (3rd) receiving 200 acres and his son John, who was married with children by this time, receiving 300 acres.

The others named in the same grant included John Ingersol (150 acres), Godfrey Peart (250 acres), Diana Callahan (150 acres), the heirs of John Godfrey (150 acres), Robert Callahan (200 acres), Nathaniel Tobin (*Tobey*), (200 acres), and Josiah (*Isaiah*) Horton (207 acres).

As would be expected, in such an isolated setting, the Cooks married into the families of the other few settlers in the area, forming intricate genealogical connections.

Within three years after the date of the grant, for every 50 acres of plantable land, the settlers had to clear and work 3 acres at least, or else clear and drain 3 acres of swampy or sunken ground. Three neat cattle were to be kept on every 50 acres. One good dwelling house was to be erected, to be at least 20 feet in length and 16 feet in breadth. No doubt all the old settlers had already fulfilled the requirements of the grants prior to them being issued.

In a few very early deeds, the settlement was referred to as Herring Cove, then as Cook's Cove. In other later deeds, it is sometimes called just "The Cove" or Guysborough Cove.

Along with the grants of land, the Cook men bought other lands as opportunity arose, for use as woodlots, and to eventually divide and share with grown children.

Along with the benefits of a new township and the large increase in population, there arose the necessity of taxation. The first assessment rolls were made in 1791. Elias Cook (3rd) was assessed 9 pounds 5 shillings 6 pence; Benjamin Cook 9 pounds 1 shilling 6 pence; John Cook, shopkeeper, 9 pounds 10 shillings 6 pence. An appeal by Elias Cook on the grounds that "he had not so many as six head of neat cattle" reduced his tax amount by 4 shillings.

By 1793, the next assessment year, there were listed 6 adult Cook men who were heads of households: Elias Cook, Senior, (3rd), Elias Cook, Junior, (4th), Elias Cook 3rd, (5th), James Cook, John Cook and Benjamin Cook.

John Cook was a shopkeeper, and kept a store at Guysborough town. He was appointed "Culler and Surveyor of Fish" in 1785. He brought action against persons caught stealing from his store to the Court of General Sessions of the Peace, on several occasions. One case, in 1791, involved the theft of "Sundry Bushels of Potatoes, the value of 14 shillings". Another, in the same year, was for the theft of "moose meat and tobacco - value of 9 shillings". In both cases the guilty parties were whipped, receiving "39 stripes on the naked back at the Public Whipping Post in Manchester" (Guysborough town), and made to either make restitution plus costs to John Cook, or, if unable to pay, be bound out for the payment of them. Justice was harsh in those days.

In his book, Guysborough Sketches and Essays, Dr. A.C. Jost has confused this John Cook with his nephew, John, son of his brother Elias. On legal documents, his nephew is referred to as John Jr., even though he was not a son of John Cook. Both John Cooks married women with the name of Elizabeth: John Cook, Sr.'s wife was Elizabeth Tobey, who was still living in 1824, when she and John sold land that she had inherited from her father Nathaniel Tobey. They lived in the Cook's Cove area, whereas John Cook, Jr., lived in the Bantry/Salmon River area. John, Jr. married Elizabeth Callahan in 1801, and he was a bachelor, not a widower, at the time of their marriage. Their six children married and settled in the communities from Salmon River Lakes through to Roachvale.

Another early court case involved Elias Cook. He was ordered to appear before the General Sessions of the Peace to answer the charge of "speaking disrespectfully of the Magistrates of the County in the Execution of their Duty", taken July 7/1786. Elias appeared on Oct. 22/1786, and "acknowledged that he believed he had said some disrespectful words, when in Liquor, that he had no ill meaning, begged the pardon of the Court and promised not to do the like again. He was dismissed."

Elias (3rd) died on March 16, 1809, and is buried in the Anglican

Cemetery in Guysborough. His son, Elias (4th) died before him, in 1797.

Elias Cook (4th) returned to live for at least a time in the U.S., for he married at Beverly, Mass., in 1769. The information given on the grant of land applied for by his children states, "Petitioners came to this province in 1789 from the U.S.A., where they were born, are all residents of Sydney County (now Guysborough County), and have received no lands. They request them on Salmon River, in the same county. Voted 1350 acres in 1808": Elias Cook (5th) with a wife and 6 children was granted 400 acres. Stephen Cook with a wife and 1 child was granted 150 acres. Ambrose Cook with a wife and 3 children was granted 250 acres. John Cook with a wife and 3 children was granted 250 acres. Edmund Cook with a wife only was granted 100 acres. Winthrop Cook with a wife and 2 children was granted 200 acres.

The area where they settled came to be known as Bantry, a community also settled by many Irish immigrants, near Erinville. The names of some of the other settlers who received grants in that area, and who had connections with the Cook family include: Matthew Hutcheson, Daniel Gerry, John Collier, John Bigsby, John Walsh, James O'Gorman, William McAllister. By 1865, Bantry was gone; its former residents moved away and settled in better populated areas.

Benjamin Cook married twice, fathering a total of thirteen children from the two marriages. In 1826, he had children, as well as grandchildren attending school at Cook's Cove. Of the 44 children registered to attend school that year, 20 of them had the last name of Cook. In 1828, Moses and Elias Cook (Benjamin's sons) and Charles Horton were school trustees.

The land for the Wesleyan chapel that was built in 1862 was given by Elias and his wife Anna.

The Cooks were connected through marriage to most of the other nine pre-loyalist settlers, most particularly with the Horton family, who settled around the part of Cook's Cove that became known as Horton's Cove.

Through the years, especially in the mid to late 1800's, there was a tendency for Nova Scotians to migrate to the United States, or to other parts of Canada, in search of better working opportunities. Many family lines are missing continuity because of this. Today, Cook descendants can be found living in every province of Canada, many of the United States, and in other countries of the world.

Genealogical Numbering System

An explanation of the numbering system of the genealogy charts is as ifollows:
1.418411) Wayne Cooke, who is
1) The first child of
1) Hugh Cooke, who was the first child of
4) Leander Cooke, who was the fourth child of
8) Charles Cook, who was the eighth child of
1) Edmund Cook, who was the first child of
4) Wintrop Cook , who was the fourth child of
1.) Elias Cook, who was a son of Elias Cook, who was our earliest known Cook ancestor to come to Nova Scotia.

Each person's descendants are followed as far as is reasonable, before proceeding with the next sibling.

Where there are ten or more children in the family, the tenth and subsequent children are so designated by underlining – 4.131 10) Charlotte (Lottie) Cook.

Elias(1st) and Joanna's Children:

Elias Cook (2nd)	bapt. Apr. 30/1699	d: May 14/1753
Miriam Cook	bapt. Sept. 22/1701	
Elizabeth Cook	bapt. Aug. 22/1703	

Elias(1st) and Abigail's Children:

Joanna Cook	bapt. June 22, 1712 Marblehead
Benjamin Cook	bapt. Sept. 30, 1716 Marblehead

Of the above:

Miriam Cook married William Tucker on June 4/1722, and had children: Elizabeth Tucker, John Tucker, Miriam Tucker and William Tucker.

Elizabeth Cook married Richard Blanch, son of Richard and Elizabeth (Taynour) Blanch of Marblehead, on Jan. 2, 1724, and had children: Elizabeth Blanch, Richard Blanch, Mary Blanch, Sara Blanch, John Blanch, Jean Blanch. (CR002a)

Elias Cook (2nd) married Sarah Haynes (b: May 14, 1710), daughter of Francis and Elizabeth (Hooper) Haynes of Marblehead, Mass., on Feb. 24/1725, at Marblehead. (CR003)

Elias(2nd) and Sarah Cook's Children:

Elias Cook (3rd)	bapt. Nov. 6/1726	d: Mar. 16/1809
Sarah Cook	b: June 7/1731(CR004a)	
Francis Cook	b: Aug. 10/1734	d: 1772 (CR004)
Benjamin Cook	b: Dec. 17/1736	d: Jan. 30/1736
Samuel Cook	b: July 22/1739	
William Cook	b: Apr. 18/1742	
Anna Cook	bapt. June 10/1744	
Ebenezer Cook	bapt. Feb. 8/1747	
John Cook	bap. June 25/1749	

Of the above children, Sarah, Francis, Benjamin and Samuel were born at Gloucester, Mass. Anna , Ebenezer, John and Elias (3rd) were born at Marblehead, Mass.

The remainder of this genealogy deals solely with the descendants of **Elias** (3rd), who married **Lydia** Searle (bapt. Aug. 6, 1722), daughter of John Searle, Jr., and Abigail (Dod) Searle, on June 18, 1747.

Children of Elias and Lydia Cook:

1) Elias Cook (4th)	bapt. Mar. 20/1748	d: Aug. 25/1797
2) John Cook	bapt. Apr.1/1753	d: Feb. 2/1840
3) Edward Cook	b: @ 1752	d: Aug. 16/1846
4) Benjamin Cook	bapt. Mar. 6/1786	d: Feb. 18/1833
5) Elizabeth Cook	b: ?	
6) Mary Cook	b: ?	No further info.
7) James Cook	b: ?	
8) Samuel Cook	bapt. May 5/1750	No further info.
9) Abigail Cook	bapt. Nov. 7/1756	No further info.
10) Lydia Cook	b: @ 1756	
11) Sarah McGuckin Cook	bapt. Nov. 20/1757	No further info.

1) Elias Cook (5th) married Anna (Cleaves) Haskoll (b: Dec. 6/1743) at Beverly, Mass., on Nov. 27/1769. Anna was a widow of Stephen Haskoll, and a daughter of Ambrose and Mary (Taylor) Cleaves of Beverly. [CR005]She was sometimes called Nancy.

Children of Elias and Anna Cook:

1.1) Elias Cook (5th)	bap. Dec. 6/1770 , Beverly, Mass.	
	d: Aug. /1825, Canso N.S.	
1.2) Lydia Cook	bap. Nov. 1/1790 U.S.A.	
1.3) Stephen Cook	bap. Oct. 3/1774 U.S.A.	d: 1844
1.4) Wintrop Cook	b: Apr. 4/1782 U.S.A.	
	bap. Nov. 1/1790	d: Jan. 2/1873
1.5) Ambrose Cook	bap. May 2/1776 U.S.A.	
1.6) Edmund Cook	bap. Oct. 8/1780 U.S.A.	
1.7) Samuel Cook	b: July 11/1784 U.S.A.	
1.8) Ann Cook	b: Nov. 5/1788 U.S.A.	
1.19) Mary Cook	b: @ 1771	d: 1825
1.10) John Cook	b: @1785 Mass., U.S.A.	

An unnamed child of Elias Cook was buried on Feb. 3, 1773, at Beverly, Mass.

1.1) Elias Cook (5th) married Deborah Godfrey on Nov. 7/1791. She was a daughter of Benjamin and Bethiah (Atwood) Godfrey, and came to Guysborough / Manchester after the death of her mother at Liverpool in 1786, to live with her grandmother, Elizabeth (Hopkins)(Godfrey) Tobey. [CR1.1]

Children of Elias and Deborah Cook:

1.11) Gideon Godfrey Cook	b: Oct. 16/1792
1.12) Elias Cook	b: Apr. 27/1795
1.13) Mary Ann Cook	b: Sept. 30/1797
1.14) Elias Cook	b: Mar. 20/1803
1.15) Ann Cook	b: Oct. 20/1805
1.16) Godfrey Milner Cook	b: Mar. 15/1812
1.17) Stephen Cook	b: July 9/1814

1.18) Elisha Henry Cook   b: Nov. 24/1816   d: Oct. 7/1904
1.19) William Cook   b: ?
There was another child - at the time of his land petition, in 1808, Elias and wife had 6 children. In 1825, Elias died. In 1826, Godfrey, Stephen, and Elias Cook were educated "Gratis" at the school at Cook's Cove, along with 8 other children who were orphans,or whose parents were too poor to pay. (CR1.1a) In 1831, Stephen Cook, age 16, attended school for the first half of the year at Boylston, as an apprentice to Mr. Thomas Hart. (CR1.1b) Deborah Cook, widow, married James Bears, widower, on Dec. 18/1827.

1.11) Gideon Cook married Elizabeth Major on Jan. 11/1820. His children were listed on the Canso School District records. He migrated to Bevely, Mass. and died there of cholera on July 27, 1854.
Children:
1.111) William Cook   b: Nov./ 1824
1.112) Elias Cook   b: Sept. 20/1824   No further information
1.113) Thomas Horton Cook   b: Sept. 22/1826

1.111) William Cook migrated to the Beverly, Mass. area of U.S.A., and was a cordwainer (leather-worker). He married Mary Pousland Sands, daughter of Stephen and Polly, on Feb. 4/1845. She died of consumption in 1875. He died before the US 1870 census.
Children:
1.1111) Mary Louisa Cook   b: June 27/1848   d: Dec. 28/1870
                                              of "fits"
1.1112) Ella Elizabeth Cook   b: Oct. 9/1849
1.1113) Benjamin Alonzo Cook   b: 1851   d: Feb. 8/1852
1.1114) Susan Augusta Cook   b: 1852   d: Dec. 19/1876
1.1115) Anita Wilton Cook   b: 1854
1.1116) Benjamin A. Cook   b: 1856
1.1117) Samuel Peart Cook   b: 1861

1.1112) Ella Elizabeth Cook married Edward Rowell, a cigar maker, on Dec. 21, 1870, at Beverly.

1.1115) Anita W. Cook married Charles G. Waitt, son of Daniel and Harriet (Crowell) Waitt, on March 6, 1879, at Beverly. They had **children**: Frederick Waitt, Leroy William Waitt, and Mary Pousland Waitt.

1.1116) Benjamin A. Cook was a dealer in wholesale produce, and then became a carpenter, in Beverly, Mass. He married **1st)** Charlotte (Lottie) Fisher, daughter of Archibald and Elizabeth Fisher of Musquodobit, NS, on July 3, 1879 at Beverly.
Children:
1.11161) William A. Cook   b: 1882 m: Ethel Haigh (Dowley) 1919 N.H.

1.11162) Arthur Blanchard Cook   b: 1883
1.11163) Viola Cook (adopted)   b: 1897

He married **2nd)** Emma Frances (Clough) Decatur, on Dec. 1, 1902 at Beverly.
Child:
1.11164) Emery Austin Cook   b: 1904 m: Mary Edna Bowen, Vermont

-

1.1117) Samuel Peart Cook never married, lived at Beverly, Mass., where he was a shoecutter.

—

1.113) Thomas Cook migrated to the Beverly, Mass. are. He was a mariner, then worked in a shoe shop in Beverly. On Mar. 13/1849, he married Hannah Jane Herrick.
Children:
1.1131) Charles Elias Cook   b: Sept. 6/1854   d: Cholera 1855
1.1132) Clara E. Cook   b: @1857
1.1133) Frederick Cook   b: 1860   d: dropsy of brain 7 mos. old
1.1134) Arthur Thomas Cook   b: Oct. 25/1867 d: Aug. 20/1869 Cholera
1.1135) George W. Cook   b: Aug. 12/1862 d: Dec./1862

1.1132) Clara E. Cook married William H. Morse, a shoemaker, of Beverly, Mass. on June 29, 1876.
Children:
1.11321) Hattie F. Morse   b: 1878   d: young
1.11322) William Horton Morse b: 1881   Married Edna May Stillman
1.11323) Lizzie F. Morse   b: 1891   No further information
1.11324) Arthur R. Morse   b: 1893   Married Catherine Julia Troop

~

1.12) Elias Cook probably died young. No further information.

~

1.13) Mary Ann Cook married James B. Richardson on Aug. 3/1820.

~

1.14) Elias Cook married Catherine Gerry (b: Oct. 26, 1807), daughter of Daniel and Sarah (Bigsby) Gerry, on Feb. 9/1831. This family lived in the Bantry, Guys. Co. area until Elias' death @1865. His widow moved with several grown children to Cedar Falls, Iowa.
Children:
1.141) George Archibald Cook   b: Jan. 22/1832
1.142) Sarah Maria Cook   b: Aug. 9/1834

1.143) Mary Gerry Cook	b: Apr. 16/1839
1.144) Daniel Gerry Cook	b: Mar. 16/1841
1.145) Elias Henry Cook	b: Oct. 11/1845
1.146) Gideon G. Cook	b: Nov. 22/1846

1.141) George Archibald Cook married Sarah <u>Jane</u> Perry (born England)

Children:

1.1411) Elias Sayles Cook	b: Mar. 16/1859	
1.1412) William Archibald Cook	b: Sept. 16/1861	No further info.
1.1413) Mary Cook	b: @ 1863	
1.1414) Sarah A. Cook	b: @ 1867	
1.1415) Daniel F. Cook	b: @ 1868	
1.1416) Arthur J. Cook	b: May/1870	
1.1417) Jennie Cook	b: @ 1873	

George A. Cook died Nov. 24, 1873. He, along with his mother, Catherine, is buried in Greenwood Cemetery, Cedar Falls, Iowa. Jane married Charles Pashby on June 27/1885. (CR1.141W)

1.1411) Elias Cook was a carpenter. He married Louisa/Lucia A. Levill late in life. She was born in Maine. They had no children of their own; she had a child from a previous marriage. He was in trouble with the law at various times throughout his life. (CR1.1411) They divorced in 1912.

1.1414) Sarah A. (Sadie) Cook married H. A. Cowan in 1891. She was a widow at the time of the 1920 census, and her brother, Arthur, divorced, lived with her.

1.1416) Arthur Cook married Anna Deere on Oct. 6, 1897, at Allison, Iowa. She had a daughter, Vera M. Carpenter. At the time of the 1900 US Census, this family lived with his mother and stepfather, Charles and Jennie Pashby in Cedar Falls, Iowa. By 1910, mother Jane and brother Arthur, who was divorced, lived with "Lias" and "Lucia" Cook.

1.142) Sarah Cook migrated to Douglas, Mass., USA, where, on April 9, 1853, she married Duty Sayles Paine, son of James and Mary (Sayles) Paine. Duty was a seaman from Rhode Island. They had three children.

Duty and Sarah Paine

Children:
1.1421) Mary Catherine Paine   b: 14 March/1854   d: 1934
1.1422) Sabrina Walling Paine   b: May 27/1856
1.1423) James Elias Paine   b: 14 June/1858
The children were born in Minnesota. Sarah died after the birth of the third child. After her death, Duty married her sister, Mary Gerry Cook.

--

1.143) Mary Gerry Cook married Duty Sayles Paine on Jan. 13/1859, at Guysborough. They migrated west, first to Minnesota, then to Iowa, settling in the Cedar Falls area for many years, later moving to Montana.
Children:
1.1431) Nathan Archibald Paine   b: Apr. 8/1860
1.1432) Sarah Paine   b: @ 1862
1.1433) Ida Anna Paine   b: Nov. 11/1864
1.1434) Laura Augusta Paine   b: May 2/1867
1.1435) Frances E. Paine   b: @ 1870
1.1436) Elisha W. Paine   b: @ 1873
1.1437) Harriet Grace Paine   b: @ 1876
1.1438) Lewellyn Basil Paine   b: Aug. 31/1877

1.1421) Mary Catherine Paine (Katie) married Charles Elias Smith (1854-1944), on Aug. 3, 1880 in Iowa. They farmed in various states.
Children:
1.14211) Sayles Elias Smith   b: 1882 d: 1950 Kelso, Washington
1.14212) Dee Forrest Smith   (Lived in Oregon)
1.14213) Park Winfield Smith   b: Jan. 26/1886 Nebraska.
1.14214) Martin Luther Smith   (Lived in Wyoming)
1.14215) Charles Lee Smith   (Lived in Vail, Washington)

1.1422) Sabrina Paine married Rev. Martin Luther Nichols (1855 – 1915), a Methodist Minister. They lived in various states, but were living in the Red Willow area of Nebraska at the time of the 1900 census. They had an adopted **daughter**:
1.14221) Grace Sabrina Nichols   b: Missouri 1885
Sabrina died on Sept. 1, 1927 in Orleans, Harlan County, Nebraska. [CR1.1422]

19

1.1423) James Elias Paine married Emily Sophia Norrish (b: England). They had **children**:

1.14231) Nathan E. Paine	b: 1884	M: Ida Nancy Cooley - 11 children
1.14232) Maud M. Paine	b: 1885	M: George. W. Morrow - 1 child.
1.14233) Sophia Ida Paine	b: 1887	
1.14234) Clara Emily Paine	b: 1900	

1.1431) Nathan A. Paine was a farmer. They lived in various states: Tennessee, the Rosebud area of Montana in 1910, and back to Tennessee by 1920, where they lived on Bear Creek Road, Franklin (near Nashville). He married Naomi Johns and had a **child**:

1.14331) Alice M. Paine   b: @ 1901

Alice Paine was a school teacher. She married Dillard Clark. They were farmers.

1.1433) Ida Anna Paine married Wellington Horace Hardy on Apr. 29/1889, at Broken Bow, Custer, Nebraska. They are buried at Kalispell, Montana [CR1.1433]

Children:

1.14331) Catherine Hardy	b: Feb. 1/1890
1.14332) Mary Frances Hardy	b: May 26/1891
1.14333) Carter Gerry Hardy	b: Mar. 23/1894
1.14334) Wellington Claude Hardy	b: Nov. 14/1897

1.1434) Laura A. Paine married Albert Snyder, son of Jacob and Ellen (Neiswanger) Snyder, on April 1/1894 at Red Willow County, Nebraska. They had a daughter: Mary Beatrice Snyder (b: 1896).

1.1435) Frances E. Paine married Nathan O. "Bud" Finch (b: New York). They lived in Montana. They had a son: Lisle Finch (b: 1894).

1.1436) Elisha W. Paine was a mechanic in Montana. He was not married by the time of the 1920 census of Rosebud, Montana.

1.1437) Harriet Grace Paine married Maurice Bentall (b: London, England), on Apr. 20, 1897 at Forsyth, Montana. They farmed in Montana for years, then migrated to Portland, Oregon by 1910, where he worked as a tailor. They had one son: Frank Maurice Bentall (b: June 15,1898 in Montana), who married Wilma Jones, daughter of William D. and Lillie Frances (Connelly) Jones, on Sept. 26, 1923 in Montana.

1.1438) Lewellyn Basil Paine married Mae Julia Sherman, daughter of Fred and Julia (Tart) Sherman. who was born in Spring Valley, Minnesota. They were married in Miles City, Custer, Montana, on Oct. 4, 1909.

1.144) Daniel Gerry Cook moved to Cedar Falls, Iowa. He married Frances Wheeler in Sept. 1869, and at the time of the 1870 US Census, he worked in a woolen mill. He became a naturalized citizen of the US in 1892.

Children:

1.144) Robert B. Cook	b: 1871	Unmarried 1920, Well Driller, Calif.
1.144) Celestia M. Cook	b: 1874	No further info.
1.144) Archibald J. Cook	b: 1876	Unmarried 1920, California
1.144) Lora M. Cook	b: 1879	No further info.
1.144) Addie C. Cook	b: 1883	m: Edward S. Lampman in 1901, 10 children

--

1.145) Elias Henry Cook. No further information. He lived in the Guysborough area @ 1866, but may have later moved to Cedar Falls, Iowa.

--

1.146) Gideon G. Cook moved to Iowa, and was living in Humboldt at the time of the 1880 census. He was a wagon maker. He married Mary L. Husted, who had two children, Allie and Jessie Husted. They had a **daughter**:

1.1461) Mary L. Cook   b: @1875

~

1.15) Ann Cook married Robert Rule on Nov. 13/1832. No futher information.

~

1.16) Godfrey Milner Cook lived at Cook's Cove, and sold property there in 1843. (CR1.16)

~

1.18) Elisha Henry Cook, mariner, married Maria Scott, daughter of Joseph and Maria Scott of Guysborough, on Dec. 19, 1844 at Beverly, Mass.

Children:

1.181) Amelia Ann Cook	b: Nov. 12/1846 Mass.	d: Nov.12/1886 Neb.
1.182) Susan F or T Cook	b: Aug. 17/1848, Beverly	
1.183) Henry F. Cook	b: Oct./1856 Minn.	
1.184) Mary E. or Maria Cook	b: 1864 Minn.	
1.185) Charles Cook	b: 1863 Minn.	
1.186) William Cook	b: Sept./1870 Minn.	
1.187) Warren Cook	b: 1872 Minn.	d: 1896

The family migrated to Minnesota, settling in Spring Grove, Houston County. Census from 1860 shows this family three houses away from Duty Paine and family, and 5 away from John G. Cook, (with wife Sarah, who were both born in NS and children born in Mass.) Although Duty and family moved on, settling in Iowa, the family of Elisha H. Cook stayed in Minnesota, first in

Spring Grove, then in Wilmington. Spring Grove was the first Norwegian settlement in Minnesota. The Minnesota State Census for 1895 gives the information that Elisha, age 70, was 40 years in the state, and was born in Manchester. The US 1900 Census for Wilmington shows an "Eliza" Cook, a word is crossed out and word Mother overwritten; this person was born Oct. 1816, Nova Scotia, living with sons William and Henry, so no doubt a mistake by the census taker. Elisha Henry Hopkins Cook died in Wilmington, Minn. on Oct. 4/1904 and is buried in Portland, Minnesota. Maria (Scott) Cook died on Nov. 17, 1886, at Wilmington.

1.181)   Amelia Ann Cook married William Hastings, on Dec. 15/1854 at Caledonia, Minnesota. He was born in Ireland (but both of his parents were born in Scotland.) They migrated to Everett, Nebraska, where they farmed. Most of the children were born in Minnesota; Eliza, Wendell and Grant were born in Nebraska. Amelia died on her 40th birthday. In 1896, William (and at least one child, Grant) migrated to South Dakota, where he also farmed.
Children:

1.1811) Maria Hastings	b: 1867	
1.1812) Sarah Hastings	b: 1869	
1.1813) Elisha Hastings	b: 1871	
1.1814) William J. Hastings	b: Nov. 7/1875	d: July 9/1952 Neb.
1.1815) Sayles Hastings	b: 1876	
1.1816) Eliza Hastings	b: 1880	
1.1817) Wendell Hastings	b: 1882	
1.1818) Grant Hastings	b: Feb. 22/1885	d: Mar. 7/1939 S. Dak.

1.1811) Maria Hastings married James Sheldon Kenaston in 1889. They migrated to Carthage, Jasper Co., Missouri. **Children:** Florence Kenaston, Alice Kenaston, Laura Kenaston, Rolla Kenaston, Helen Kenaston, Harold Kenaston.

1.1814) William J. Hastings was a rancher at Springview, Keya Paha County, Nebraska. He married Lenna Pense. **Children**: Lenna M. Hastings, Joy A. Hastings, Alice Hastings, Esther Hastings.

1.1818)   Grant Hastings married Edna Vinnard in 1910 in South Dakota, although they later divorced. **Children:** Kenneth Hastings, Homer O. Hastings m: Marlys Anderson), Ralph Hastings, Minnell? Hastings.

--

1.182) Susan Cook married Charles Tompkins on July 6, 1885. They lived in Caledonia, Minnesota. They had no children.

~

1.2) Lydia Cook married William Horton, son of Isaiah and Anna (Wood) Horton, on Oct. 2/1791. **Children:**

1.21) William Horton	b: Jan. 31/1792
1.22) Ambrose Horton	b: Oct. 28/1793 d: Sept. 14/1873
1.23) George Horton	b: Oct. 25/1795
1.24) Hannah Cleeves Horton	b: Aug. 25/801
1.25) John Stephen Horton	b: July 25/1799
1.26) Mary Horton	b: Aug. 24/1809
1.27) James Edward Horton	b: June 24/1812
1.28) Sarah Dorcas Horton	b: May 15/1814
1.29) Lydia Horton	b: ?
1.2 10) Priscilla Horton	b: ?
1.2 11) Thomas Horton	b: ?

1.21) William Horton married Hannah Ryder on Jan. 26/1813. They had five **children:** George Henry Horton, William Mariner Horton, Valentine Horton, Ambrose Cleeves Horton, and Nancy Horton.

--

1.22) Ambrose Horton married Dorothy Ryder on Dec. 27/1814. They had a **daughter**: 1.221) Lydia Horton.

--

1.23) George Horton married Mary Whitman. They had no children.

--

1.24) Hannah Horton married William Cook (# ?).

--

1.25) John S. Horton married Elizabeth Russel on July 31/1823. They had nine **children**: Ann Horton, Elizabeth Horton, James Horton, John Horton, Sarah Jane Horton, Susan Horton, Thomas Horton, Reuben Horton, and Lydia Maria Horton.

--

1.27) James E. Horton married Mary Ann Gammon on Dec. 15/1836. They had 13 **children** in 26 years: Mary Horton, William Archibald Horton, Ambrose Horton, Naomi Caroline Horton, Lucinda Maria Horton, Jeremiah Jost Horton, Eliza Dorcas Horton, Eleanor Jane Horton, Hezekiah H. Horton, Mahala Jemima Horton, George Whitfield Horton, Thomas Henry Horton, and Sydney Smith Horton.

--

1.28) Sarah D. Horton married John William Bigsby (b: Nov. 17/1807), on Aug. 31/1839. He was a son of John and Rachel (Critchett) Bigsby, who lived in the area of Cook's Cove that came to be known as Bigsby's Head.

--

1.29) Lydia Horton married Robert Burns on July 13/1828.

--

1.2 11) Thomas Horton married Mary Cook (#1.53) on Jan. 19/1830. See children under this number.

~

1.3) Stephen Cook married Sarah Demas in 1800. She was born in the U.S., as noted on the 1817 census.

Children:

1.31) Demas Francis Cook	b: May 11/1801	d: Apr. 13/1856
1.32) Son	b: ? (On the 1817 census - no further info)	

1.31) Demas Francis Cook lived in the Salmon River area. He was a carpenter. He married Ann Russell on Jan. 21/1824. She was b: 1806, d: Apr. 15/1881. In 1867, they migrated to Bradford (Haverhill) Mass, U.S.A., with several of their younger children.

Children:

1.311) William Alexander Cook	b: Jan. 29/1825	
1.312) Demas Francis Cook	b: July 1/1827	
1.313) Sarah Ann Cook	b: Jan. 27/1829	
1.314) Elizabeth Jane Cook	b: Jan. 27/1831	No further info.
1.315) James Brown Cook	b: Mar. 31/1833	
1.316) Emmeline Marshall Cook	b: Dec. 12/1835	
1.317) Stephen Charles Cook	b: Apr. 11/1839	d: 1910
1.318) Susan M. Cook	b: Sept. 4/1841	
1.319) Thomas Russell Cook	b: Oct. 18/1844	d: Feb. 2/1918
1.31 10) Christopher Columbus Cook	b: Dec. 28/1846	d: May 29/1926
1.31 11) Joseph D. Cook	b: Dec. 24/1849	d: Jan. 15/1912

1.311) William Alexander Cook was a ship carpenter, at Cook's Cove . He married **1st)** Armenia McDonald on Jan. 18/1851. Armenia died at age 38, on April 29/1870, of consumption.

Children:

1.3111) Harriet (Hattie) Augusta Cook	b: 1853	d: 1919
1.3112) Ernest Cook	b: 1864	Never married

He married **2nd)** Harriet Aitkens, widow, from Salmon River, on Dec. 8/1870. She was the daughter of William and Ann Spanks.

1.3111) Hattie A. Cook married Charles W. Peart @ 1872, son of Godfrey and Martha (Scott) Peart. They had a **son** Arthur J. Peart, and brought up a nephew, George Peart.

--

1.312) Demas Francis Cook migrated to P.E.I. He was a shipbuilder and a farmer in the Murray River area. He married Rebecca Elizabeth Bears, daughter of David and Dorcas (Whitman) Bears, in Aug./1853. Demas died on Nov. 7, 1908 and is buried in Murray River Cemetery. (CR1.312)

Children:

1.3121) James Alexander Cook	b: Jan. 21/1857	d: Oct. 29/1859
1.3122) Lelia Ada Cook	b: Dec. 17/1860	d: 1927

1.3123) Leonard <u>Thomas</u> Cook   b: June 2/1861   d: 1938
1.3124) J. Francis (Frank) Cook   b: @ 1872 adopted

Demas Francis Cook   **Rebecca Bears Cook**

1.3122) Lelia Cook married Matthew Morris MacLeod on March 12, 1889, at Murray River, PEI.
<u>Children</u>:

1.31221) Isabella MacLeod	b: Feb. 14/1890
1.31222) Margaret MacLeod	b: Nov. 16/1895
1.31223) William F. MacLeod	b: Jan. 22/1901

1.3123) Leonard <u>Thomas</u> Cook was retail merchant in Murray River, P.E.I. In politics, he was Liberal, and ran for Councillor in the Electoral District of 4th Kings in 1904, receiving 310 votes, or 45.99%. He was beaten by Murdock MacKinnon, who received 364 votes, or 54.01%. Thomas married Jane Munn (CR4.793) (1872-1964). They had **children**:

1.31231) Francis Russell Cook	b: June 16/1894	d: young
1.31232) Thomas William Cook	b: Jan. 12/1895	d: 1958
1.31233) Ewart Gladstone Cook	b: June 2/1898	d: young
1.31234) Lillian Ada Cook	b: Mar. 24/1900	d: 1978
1.31235) Rebecca M. Cook	b: Mar/1902	d: 1990
1.31236) Jessie E. Cook	b: Feb 1904	d: 1991
1.31237) Emma Cook	b: Feb 1906	d: 1991
1.31238) Henrietta Cook	b: Feb 1908	d: 1985
1.31239) Jennie Cook	b: Apr 1910	d: 1991

1.31232) Thomas Cook attended Acadia University, then Yale University for his Ph.D. He taught at Acadia, University of Toronto, University of Saskatchewan, then accepted a position with the Defence Research Board of Canada. He married Dorothy Cochran in 1925.

25

1.31234) Lillian Cook married David Percy Sharam in 1933.

1.31235) Rebecca Cook married Wallace E. Scantlebury in 1930.

1.31236) Jessie Cook attended Acadia University, then the Royal Victoria School of Nursing in Montreal, becoming a RN in 1937, and receiving a certificate in Teaching and Supervision. She taught in Montreal for many years.

1.31237) Emma Cook was a nurse. She married Alfred E. Innocent in 1939.

1.31238) Henrietta (Etta) Cook married Stirling Giddings in 1933.

1.31239) Jennie Cook attended Acadia University, receiving a B.Sc., with a major in Home Economics. She taught Remedial Reading/Speech Therapy at the Murray River and Southern Kings schools. She married Malcolm MacKinnon in 1935.

--

1.313) Sarah Ann Cook married James Cohoon, a mariner from Canso, in 1853. He worked his way through the seafaring ranks, beoming a Master Mariner. They lived in various places, including Canso and Pictou, then settling in North Sydney, Cape Breton, where he owned a hardware store. Sarah Ann died aged 92 years, 5 months in 1921.

Children:

1.3131) Harvey Cohoon	b: @1855
1.3132) Reuben Cohoon	b: Dec. 3/1855
1.3133) William Havelock Cohoon	b: Mar. 5/1860
1.3134) Laura A. Cohoon	b: @1863
1.3135) Carrie M. Cohoon	b: June 4/1866
1.3136) Sarah (Sadie) Emma Cohoon	b: Nov. 17/1869

1.3131) Harvey Cohoon was a merchant, first at Pictou, then at North Sydney. He married three times, all in Pictou County, his wife dying within a few years of their marriage each time. He married **1st)** Eliza A. Arthur in 1885. He married **2nd)** Jane A. Grant in 1886. **Children**: Sadie and Eliza. He married **3rd)** Sadie C. Smith in 1889. At the time of the 1891 census, his sister, Carrie Cohoon lived with the family.

1.3132) Reuben Cohoon was a miner for a time, then worked as a house carpenter, then was a grocer, all at North Sydney. He was not married at the time of the 1911 census, but lived with his widowed mother.

1.3133) William Havelock Cohoon migrated to Quincy, Mass., where he worked as a typesetter. He married **1st)** Caroline (Ferguson) Rogers, who was also born in Nova Scotia, a daughter of John and Eliza (Thompson) Ferguson, on Apr. 17, 1895, at Boston. She died in 1907. He married **2nd)** Hattie F. ___, who was born in Massachusetts, but whose parents were born in   Canada. There were no children from either marriage.

1.3134) Laura A. Cohoon married John A. McKenzie, merchant, son of Roderick and Sarah McKenzie, (who was the postmaster at Grand River) on July 18, 1889, at North Sydney. **Children**:

1.31341) Sadie C. MacKenzie	b: @1890
1.31342) Annie C. MacKenzie	b: June/1892
1.31343) Harvey Shaw MacKenzie	b: Dec. 3/1893
1.31344) Marjorie J. MacKenzie	b: Sept./1895

1.3136) Sadie Cohoon married Fenwick Kelly, son of James and Rachel Kelly of North Sydney on Jan. 24/1893. He was a broker in a ship chandlery at North Sydney. They had a **son**:
1.31361) Shirley Kelly

--

1.314) Elizabeth Jane Cook married Noah B. Church, a ship carpenter. They lived in Newburyport, Mass. **Child**:
1.3141) Charles A. Church   b: Aug./1857
He Married Amelia R. Logan, daughter of William and Margaret (Boon) Logan, of Caswick, N.B., at Newburyport, Mass. on Aug. 2/1882. He died of tonsil cancer in 1909.

--

1.315) James B. Cook lived at Cook's Cove. He was a Ship Carpenter. He married Jeanette Maria Grant from Oyster Ponds on Sept. 29/1864. She was b: @ 1846, died before 1881.
Children:

1.3151) Annie Maria Russell Cook	b: June 29/1865
1.3152) Alexander Hanlock Cook	b: Feb. 3/1867
1.3153) Francis Murray Cook	b: @ 1869
1.3154) William Evans Cook	b: Sept. 15/1874
1.3155) Mary Elizabeth Cook	b: Jan. 4/1872

1.3151) Annie R. Cook married Arthur C. Ford, a shoe manufacturer, son of Charles T. and Sophronia (Carleton) Ford on Aug. 2/1892, at Bradford, Mass.

1.3153) Frank M. Cook married **1st)** Josie Mary Jones, daughter of John and Caroline Jones, on Jan. 13/1902, and **2nd)** Grace E. Stearns, daughter of Simon Luther and Jerusha (Bigsby) Stearns in 1927.

1.3155) Mary Elizabeth Cook (or Elizabeth Marie) was a trained nurse. She married Asher Burton Arnold, a leather dealer, son of John W. and Mary (Grimstone) Arnold, on June 26, 1901, at Haverhill, Mass. They had a **daughter**: Mary E. Arnold.

--

1.316) Emmeline Cook married Leonard Choate[CR1.316H], a Ship Joiner from Newburyport, Mass.

Children:

1.3161) Anna R. (Annie) Choate	b: 1859
1.3162) Mary J. Choate	b: 1860
1.3162) Henry M. Choate	b: Aug. 1861
1.3163) Elizabeth J. Choate	b: 1865
1.3164) Frank W. Choate	b: 1867

1.3161) Annie Choate married Joseph Noyes and had **children**: James C. Noyes, Henry B. Noyes, Walter O. Noyes, Gladys B. Noyes. Mother Emmeline lived with this family in 1920.

1.3162) Henry M. Choate married Lydia A.B. (Brackett)Washburn, a widow, on Jan. 2, 1898. She was a dressmaker from No. Hermon, Maine, the daughter of Joshua and Lydia (McKenny) Brackett.

1.3163) Elizabeth J. Choate married Edward E. Rose. They had no children. They lived in New Haven, Connecticut. After Edward's death, she moved in with her widowed brother Henry Choate in Newburyport, Mass., and was living there in 1930.

1.3164) Frank W. Choate was a shoe cutter in a factory in Newburyport in 1900, but by 1910, he was a patient at the Gardner State Colony.

--

1.317) Stephen Cook migrated to the Haverhill, Mass., area, where he was a carpenter. He married Francette P. Poor, (b:1849), daughter of William and Charlotte F. (Robison) Poor, of Nova Scotia, on Feb. 28, 1868, at Amesbury, Mass.

Children:

1.3171) Emma A. Cook	b: June/1869	
1.3172) William H. Cook	b: 1870	
1.3173) Mary Belle Cook	b: 1872	
1.3174) Cora F. Cook	b: Sept./1873	
1.3175) Hattie L. Cook	b: 1876	d: Aug. 29/1894
1.3176) Fred Sumner Cook	b: March 27/1877	
1.3177) Susan C. Cook	b: Sept./1882	

1.3171) Emma A. Cook did not marry. She lived with her sister Susie and family in 1920.

1.3172) William H. Cook married Hattie Spanks, daughter of Elias and Charity Spanks (#1.531) of N.S., on Aug. 24, 1890, at Haverhill, Mass.

Children:
1.31721) Pearl Horton Cook   b: March/1891
1.31722) Marion <u>Hope</u> Francette Cook   b: June 29/1897   d: 1987
1.31723) Charles C. Cook   b: 1902

1.31721) Pearl Horton Cook married Roland Edmond Pettingill, a tinsmith, son of Edmond and Lizzie (Fletcher) Pettingill, on Sept. 30/1912, at Merrimac, Mass. **Children**: Charles Pettingill, William Pettingill, John Pettingill.

1.3173) M. Belle Cook married W. Biron Hutchings, son of Frank B. and Nellie E. Hutchings of Marlborough, on Sept. 7, 1890.

1.3174) Cora F. Cook   married Albert G. Eames, a carpenter, son of John and Helen (Stearns) Eames of Maine, on Sept. 26, 1901.
Child:
1.31741) Alice Louise Eames   b: Aug. 5/1903

1.3176) Fred S. Cook married **1st)** ?   **2nd)** Helen M. Seelye, in 1896.
Children:
1.31761) Fred S. Cook   b: 1898
1.31762) Florida Francette Cook   b: July 24/1910   d: 1997
1.31763) Seelye F. Cook   b: 1918

--

1.3177) Susan (Susie) Cook married Herbert Milton Ford.
Children:
1.31771) Stephen H. Ford   b: 1905

--

1.318) Susan Cook married John P. Evans, a Ship Joiner from Newburyport, Mass.
Children:
1.3181) Joseph O. Evans   b: 1876
He was an electrician in a silver shop in Newburyport. He married Addie Frances Safford, daughter of Charles N. and Addie (Pierce) Safford, on Nov. 16, 1898. They had **children** Ralph R. Evans, Ruth F. Evans and Doris S. Evans.

--

1.319) Thomas R. Cook was a carpenter, and became a building contractor in Haverhill, Mass. He married **1st)** Luella S. Cogswell on Oct. 21, 1874, at Haverhill. She was born in Canaan, NH, a daughter of Jonathan and Louisa Cogswell. She died on March 11, 1875, of spinal meningitis. He married **2nd)** Sophia P. Hills, daughter of Elisha & Arvella Hills of Winchester, NH, on Mar. 18, 1876 at Haverhill. She died on Jan. 11, 1877 or Puerperal Fever.

Child:
1.3191) Annie S. Cook   b: Jan. 2/1877   Never married.   She was a music teacher in 1900, a dressmaker 1910-1930.

Thomas R. Cook married **3rd**) Caroline E. Cook (#4.86), daughter of William and Esther Cook, on Nov. 2, 1878. (She was a widow at the time of the 1920 US census.)

Children:
1.3192) Minnie Susan Cook   b: June 1879 - She became a bookkeeper.
1.3193) Lillian A. Cook   b: Oct. 7/1880   d: age 94
1.3194) Carolyn F. Cook   b: Sept. 1884 - She became a teacher.

1.3192) Minnie S. Cook married Harry William Hale, son of Frank E. and Julie A. (Bourne) Hale, on Oct. 14, 1903, at Merrimac, Mass.

1.3193) Lillian A. Cook married Perley A. Carleton, son of George F. and Millie Perley, on Oct. 26, 1911 at Haverhill, Mass. They had one **child:**
1.31911) George Thomas Carleton   b: Aug. 29/1915
                                  He lived at Beverly, Mass.

--

1.3110) Christopher Cook was a contractor and builder at Bradford (Haverhill), Mass. He was an alderman for that town in 1916, and was commissioner of public property during his term. He founded the Master Carpenters' Association in Haverhill. He was a member of Merrimack Lodge of Masons [CR1.3110]. He married Ella J. Pressey, daughter of Eben G. and Hannah H. Pressey (1847-1922), on Nov. 17/1870, and they celebrated their fiftieth wedding anniversary two years before her death in 1922.

Children:
1.3110 1) Harry R. Cook   b: 1871
1.3110 2) Lena B. Cook   b: 1873
On the 1900 US Census, Christopher and Ella lived in Bradford with daughter Lena. The census gives us the information that Ella was the mother of four children, two of whom were living at the time of the census.

1.31 10 1) Harry R. Cook married Annie McGibbon and had 3 **sons:**

1.31 10 11) Forrest Russell Cook (1895-1974) who was head of the leather department for Filene's, Boston, and who served with the Yankee division in France. He was awarded the Croix de Guerre, and a special citation for bravery. He married Priscilla Fuller (1900-1979). [CR1.31 1011] They had at least one child, a daughter, Barbara A, as shown on the 1930 census.

1.31 10 12) Harold M. Cook, Lynn, Mass., who was a cashier at Burr & Co., bankers, of Boston.

1.31 <u>10</u> 13) Howard C. Cook, Lynn, Mass., who was an electrician. Neither Harold nor Howard were married at the time of the 1930 census. At that time, mother Annie, a widow, lived with them.

1.31 <u>10</u> 2) Lena B. Cook married Justin Stickney, from New Hampshire. They had no children.

--

1.31 <u>11</u>) Joseph Cook was approx. 20 years old when he went to the U.S.A. with his parents. He became a prominent builder and contractor of Haverhill, Mass., for forty years. His firm, J.D. Cook and Son, built many houses and businesses in the area. Among other organizations, he was a member of the I.O.O.F. He married Alice Mitchell, daughter of Elijah and Urania Mitchell, from Haverhill, Mass. in Sept., 1879. **Children:**

1.31 <u>11</u> 1) Josie Alice Cook	b: Feb. 6/1880	d: Aug. 21/1880
1.31 <u>11</u> 2) Twin who died at birth	b: Feb. 6/1880	d: Feb. 6/1880
1.31 <u>11</u> 3) Albert Henry Cook	b: Dec. 28/1881	d: Dec. 1/1950
1.31 <u>11</u> 4) Bertha Russell Cook	b: Oct./1883	
1.31 <u>11</u> 5) Eben Mitchell Cook	b: July 28/1886 Never married	d: Dec. 16/1939
1.31 <u>11</u> 6) Joseph Tenney Cook	b: Apr. 1/1890	d: Sept. 29/1936

1.31 <u>11</u> 3) Albert Cook was the county bridge tender at Haverhill, Mass., for 35 years. He married Alice Ada Abbott in 1902.
Children:
1.31 <u>11</u> 31) Arthur Joseph Cook   b: 1903
He was a welder. He married Florence L. ____. They lived at Watervliet, New York, at the time of the 1930 census.
1.31 <u>11</u> 32) Doris Bertha May Cook   b: 1906
Married __ Belmont.   Lived at Lenox, Mich.
1.31 <u>11</u> 33) Wilbur Francis Cook   b: 1907
          Lived at Brooklyn, New York

1.31 <u>11</u> 4) Bertha Cook married Edward Z. Gerah, from Lynn, Mass., on June 20, 1912 at Haverhill. They had no children.

1.31 <u>11</u> 5) Eben M. Cook carried on the J. D. Cook and Son contracting business after his father's death. He was a member of all the Masonic orders, including Merrimack Lodge, A.F. and A.M., Aleppo Temple, and Order of the Mystic Shrine, Boston.

1.31 <u>11</u> 6) Joseph T. Cook married Eva Beatrice Montminy. They lived in Plaistow, N.H. , where he worked as a chemist in a tonic factory.
Children:

1.31 <u>11</u> 61) Joseph T. Cook, Jr.   b: Apr. 11/1919   d: Mar. 8/1962
1.31 <u>11</u> 62) Eben Bernard Cook   b: Jan. 3/1921   d: June13/1976
1.31 <u>11</u> 63) Joan B. Cook   b: Jan. 15/1925

The Isaac's Harbour/Country Harbour Cookes

The Cooks who lived in the Isaac's Harbour and Country Harbour area were descendants of Wintrop Cook. Wintrop's father, Elias, had moved back to the U.S., where he married, and had a large family. Most, if not all, of his children returned to the Guysborough area in 1789. Elias Cook died in 1797.

Wintrop was born in the United States in 1782. It is not known whether he was one of the sons who came to Guysborough in 1789, for he married at Marblehead, Mass., in 1804, although he, too, could have returned to the U.S. for a while. Several of his children were also born in the U.S., and several more in Manchester, N.S. The three youngest were born at Stormont.

Wintrop, and some of his brothers and married sisters, received land grants in the Salmon River Bridge (or Bantry) area, along the road leading from Guysborough to St. Mary's. The grants were applied for in 1808, and received in 1810. Wintrop was a cooper (barrel maker), and several of his sons followed him in this trade. The settlement at Bantry / Salmon River Bridge did not prosper, and many of the residents moved elsewhere. Stormont, at that time, was considered a booming town, and so the Wintrop Cook family moved there. They had at least nine children, and perhaps even more:

. . . . Their first child was a son, Edmund, who married Elizabeth Mars (Marr) of Country Harbour. From Stormont, Edmund and Elizabeth moved to Isaac's Harbour.

. . . . The second child was a daughter, Rebecca (Becky), who married Jonathan Hayes [CR1.422] and moved to Isaac's Harbour.

. . . . The third child was a son, John, who probably died young, as there was another son born later who was also named John.

. . . . Samuel was the next child. He married Elizabeth Haine (Hayne), and later moved to Fisherman's Harbour.

. . . . The fifth child, and second daughter, was Lydia. She married George Mason, and they also moved to Fisherman's Harbour.

. . . . The sixth child was a son, John, who married Maria Jane Hallett. John and Maria lived at Country Harbour.

. . . . . . The seventh child was another son, Wintrop. He married Sarah Ann Beiswanger and they lived at Stormont.

. . . . James was the eighth child. He married Charlotte Eve Beiswanger, a sister of Sarah Ann Beiswanger, who married Wintrop Cook, Jr. James and Eve lived at Stormont.

. . . . . Francis Cook was another son. Francis married Sarah Ann Hallet, and lived at Country Harbour, although in the early 1850's, they lived at Halifax. Sarah Ann Hallet was a sister of Maria Jane Hallett, who married John Cook.

. . . . . .(Perhaps) Louisa Cook [CR1.4]

The Isaac's Harbour/Country Harbour men were farmers and fishermen. Some of them followed the sea all of their lives, becoming captains of ships sailing the world, until the time of the great sailing ships ended. After that, shipping companies working the Great Lakes of Canada offered seafaring employment, which continues today.

A large number of Cook(e) men and their descendants became miners, for the gold mines in Goldboro, Country Harbour, Wine Harbour, Forest Hills, and elsewhere, gave Guysborough County much prosperity in the late 1800's. Gold mining ended in the 1940's, and many of these experienced miners found jobs in other mines all over Canada, including the New Glasgow area, Cape Breton, and Ontario.

1.4) Wintrop Cook married Lydia Collier (#10.2) on Apr. 17, 1804, at Marblehead, Mass. She was born at Marblehead, @ 1788, the daughter of John and Lydia Collier. At the time of the 1817 census, they lived in the Guysborough area. Lydia was a midwife for the Stormont area for many years. Wintrop died at Stormont, aged 91, on Sept. 23/1867. Lydia died , aged 85, on Jan. 2/1873, at the Isaac's Harbour home of her daughter, Becky Hayes.

Children of Wintrop and Lydia Cook:

1.41) Edmund Cleeves Cook	b: Oct. 28/1804 USA
1.42) Rebecca Cleeves Cook	b: Oct. 9/1806 USA
1.43) John Cook	b: June 7/1808
1.44) Samuel Cook	b: Apr. 8/1809
1.45) Lydia Cook	b: June 4/1811
1.46) John Cook	b: Oct. 14/1813
1.47) Wintrop Cook	b: Feb. 28/1818
1.48) James Cook	b: Oct. 13/1820
1.49) Francis Cook	b: @1817

1.41) Edmund Cook married Elizabeth Mars of Country Harbour on Feb. 10/1830, by Rev. Lewis. Elizabeth was born on March 5, 1809, to John and Sophia Mars. Edmund was a farmer and a fisherman. They lived on the East side of Stormont (Township Lot #66), and later moved to Isaac's Harbour. On the 1891 census, Elizabeth was 87, a widow, and living with her son Samuel and family. It also notes that her parents were born in Scotland. I have not been able to find any other information on this Mars family of Nova Scotia, but Mars was a fairly common name in early Maine.

Children of Edmund and Elizabeth Cook:

1.411) Mary Ann Cook	b: Apr. 6/1831
1.412) John Joseph Marshall Cook	b: Jan/1833
1.413) Martha Arabell Cook	b: June 15/1837
1.414) Louisa Caroline Cook	b: Jan. 10/1840
1.415) Maria Jane Cook	b: July 28/1844
1.416) Lydia E. Cook	b: @ 1852
1.417) Elias Foster Cook	b: March/1831
1.418) Joseph Charles Cook	b: Apr. 12/1849
1.419) Samuel Cook	b: @1835
1.41 10) Sarah Cook	b: ?

1.411) Mary Ann Cook married John Frederick Robar [CR1.411] of St. Mary's. They were married by the Rev. Mr. Uniacke on Oct. 27/1853. They lived in Isaac's Harbour North. **Child**:

1.4111) David James Robar   b: Jan. 14/1854

He married **1st)** Martha Davidson, daughter of James and Isabella Davidson, in 1879. He married **2nd)** Margaret Jadis, daughter of Charles and Rebecca (Dolliver) Jadis, in 1887.

Children:

1.41111) Mary (Minnie) Sarah Robar	b: June 16/1893
1.41112) John Charles (Jack) Robar	b: Dec. 8/1904
1.41113) James Alfred Robar	b: Mar. 16/1908
1.41114) William McAndrew Robar	b: @ 1890
1.41115) Lydia Robar	b: No further information
1.41116) Roney Starrett Robar	b: Mar. 31/1895
1.41117) Valentine Harry Robar	b: Feb. 14/1899
1.41118) Rhoda Robar	b: May 31/1903

1.41111) Minnie Robar married Arthur N. Barmby.

1.41112) John C. Robar migrated to Royal Oak, Michigan. He was a member of the Masonic order. He married Margaret Pender.

1.41113) James Robar served overseas in WWII. He was a contractor and builder in Saint John prior to migrating to Saskatoon, Sask. He married Dorothy Dugay.

1.41114) William Robar was a veteran of WWI, serving in the Merchant Marines. He married Leona Hayes, daughter of Marshall and Annie (Davidson) Hayes. {Marshall was a son of Edmund C. Hayes and Louisa (Cook) Hayes}.

1.41116) Roney Robar was a seaman in his younger years. He migrated to Kirkland lake Ontario. He was a veteran of the Royal Navy in WWI., and a member of the Masonic Lodge. He married Katherine Pride of Sonora, N.S.

1.41117) Valentine Robar was a seaman. He migrated to Royal Oak, Michigan, and became a naturalized citizen of USA in 1936.

1.41118) Rhoda Robar married Archibald Milton Darrach.

--

1.412) No further information - probably died young

--

1.413) Martha Cook is shown as a tailoress on the 1871 census. She married Josiah Jordan, a carpenter, at Trinity Church in Halifax, on Nov. 22/1871 (CR1.413). He was a son of William and Mary Jordan of Halifax. She was widowed by the 1891 census, which showed she worked as a nurse.
Children:
1.4131) Maude A. Jordan	b: @1873	d: 1907
1.4132) William Edmund Jordan	b: Apr. 15/1876	d: Aug. 3/1922

Martha and children migrated to Providence, Rhode Island, USA in 1892. Maude died there, unmarried, on April 10, 1907. Martha died on Nov. 23, 1908. William Edmund Jordan married Annie Henrietta Ralph at Providence, on July 14, 1903. William was in the US Armed Forces for a time, and was a 1st Sergeant in 1900, stationed at Cavite, Philippine Islands. By the 1910 US

36

census he was a machinist, and his WWI Draft Reg. card gives the information that he was a Machinist for Brown & Sharpe Mfg. Co. In 1920, he and his children, William and Dorothy, lived alone with Hattie M. Lintlop, a servant (widow of James Lintlop, she was born Hattie M. Langley, daughter of William B. and Susan G. Langley. She and her husband James and their family also migrated to the Rhode Island area, where he was a sailor and she, a dressmaker).

Children

1.41321) William Harris Jordan	b: Aug. 2, 1903	No further ino.
1.41322) Louise Maude Jordan	b: 1905	d: 1973
Married Adolph Vespia, 5 children, 3 still living		
1.41323) Dorothy E. Jordan	b: 1907	Married Wallace E. Wood

--

1.414) Louisa Cook married Edmund Hayes (#1.422) on Feb. 17/1857.

Children:

1.4141) Mary Ann Hayes	b: @ 1860
1.4142) Harriet Jane Hayes	b: @ 1863
1.4143) Priscilla (Ella) Hayes	b: Jan./1867
1.4144) Leanis Mahala Hayes	b: Dec. 3/1870
1.4145) Marshall Weeks Hayes	b: Sept. 19/1872
1.4146) Sarah Elizabeth Hayes	b: June 25/1875
1.4147) Jessie Lois Hayes	b: Oct. 28/1880

1.4141) Ann Hayes married Samuel Joy, a farmer, who was born in Maine. They lived in Methuen, Mass., USA. She was a widow at the time of the US 1920 census. They had no children.

1.4142) Harriet (Hattie) Hayes married John H. Myers, son of John and Amy (McMillan) Myers. They had **children:** Othilda Myers (m: Harry McDonald), Adelaide Myers (m: Graham Giffin), and Ashley Solomon Myers (b: 1888, d: 1865, m: Eva Hadley, who lived to be 106).

1.4143) Ella Hayes married David Shiers. They had no children.

1.4144) Leanis Hayes married George Myers, son of Stephen and Emma (Latham) Myers, and brother of Dellis and Effie Myers and had **children:** Reginald Bertram Myers (m: Gladys Mae Smith), Lydia Myers (m: Albert McKenna – lived at Lawrence, Mass.), Stephen Edmund Myers (m: Helen Langille), Robert Marshall Myers (m: Alice Blair), Maud Othilda Myers (m: George Burke Mason), George Ashford Myers (killed in a mining accident in Ontario. His mother found out about the tragedy from a newspaper article about the event).

1.4145) Marshall Hayes married Annie Davidson (b: 1875, d: 1907). He owned and operated a general store at Isaac's Harbour North. Later he sold it to Truman Giffin. **Children:** Iris Hayes (d: a baby), Leona Anne Hayes (m: Billy Robar), Harriet Hayes (m: Bob Malloy; she spent two years at the Kentville Sanatorium and died several months after returning home. Many years later, Bob married Ina Smith), Grace Hayes (b: 1902, d: 1904).

1.4146) Sarah Elizabeth Hayes (Bessie) married Marcus Cooke (#1.4181). See children under that number.

1.4147) Jessie Hayes married Stanford Giffin, son of Zeba and Annie (Blakeley) Giffin, and had **children:**
Oswald <u>Knowlton</u> Giffin (m: Dorothy MacIntosh), Annie Louisa (Louise) Giffin (m: John Little), Irma Giffin (m: Edgar Leslie).

Stanford and Jessie Giffin

--

1.415) Maria Cook never married. She moved to U.S.A. while quite young.

--

1.416) Lydia Cook married Joseph Hayes (#1.425) on Jan. 16/1873, at Melrose. She died before 1884, when he remarried and had more children (See #1.425).
Children:

1.4161) Alfred Charles Hayes	b: Jan. 26/1878	d: 1955
1.4162) Leonard Whitman Hayes	b: June 16/1875	d: 1954
1.4163) Eugenia Hayes (Jean)	m: Alfred Percival	

--

1.417) Elias Foster Cook married Priscilla McConnell (b: @ 1841, d: Aug.8/1897) on Jan. 15/1860, at St. Mary's. Elias and Priscilla lived at Stormont, on the East side, facing the harbour, and for a time, at Wine Harbour, where Elias mined gold, and where some of the children were born. (CR1.417) *There are discrepancies in the birthdates from birth records and census records for many of this family group.*
Children:

1.4171) Tyrus Cook	b: Oct. 2/1862
1.4172) Louisa Caroline Cook	b: Sept. 30/1866
1.4173) Edmund Cook	b: Mar. 1873
1.4174) Elias <u>Foster</u> Cook	b: May 22/1871

1.4175) Russell Cook	b: Apr. 8/1869	
1.4176) William B. Cook	b: Aug. 2/1871	No further info.

1.4171) Tyrus Cook was a gold miner. He married @ 1892, Mary Dellis (or Dellice) Myers (b: Oct. 27/1873). She was a daughter of Stephen and Amy (Latham) Myers of Goldboro. She died of breast cancer in 1940. Tyrus died of stomach cancer in 1928. **Children**:

1.41711) Carrie Lee Cook	b: Sept. 17/1893	d: July 30/1955
1.41712) Eddy Cook	b: Jan./1897	d: Apr. 29/1897
1.41713) William Cook	b: July 7/1898	d: Dec. 8/1904
1.41714) Effie May Cook	b: Dec. 23/1900	d: May 25, 1911
1.41715) Amy Alfreda Cook	b: June 6/1903	d: 1979
1.41716) Mildred Cook	b: 1906	
1.41717) Clarence Cook	b: 1907	
1.41718) Warren E. Cook	b: Oct. 1915	d: June 8, 1916

1.41711) Carrie Lee Cook married Warren Everett Pace, a mariner from West Liscomb, on Oct. 7/1915. She died in 1955 and is buried at Indian Harbour Lake.

1.41714) Effie May Cook died on May 25, 1911 of Diptheria, and is buried at Isaac's Harbour North. *In January, 1877, a Diptheria epidemic caused the death of many children throughout the eastern shore, to the Country Harbour, Stormont, Isaac's Harbour area and beyond. When the disease entered a home, it usually took away all the small children of the family. Stephen and Lucinda Fenton lost two children, James Orris, aged 5 and Sarah, aged 2 1/2. Charles and Betsy Cook lost two year old Zuleika. Spencer and Susan Giffin lost three children in the first week of January, 1877.*

1.41715) Amy A. Cooke married Thomas David James Bennett, son of Andrew and Martha (Jordan) Bennett of Indian Harbor, on Nov. 20, 1928. He died of TB on Jan. 6, 1935, aged 40. He is buried in Sunset Rest Cemetery, Indian Harbour.

1.41716) Mildred Cook married Arnold Edison Jordan, a widower from Jordanville in 1928.

1.41717) Clarence Cook married Mable Riley of Indian Harbour, daughter of Joseph and Alice (Pickett) Riley, on Sept. 11, 1928. She died of tuberculosis on June 28, 1934, aged 31.

1.4172) Louisa Cook married Wentworth Mason (#1.4514), at Halifax, on Nov. 1, 1886. On various documents, he is also called either Wintrop or Winthrop. They lived at mining towns, incuding Springhill, eventually settling in MacPherson's Mills. He was a coal and gold miner and a farmer. He died at

MacPherson's Mills on Apr. 21, 1923, of tuberculosis. Louisa migrated to the Timmins, Ontario, area with several of her grown children and their families, and was living there in 1949.

Children:

1.41721) Stanley Edward Mason	b: Nov. 22/1887
1.41722) Violet Belle Mason	b: Apr. 17/1891
1.41723) Leslie Seymour Mason	b: Jan. 12/1895
1.41724) Blanche Lydia Mason	b: July 8/1894
1.41725) Edna May Mason	b: Sept.25/1896
1.41726) Abner Mason	b: Apr. 25/1898

1.41721) Stanley Mason married Alma Clyburne, daughter of David and Alma/Emma (Fenton) Clyburn on March 27, 1908 at Isaac's Harbour. They lived in Stellarton, NS. He was killed in an accident in 1927, at age 40. Alma died at Stellarton in 1944. They had children, including a son, Stanley Edward, who died in 1940 of tuberculosis, age 30.

1.41722) Violet Mason married Harry M. Feltmate, (b: 1893) son of Ephraim C. and Elceba (Croft) Feltmate, Whitehead, N.S., on Nov. 4, 1913. This family migrated to the Timmins, Ontario area.

Children:

1.417221) Seward Stanley Feltmate	b: Jan. 27/1914
1.417222) Albert Leslie Feltmate	b: Dec. 24/1916
1.417223) Lawrence Murdoch Feltmate	b: Jan. 1/1921

1.41723) Leslie Mason married Phyllis Elizabeth Wilford in Edinburgh, Scotland on Feb. 12, 1919.

1.41724) Blanche Lydia Mason married Donald Allen Fraser, a miner, on Nov. 23, 1920, at MacPherson's Mills, NS.

1.41725) Edna Mason married Kenneth George Croft, son of Robert and Janie Croft in 1918. (Robert was a farmer, born at White Head). Kenneth was a steelworker at Trenton.

1.41726) Abner Mason was a coal miner at the Vipond Mine. He never married. He died of consumption, age 28, on Feb. 11, 1927, at Muskoka Hospital for Consumption, Gravenhurst, Ontario.

1.4173) Edmund Cooke married Bessie B. Latham, daughter of John and Jane Latham, Isaac's Harbour, on Nov. 14/1900. She died on May 14, 1918, at Joggins Mines, age 35. She is buried at Isaac's Harbour. Edmund died in St. Martha's Hospital, Antigonish, on Aug. 18, 1940.

Children:
1.41731) Gertrude Cooke   b: Jan., 1901
1.41732) John C. Cooke   b: 1905
1.41733) Ina Leola Cooke   b: @1907
1.41734) Zelma Bessie Cooke   b: Aug. 24/ 1910 d: July 29/1996
1.41735) Priscilla Jane Cooke   b: @1911
1.41736) Edith Corabelle Cooke b: 1916

1.41731) Gertrude Cooke married Abraham Hennessey (born Newfoundland) in 1919. He was killed in the Allan Mine explosion in April, 1935. [CR1.41731]

1.41733) Ina Leola Cooke married Daniel McIntosh, Lumberman, son of William and Olive McIntosh of Stillwater. They were married on Feb.3, 1927, at St. James' Manse, Antigonish.

1.41734) Zelma Cooke married Kenneth C. McGillivary in 1928.

1.41735) Priscilla Cooke married Ellis Murray Davidson, son of John C. and Emma (Hingley) Davidson of Sherbrooke, on Sept. 21, 1929 at New Glasgow.

1.41736) Edith Cooke married Almon Roy Langille, son of Winton and Odessa (Stevens) Langille, in 1935.

1.4174) Foster Cook married Martha Jane (Janie) Silver, daughter of Clayton and Martha (Luddington) Silver on Dec. 22, 1921. [CR1.4174] Janie died young. Three of their daughters, Margaret, Daisy, and Olive, lived with John and Elsie Hayne, Country Harbour, until they were able to be on their own. [CR1.4174a]

Children:
1.41741) Gladys Cook   b: 1921
1.41742) Mary Cook   b: ?
1.41743) Margaret Elizabeth Cook b: Mar.14/1925 d: Mar. 12/1995
1.41744) Daisy Belle Cook   b: @ 1927
1.41745) Olive Cook   b: 1928   d: 1989
1.41746) Tyrus Cook   b: 1930   d: 1999
1.41747) Louise Cook   b: 1923   d: 1936

--

1.4175) Russell Cooke married Laurilla Maria Langley on Dec. 9/1893. She was born July 3/1874 at Shubenacadie, and was a daughter of Moses and Margaret Eliza (Silver) Langley. Russell went to sea at age 12 as Ship's cook, running between the West Indies, U.S.A., and Canada. In his early 20's, he left the sea, and became a miner for a good number of years. They lived in various mining communities throughout eastern Nova Scotia. He later settled at Springville, Pictou County. Russell was also well-known for "witching" water (predicting where water was located underground for wells). He was interested in sports, played hockey and skated at an advanced age. He died on Dec. 25, 1952. Laurilla died on Aug. 15, 1958.

Russell and Laurilla Cooke's Children:

1.41751) Orris Stephen Cooke	b: June 17/1895	d: Sept. 1/1971
1.41752) Byron Foster Cooke	b: Oct. 25/1895	
1.41753) Edward Charles Cooke	b: Oct. 12/1898	d: Mar. 4/1968 Vancouver, BC
1.41754) Brenton Cooke	b: Apr. 20/1900	
1.41755) Roland Lea Cooke	b: 1907 Goldbrook, NS	
1.41756) Edith Cooke	b: Nov. 18/1909	
1.41757) Hugh A. Cooke	b: 1912	d: Dec.3/1994 Never married
1.41758) Daisy Cooke	b: Nov. 16/191	d: Feb./2011
1.41759) Florence Cooke	b: ?	d: a baby
1.4175 10) James Spurgeon Cooke	b: Nov. 16/1902	d: 1980

1.41751) Orris Cooke lived at Springville, Pictou Co. He became a carpenter. He was a First World War veteran and enlisted as a member of the 78th Pictou Highlanders, 15th Battalion, later transferring to the 17th Battalion of the 48th Toronto Highlanders. He was wounded a few times, last at Vimy Ridge and sent home. He was a Scoutmaster for close to 20 years. He married **1st)** Vera Langley (#1.41971). She died on Aug. 25,1952, and Orris married **2nd)** Florence Davidson.

Orris Cooke

1.41752) Byron Cooke was a veteran of WW I. He lived at Trenton, N.S. He married Etta Arbuckle in 1919.

1.41753) Edward Cooke was a machinist. He served in the 82nd Regiment, C.E.F., and for many years with the Cdn. Merchant Marines in WWII.

1.41755) Roland Cooke was a veteran of WW II. He married Ada Isabel Buck. They lived at Irish Mountain, Pictou Co., N.S., and in the U.S.

1.41756) Edith Cooke married Jack Robertson.

1.41758) Daisy Cooke married **1ˢᵗ)** W.F. Brennan, and **2ⁿᵈ)** Clarence MacDonald.

1.4175 <u>10</u>) James Spurgeon Cooke married Rachel Gilmen Grant (b: Glasgow, Scotland) on Dec. 13, 1924, at New Glasgow. He was a Machinist, resided in Springville.

--

My great-great grandfather, Capt. Charles Cooke

1.418) Charles Cooke followed the sea all of his life, working as a fisherman out of Stormont, then as a crewman aboard a schooner. He eventually became a Captain and owned several schooners at different times, including the *Ella May, Gentile, and Dark Secret.* Charles married Elizabeth Macbeth Findlay (Betsy), (b: Oct. 2/1855, d: 1910), on Feb. 15/1872, at the Anglican Church, Country Harbour. Betsy was the 17 year old daughter of William and Margaret (Addison) Findlay, who immigrated from Banff, Scotland in 1867. The Findlays (CR1.418w) settled on the west side of Country Harbour. Betsy died on Jan. 15, 1909. Charles died, aged 73, on Jan. 8, 1923. Betsy died on Jan. 15, 1909 at age 52, after suffering from a stroke for three years.

<u>**Children**</u>:
1.4181) William <u>Marcus</u> Cooke   b: Aug. 15/1872   d: Nov. 19/1950
1.4182) Zelda <u>Zuleika</u> Cooke   b: Aug. 22/1874   d: Jan. 6/1877
1.4183) Hugh Allen Cooke   b: 1877   d: 1906
1.4184) Leander John Cooke   b: Mar. 12/1883   d: Mar. 27/1969
1.4185) Tremaine Hollis Cooke   b: Mar. 5/1890   d: Aug. 11/1964
1.4186) Winifred Marcella Cooke (adopted) b: @1900   d: ?
See (CR1.418) for notes on this family.

1.4181) Marcus Cooke worked his way up through the ranks of seafaring vessels, and became a Master Mariner, then Captain of various ships. One well known schooner he was Master of was the tern *John A. Beckerman*, 241 feet long with 2 decks. It carried mostly lumber to New York, Boston and other New England ports. (CR1.4181) He married Sarah Elizabeth (Bessie) Hayes (#1.4146).

Marcus Cooke

Children:

1.41811) Bertram Allen Cooke	b: July 28/1898	d: Sept. 27/1941
1.41812) Harold Addison Cooke	b: July 19/1902	d: Aug. 16/1956
1.41813) Adelaide Cooke (adopted)	b: 1914	d: TB age 16

Mark and Bessie also brought up Ruth Deal, who married C. Ritson Durling, Annapolis Royal.

Bert Cooke

1.41811) Bert Cooke married Annabelle Davidson. They had no children. He was killed in an accident at Seal Harbour Gold Mines. He was struck across the chest by a heavy steel cable when an electric hoist clutch band broke. The cable pierced his heart, and brought death almost instantly. Annabelle later married an Armstrong. She died in 1992.

1.41812) Harold (Hal) Cook married Alberta Elora Kirby (b: Apr. 14, 1909, d: Dec. 30, 1996) on June 20, 1927, daughter of Burton and Marjorie (MacKenzie) Kirby of Upper Whitehead. Many years after Hal died, she married Charlie Cook (#1.4721).

Hal Cooke

1.4182) Zuleika Cooke died at age 2, during a diptheria epidemic. She is buried near the old Stormont Commons.

1.4183) Hugh Allen Cooke was killed in a mining accident at Stellarton, NS. [CR1.4183] He was 28 years old and engaged to be married.

Hugh Allen Cooke

1.4184) Lea Cooke became a Master Mariner at the age of 19, and captained various vessels, including the *Lewis* and the *Albertha*. He survived several shipwrecks; one noteable experience involved being torpedoed by a German submarine in 1917. He married Margaret Martin (Maggie, b: 1883, d: 1968) on Jan. 26, 1910. She was the daughter of Capt. John and Elizabeth (Donovan) Martin of Dartmouth, NS, and was a sister of John Martin who married Winnifred Cook (#1.4186). Although they were married by Rev. Y.O. Weeks, a Baptist minister, at Isaac's Harbour, Maggie remained true to her RC faith, and is buried in St. Peter's Cemetery, Dartmouth. Lea is buried in the cemetery at Isaac's Harbour.

Leander Cooke

Children:

1.41841) Elizabeth Thelma Cook	b: May 24/1909	d: Aug. 13/1909
1.41842) Hugh Allen Cooke	b: Oct. 27/1910	d: Jan. 1/1997
1.41843) Leo Martin Cook	b: Nov. 1/1912	d: Oct. 31/1975
1.41844) Lawrence Addison Cooke	b: July 29/1917	d: 1957

1.41845) Daughter, who d: soon after birth, unnamed. Buried in Pioneer Cemetery, Isaac's Harbour. Lea and Maggie also brought up Gerry Martin (b: July 13/1920).

1.41842) Hugh Cooke married Dorothy Whitman. They had 6 children.

Hugh Cooke

Leo Cook

1.41843) Leo Cook married **1ˢᵗ)** Helen Jollimore, **2ⁿᵈ)** Audrey Emeno. Leo and Helen had a daughter; Leo and Audrey had two sons.

1.41844) Lawrence Cooke married Dorothy <u>Jean</u> Harvey (1917-1972). He was killed in a car accident in 1957 in Ontario. They had two daughters: Catherine Jean (m: John Seddon), Harlene Ann (m: Mervin Rowe).

Lawrence Cooke

--

1.4185) Tremaine Cooke was a veteran of both World Wars. During WWI he was a Machine Gunner, 85ᵗʰ Battalion, Canadian Expeditionary Forces. In WWII, he was a cook in the RCN at HMCS Stadacona. He married Lena Mae Langley (#1.49141), daughter of Arthur and Bertha Langley, on Nov. 25, 1912. Tremaine was the lighthouse keeper on Green Island (now Country Island), in 1929. He and Lena divorced, and all the children except Frank were placed in foster homes. The youngest daughter, Irene, was adopted by an Andrews family in Cape Breton.

Tremaine Cooke

Tremaine moved to Milton, Queens County. Both Tremaine and Lena remarried (He married Zelma Foster on July 17, 1930, and she married

George Mason #1.4513), but reunited after the deaths of their 2nd spouses and remarried again on Sept. 26, 1953.

Children:

1.41851)	Zelma Zuleika Cooke	b: Jan. 15/1913	d: Jan. 1/1971
1.41852)	Frank Cochrane Cooke	b: Apr. 16/1915	d: Mar. 25/1965
1.41853)	James Spurgeon Cooke	b: Apr. 6/1919	d:
1.41854)	Charles Arthur Cooke	b: Nov. 12/1922	
1.41855)	Irving MacGregor Cooke	b: May 31/1924	d: Mar. 4/2004
1.41856)	Irene June Cooke	b: June 6/1926	d: Jan. 10/2007
1.41857)	Kenneth Tremaine Cooke	b: Aug. 10/1927	
1.41858)	Bertha Elizabeth Cooke	b: Dec. 16/19__	d: at 3 mos.

1.41851) Zelma Cooke married **1st)** Frank DeWolfe, **2nd)** George Zwicker. No children from either marriage.

1.41852) Frank Cooke never married.

1.41853) James Cooke never married.

1.41854) Charles Cooke was born in Timmins, Ontario. While serving with the Canadian Armed Forces in Glasgow, Scotland, during WWII, he met Florence MacKay, and married her on Sept. 14. 1945. They had 7 children. Charles lives in Milton, N.S.

1.41855) Irving Cooke married Annie Matthews. They had 3 children.

1.41856) Irene Cooke was adopted by Clarence Henry Andrews and Mayme Margaret (MacDonald) Andrews of Coxheath, Cape Breton. She married Alfred James Davis (Al), also of Sydney and Inverness, Cape Breton. Irene and Alfred lived in Strathlorne and Inverness, where they owned and she managed, the Inverness Lodge and Motel.
They had two children.

1.41857) Kenneth Cooke married Lilly G. Barnes (b: Sept. 11, 1918). They lived in B.C. They had 2 children.

--

1.4186) Winnie Cooke married John James Martin, son of John and Elizabeth (Donovan) Martin. They had two daughters, Iris and Lorraine.

--

1.419) Samuel Cook was a fisherman at Isaac's Harbour. He married Annie J. Hayes, daughter of Jonathan and Rebecca (Cook) Hayes (b: 1839), on Oct. 15, 1860, at Country Harbour. Annie was only 40 years old when she died in 1879.

Children:

1.4191) Leander S. Cook	b: Jan. 7/1861	
1.4192) Martha Arabella Cook	b: Apr. 12/1863	d: 1936
1.4193) Olivia Alice Cook	b: Jan. 24/1865	
1.4194) John Charles Cook	b: Oct. 14/1866	
1.4195) Maria Jane Cook	b: Dec. 7/1868	
1.4196) Laurella Ann Cook	b: Oct. 6/1869	d: 1960
1.4197) Florence Cook	b: Jan. 22/1874	
1.4198) Robert Emmit Cook	b: Nov. 13/1874	
1.4199) Samuel Bruce Cook	b: Nov. 2/1876	d: Oct. 6/1955

1.4191)   Leander S. Cook married Effie Jane Myers (b: 1871), daughter of Stephen and Emma (Latham) Myers. She died in 1897, age 26.

1.4192)   Martha Arabella (Belle) Cook married William Leretus Hines on Jan. 30, 1884 at Isaac's Harbour.

Child:

1.41921) Winnifred Hines   b: Oct. 18/1886
Married William H. Foxley at Halifax, in 1910. He was born in London, England. They had a **daughter**, Helen (b:1911, St. John NB)

1.4193)   Olivia Alice Cook married George Stewart. They migrated to Cambridge, Mass.

Child:

1.41931) Esther Gladys Stewart   b: Apr. 25/1896
She became an R.N. She married Clarence M. Perkins and had **children**: Robert S. Perkins, Charlotte A. Perkins, Rosamond E. Perkins.

1.4194)   John Charles Cook married Varina Belle Davidson, daughter of James and Mary Davidson, on July 13, 1895. They lived at Isaac's Harbour North, on the lot where Paul and Patsy MacIsaac have their home today. They had no children.

1.4195) Maria Jane Cook married George Myers Clyburne (b: Mar. 11/1868), son of Jane (Myers) Clyburne. They lived in Argyle, Guys. County, where he had been brought up by John and Janet Kennedy. When he was an infant, he was bound out by the Overseers of the Poor for the township of Stormont, as an apprentice to the Kennedys until he was 21, for $16.00. The Kennedys had no children of their own. George and Maria married in 1903. On the 1911 Census, nephew Verne Langley lived with them.

1.4196) Laurella Ann Cook married Ira Lewis Fenton (1.4413).
Children:
1.41961) Lola Deferris Fenton   b: Oct. 31/1894
1.41962) Effie Belle Fenton   b: Dec. 3/1897
1.41963) Alice Yvette Fenton   b: Oct. 20/1902   d: 1925

1.41961) Lola Fenton married Stewart Baker. They migrated to Kirkland Lake, Ontario. They had four **children**: Norma, Hilda, Iris and Cyril.

1.41962)   Effie Fenton married Samuel George Billard and had three **children**: Lewis, Gloria and Arthur.

1.41963) Alice Fenton married Garfield Peitzsche and had one **child**: Doris Marie Peitzsche. Alice and Garfield both died of tuberculosis. Marie was brought up by her grandmother, Laurella ("Lell") Fenton. Marie married Fred Ward, a miner from Reserve Mines, Cape Breton. They had two daughters.

1.4197) Florence Cook married Harvey B. Langley on July 15/1893. He was the son of Moses and Margaret Langley, and a brother of Laurilla Langley, who married Russell Cooke (#1.4175). Florence died of TB, age 37, in 1909. Harvey was killed by a falling limb of a tree at Upper Caledonia in 1911.
Children:
1.41971) Vera M. Langley   b: Feb. 10/1895
1.41972) William Vernon Langley   b: June 13/1897

1.41971)   Vera M. Langley married Orris Cooke (#1.41751), son of Russell and Laurilla Cooke.

1.41972)   Vernon Langley was a veteran of WWI, and was part of the Canadian Expeditionary Forces overseas.   He was a cook aboard sea vessels. He migrated to the US, living in Chelsea, Mass. in 1939, the date of his Naturalization papers.

1.4198) Emmit Cook never married.

1.4199)   Bruce Cook married Eliza Alice Clyburne, daughter of Simon and Annie Clyburne, on June 25, 1904.
Children:
1.41991) Joyce Cooke   b: Sept. 1/1901   d: 1985
1.41992) Samuel Howard Edison Cooke   b: 1905   d: Apr.3/1970
1.41993) Annie Rita Cooke   b: Sept. 18/1910   d: 1946
1.41994) Errington Cooke   b: Nov. 25/1913

Opposite:
Errington, Edison and Bruce Cooke

1.41991) Joyce Cooke married Stanley MacKenzie.

1.41992)   Edison Cooke married Bertha Langille (b: 1911), daughter of Winton and Louise (Stevens) Langille, on Feb. 4, 1928. They had 15 children.

1.41993) Rita Cooke   married Aubrey Gifford Carroll, on Dec. 18, 1928, at Halifax.

1.41994) Errington Cooke married Martina Grace @ 1904. They had a large family.

--

1.41 <u>10</u>) Sarah Cook married Henry Robar, a fisherman from St. Mary's River in January, 1862[CR1.41<u>10</u>], at St. Mary's River.
Children:
1.4 <u>10</u> 1) Ida <u>May</u> Robar   b: Apr. 29/1867
1.4 <u>10</u> 2) Charles Colens Robar   b: Sept. 4/1865 No further info.

1.4 <u>10</u> 1) Ida May is shown on the 1881 census in the family of Charles and Betsy Cooke, Isaac's Harbour. She migrated to the USA, where she married Charles E. Saunders in Rhode Island in 1894. He was born in Rhode Island, as was his mother; his father was born in England. He was a State Manager for an Insurance company. They later migrated to New Hampshire, where she died on Sept. 26, 1919, of complications following a hysterectomy (multiple fibroid tumors).
Children:

1.4 <u>10</u> 11) Ernest Robar Saunders   b: Jan. 25/1895
1.4 <u>10</u> 12) ?   The 1900 US census noted that Ida had 2 children, only 1 was living at that time.

1.4 <u>10</u> 11) Ernest R. Saunders was an electrician. He married Beatrice A. Cheever, daughter of Lewis and Harriet (Clarke) Cheever, at Manchester, New Hampshire on June 2, 1916.

~

1.42) Rebecca Cleeves Cook married Jonathan Hayes.
Children:
1.421) Andrew Joseph Hayes   b: Nov. 3/1826
1.422) Edmund Cook Hayes   b: Apr. 9/1829
1.423) John Hayes   b: Jan. 14/1832
1.424) Abigail Hayes   b: May 24/1837
1.425) Joseph Elliot Hayes   b: Aug. 26/1844
1.426) Ann J. Hayes   b: July 10/1845
1.427) William Hayes   b: Nov/1851

1.421) Andrew Joseph Hayes probably died young.

1.422) Edmund Cook Hayes married Louisa Cook (see #1.1414).

Edmund Hayes

1.423) John Hayes - No further information.

1.424) Abigail Hayes married David Brydle of St. Mary's, and had
children:
1.4241) William H. Brydle   b: 1860
1.4242) David Edmund Brydle   b: 1861
1.4243) Harriet Ann (Hattie) Brydle   b: 1865
1.4244) Mary <u>Ella</u> Brydle   b: 1868

1.4245) Frederick B. Brydle   b: 1870
1.4246) Charles L. Brydle   b: 1873
1.4247) Joseph S. Brydle   b: 1874

1.4241) William H. Brydle migrated to Cambridge, Mass., USA. He married Alma J. Langley, daughter of James and Eliza Langley, on Oct. 28, 1890. They had 3 **daughters**: Mildred Bell Brydle (b: 1892), Gertrude Brydle (b: 1895) and Mabel Augusta Brydle (b: 1891).

1.4242) David Edmund Brydle never married. He died in 1936.

1.4243) Harriet V. (Hattie) Brydle married Christopher Chisholm, son of William and Ann Chisholm of Ogden in 1885. They had a large family.

1.4244) Ella Brydle married John Lintlop, son of William and Isabella Lintlop of Isaac's Harbour, in 1895.

1.4245) Frederick B. Brydle married Melvina J. Davidson, daughter of Duncan and Mary Davidson of Isaac's Harbour in 1896.

1.4246) Charles L. Brydle married Eliza McDonald, daughter of Kenneth McDonald of Wine Harbour in 1905.

1.4247) Joseph S. Brydle was a gold miner. He never married. He died at Isaac's Harbour in 1951.

--

1.425) Joseph Hayes was a sailor. He married **1st)** Lydia Cook (See #1.416 for their children) in 1873 . He married **2nd)** Mary S. (Shiers) Hallett, widow, in 1884. She was a daughter of Jacob and Mary (Myers) Shiers, and a sister to David Shiers, who married Ella Hayes (#1.4143).
Children from his **2nd** marriage:
1.4251) Minnie Hayes   m: Guilford MacDonald
1.4252) Winnifred Hayes   m: George Wamboldt

--

1.426) Ann Hayes married Samuel Cooke (# 1.1419).

1.427) William Hayes was a mariner, and worked as a cook on board schooners. He never married. He is shown on the 1911 census, age 59, at Isaac's Harbour with his nephew Alfred Hayes living with him.

~

1.44) Samuel Cook married Elizabeth Haine (b: Sept. 10, 1819), daughter of Johan George and Louise (Sarty) Haine, on Jan. 26/1837. Elizabeth was born at LaHave, N.S. @ 1817. Elizabeth became ill, and had to be taken care of outside the home. Some of the younger children were brought up by various relatives in the area. Samuel and family moved to Fisherman's Harbour. Elizabeth died on Oct. 11, 1864, at Guysborough.

Children:

1.441) Elizabeth White Cook	b: Feb. 2/1838
1.442) Ambrose Cook	b: Nov. 25/1842
1.443) Desire Cook	b: Oct. 16/1844
1.444) Eunice Cook	b: June 16/1845
1.445) Lucinda Cook	b: May 31/1846
1.446) Sophia Matilda Cook	b: Mar. 31/1852
1.447) Priscilla Cook	b: July 18/1855
1.448) Rebecca Cook	b: Mar. 6/1858
1.449) Elias Cook	b: June 16/1861 d: Oct. 20/1928

1.441) Elizabeth Cook married Joseph <u>Charles</u> Fenton from Fisherman's Harbour on Jan. 5/1862, at Country Harbour. She died of consumption at age 37 on April 13/1874. The younger children were brought up by other families.

Children:

1.4411) Lydia <u>Lorella</u> E. Fenton	b: Aug. /1870
1.4412) Hezekiah <u>Charles</u> Fenton	b: Nov. 17/1873 d: Aug. 13/1945
1.4413) Ira Lewis Fenton	b: Dec. 8/1868
1.4414) Martha A. Fenton	b: 1860 (CR1.4414)
1.4415) James E. Fenton	b: @ 1864 No further information

1.4411) Lorella Fenton lived with the family of John and Amy Myers at Isaac's Harbour in 1881. She married David Thomas Walsh (#1.4434), son of John and Desire (Cook) Walsh, in 1893 at Isaac's Harbour.

1.4412) Charles Fenton married Estella Mason (b: 1883), daughter of Albert and Victoria A. (Horton) Mason, on July 30, 1924. **Estella lived to be 108 years old**. *On the record of his birth, his name is given as Hezekiah C. Fenton, however, on his marriage license, he gives his name as Charles Arthur Fenton. There is also a one year discrepancy in his age, the birth record states Nov. 17, 1873, and the death record gives his birthdate as Nov. 17, 1874.

1.4413) Ira L. Fenton married Laurella Cook (See # 1.14196 for information on descendants).

--

1.442) Ambrose Cook was a boat builder at Fisherman's Harbour. He married Charlotte Taylor, (CR1.442W) daughter of George and Elizabeth (Jarvis) Taylor, at

Stormont, on April 10/1866. She died at age 23 of consumption, on Dec. 6/1867.

Child:
1.4421) Catherine (Cassie) Cook   b: Mar. 21/1867
She married William S. MacDonald, Fisherman's Harbour, on Aug. 10/1893. He was born at Coddles Harbour, a son of John and Mary (Mason) McDonald.
Children:
1.44211) Norman Leslie MacDonald   b: May 13/1894
1.44212) Arthur Roy MacDonald   b: July 28/1895
1.44213) Jessie G. MacDonald   b: July 21/1899
Cassie died in a fire on Jan. 3/1909. William remarried, to Ada (Hull) Crooks, a widow.

--

1.443) Desire Cook married John Walsh, Jr., son of John and Mary Walsh, (CR1.443) from Forks of St. Mary (now Glenelg). John Sr. was born in Ireland. John, Jr. was a widower by 1891. In 1894, he married Sarah Jackson, a 39 year old widow.
Children:
1.4431) Henry H. Walsh   b: @ 1862
1.4432) Margaret Walsh   b: @ 1867 No further information
1.4433) Rosannah Walsh   b: @ 1869
1.4434) David Thomas Walsh   b: June 16/1872
1.4434) John S. Walsh   b: @ 1875
1.4434) Melissa Walsh   b: @ 1879 No further information
1.4434) Olive Walsh   b: @ 1883
1.4434) Levi Walsh   b: @ 1885

Of the above:
Henry Walsh married Lottie M. Whitman, daughter of Levi and Sophia Whitman of Canso. They lived in the Fall River area of Halifax County. They had children Charles W. Walsh, Muriel M. Walsh, Reginald E. Walsh, Frank Ernest Walsh, Jean Alberta Walsh, H. Fred Walsh.
Rosannah Walsh married John Henry Hallet of Stormont. They had children Harry Bruce Hallett, Jerusha M. Hallett, Verena Rose Hallett, Grace Eliza Hallett, Walter Douglas Hallett, Clara Lillian Hallett.
David Thomas Walsh married Lorella Fenton, daughter of Charles and Elizabeth Fenton. They had children James Walter Walsh, Mary Agnes Walsh, Margaret Pearl Walsh, Christina Walsh, Simon F. Walsh, Catherine Walsh.
John S. Walsh married Annie ? and had children George H Walsh and Frederick Walsh.
Olive Walsh married Robert Henry Kenney, son of Robert and Ann Kenney.
Levi Walsh married Margaret Kenney.

--

1.444) Eunice Cook
Children:
1.4441) Sophia Matilda Cook   b: Jan. 7/1872
1.4442) John Cook   b: May 20/1874
1.4443) Alexander Cook   b: March 19/1880
1.4444) Edna Alice Cook   b: Feb. 8/1885

1.4441) Sophie Cook married Caleb Mason, son of Edward and Jane (Fenton) Mason of Country Harbour on Dec. 18/1903.
Children: Laurence Mason (m: Hilda Johnstone), Alma Mason (m: Walter Mason), and Lois Mason (m: MacLean Sutherland).

**Opposite -
Caleb and Sophie Mason**

1.4442) John Cooke never married. He lived with his brother Alex Cooke and family for over 30 years. He died, age 77, at Fisherman's Harbour in March/1951. His brother Alex died three days before him.

1.4443) Alexander Cooke married Verena Jane Bingley (b: July 19, 1889, d: 1982), daughter of John and Minnie Bingley. **Children**: Lois Edna Cooke (m: Harnish of West Dover, NS), Hilda Elizabeth Cooke (m: Walter R. Siteman), Cora Lee Cooke (m: Malcolm W. MacDonald), Mary Marguerite Cooke (m: Ralph Giffin).

1.4444) Edna Cooke married Walter Archibald Kaiser, Port Bickerton, on Aug. 15/1903. They had a **daughter**, Rebecca b: 1908.

--

1.445) Lucinda Cook
Child:
1.4451) William Abner Cooke   b: @ 1864 [CR1.4451]   d: 1931
Lucinda married **1st)** Stephen Fenton, son of Jacob and Elizabeth Fenton on April 12/1872.
Children:
1.4452) Margaret Ann Fenton   b: June 4/1870
1.4453) Sophia Catherine (Katy) Fenton b: June 4/1869
1.4454) James Orris Fenton   b: @ 1872   d: 1877

1.4455) Selvina Fenton	b: Aug. 1/1872	No further info.
1.4456) Sarah Elizabeth Fenton	b: @ 1874	d: 1877
1.4457) James Charles Howard Fenton	b: Jan. 5/1877	d: 1956
1.4458) Charlotte (Lottie) Fenton	b: Aug. 20/1881	
1.4459) Iva Nora Belle Fenton	b: 1886	
1.445 10) Olive Fenton	b: 1887	
1.445 11) Love Maud Fenton	b: Nov. 4, 1891	

Lucinda married **2nd)** James Henry Mason, (#1.4517) son of William and Mary Mason, on Aug. 27/1898, at Country Harbour. Henry Mason was the older brother of her daughter Maggie's husband. He was 32, she was 47, at the time of their marriage. Lucinda died at Eight Island Lake on July 19, 1912, age 64.

1.4451) William Abner Cooke was brought up in the Whitman Giffin household, from a small child until at least the age of 16. He married Margaret Emma Harris on Sept. 18/1889, at Cambridge, Mass., U.S.A. **Children:**

1.44511) Emma May Cooke	b: Aug. 26/1890	d: 1965
1.44512) William Wallace Cooke	b: July 26/1892	d: 1981
1.44513) James Howard Cooke	b: Aug 23./1894	d: 1960
1.44514) Lillian Florence Cooke	b: Oct. 17/1896	d: 1897
1.44515) Catherine Mabel Cooke	b: June 29/1898	
1.44516) Alice Cornelia Cooke	b: Sept. 24/1900	
1.44517) Gladys Lucinda Cooke	b: Dec.10/1902	
1.44518) Hugh Allan Cooke	b: May 22/1905	d: 1992
1.44519) Lorne Edison Cooke	b: Oct. 31/1907	d: 1999

1.44511) Emma May Cooke married George Samuel Jarvis and had two sons.

1.44512) William Wallace Cooke married **1st)** Eva Marion Johnston; **2nd)** Jean Harpell. No children from either marriage.

1.44513) James Howard Cooke married Mildred Scott and had three sons.

1.44515) Catherine Mabel Cooke married **1st)** Jack Hart (One son), married **2nd)** Walter McDougall (One son), married **3rd)** Norman Adams (Five children)

1.44516) Alice Cornelia Cooke married **1st)** John W. Fraser (Four children), married **2nd)** Bill Hoeg.

1.44517) Gladys Lucinda Cooke married John Vincent MacPherson (Adopted son).

1.44518) Hugh Allan Cooke married Evelyn A. McInnes (One daughter).

1.44519) Lorne Edison Cooke married Ruby Evelyn Burke (5 children).

--

1.4452) Annie Fenton married George Mason (1.4513), son of William and Mary Mason, on Nov. 24/1891. They had **children**: Lottie Mason (married Currie Feltmate), Stephen Mason, George Mason.

1.4453) Katy Fenton married William Clyburn, son of Jesse and Sarah Clyburne, on March 30/1891, as his first wife. He was a widower by 1898. **Child**: Georgina Clyburn, who was brought up for a while by Moody and Lottie Clyburn (She married Amos Childs).

1.4457) James Fenton [CR1.4457] was a miner. He married **1st)** Edna Luddington, daughter of William and Henrietta Luddington of New Harbour in 1911. She died of TB in 1915. He married **2nd)** Annie (Feltmate) Hendsbee, widow of Delbert Hendsbee of Eight Island Lake in 1917. She was the daughter of George and Maud Feltmate of Whitehead, N.S.

1.4458) Lottie Fenton married **1st)** Moody Clyburn, son of William and Betsy Clyburn, on Feb. 6/1901, at Isaac's Harbour, and **2nd)** David E. Johnston, son of Thomas and Priscilla (Cook) Johnston (#1.447), in 1908. **Children**: a daughter, b: @1900, David Johnson, Howard Lawson Johnson, George Warner Johnson.

1.4459) Iva B. Fenton married John F. McDonald on March 28, 1908, at Isaac's Harbour. He was a miner, son of Alexander and Addie McDonald, of East River, Sheet Harbour, Hfx. County.

1.445 10) Olive Fenton lived with her sister Annie Mason and family in 1911, along with two Fenton **children**, nephews of Annie: Howard Fenton and Clarence Fenton.

1.445 11) Love Maud Fenton married Henry (Harry) Hattie on Oct. 2, 1909. He was a son of Alexander Henry and Lydia (Mason) Hattie (#1.4516). **Children**: MacIntosh Hattie (d: a baby), James Athol Hattie (m: Martha Grace), Douglas McKay Hattie (d: age 5), more?

--

1.446) Sophia Matilda Cook married John Henry Kaiser on Aug. 8/1877, at Port Bickerton.
Children:
1.4461) Mortimer Kaiser   b: @ 1869
1.4462) Jacob Kaiser   b: @ 1878

1.4463) Ira Whitman Kaiser	b: Feb. 1/1879	d: May 15, 1953
1.4464) Nancy Jane Kaiser	b: June 4/1880	
1.4465) Ralph Livingstone Kaiser	b: July 7/1882	d: Jan. 9, 1950
1.4466) Elmira May Kaiser	b: Apr. 27/1884	
1.4467) Seymore Kaiser	b: Mar. 15/1886	
1.4468) Bessie Amanda Kaiser	b: Mar. 14/1888	
1.4469) Stillman Kaiser	b: Jan. 27/1890	
1.446 10) Della Kaiser	b: Dec. 16/1891	
1.446 11) Percy Elias Kaiser	b: Aug. 24/1893	
1.446 12) Alexander Foster Kaiser	b: Jan. 9/1897	

1.4461) Mortimer Kaiser married Lottie (Charlotte) Keizer, daughter of Nathaniel Keizer of Fisherman's Harbour, on May 3, 1898. They had a son, William Harold Kaiser, born 1898 (Lived in Kirkland Lake, Ontario in 1946).

1.4462) Jacob Kaiser married Jane Avery, daughter of Charles and Annie Avery, of Larry's River, on June 17, 1898. They lived in various places, including Cape Breton. Their son, Lester Ellsworth Kaiser (b: 1903), was a miner, b: Sydney. He married Marie Harrigan of Springhill in 1929. Another son, Marshall Courtney Kaiser was born in 1899, Port Bickerton. Son Rolland Stanley Kaiser was born in 1905, Port Bickerton (married Margaret Lillian MacDiarmid). A daughter Lena Doris Kaiser, married Vernon Francis Corkum, but later divorced.

1.4463) Whitman Kaiser was a boatbuilder and fisherman. He married Annie May Williams, who was born in Birmingham, England. They had children: Irvin, John Havelock, Lucy Winona (married Ansel Russell). Annie died on June 8, 1955.

1.4464) Nancy Jane Kaiser married John Samuel Taylor, son of Thomas and Rebecca Taylor, on Sept. 29, 1902.

1.4465) Ralph Kaiser married Theresa Harpell, daughter of Jeremiah and Louisa Harpell, on Nov. 11, 1913.

1.4466) Elmira May Kaiser married Stanley Howard Langille, son of Edwin and Victoria Langille, at Tancook, on Oct. 13, 1904.

1.4467) Seymore Kaiser married ? He drowned on March 24, 1926, aged 40, and is buried in Port Dufferin.

1.4468) Amanda Kaiser married Garfield Horton, son of E.F.C. Horton, on Nov. 2, 1911. They had children: Rhoda Frances (m: Asa L. Harpell).

1.4469) Stillman Kaiser married Nina Rudolph, daughter of Herbert Rudolph, on Feb. 9, 1911.

1.446 10) Della Kaiser married Theodore Harpell, son of Jeremiah Harpell, on Aug. 27, 1910.

1.446 11) Percy Kaiser married Florence Hannah Wilson, daughter of Lewis and Mary Matilda Wilson of Spanish Ship Bay, on Feb. 12, 1919.

1.446 12) Alexander Foster Kaiser married Eva May McDonald, daughter of David and Agnes McDonald, on Oct. 11, 1919 at Port Hilford.

--

1.447) Priscilla Cook married Thomas Johnston, Country Harbour Mines.
Children:

1.4471) David E. Johnston	b: 1880
1.4472) Mary C. Johnston	b: 1885
1.4473) Samuel Johnston	b: 1889
1.4474) Elgrada Johnston	b: 1893
1.4475) John A. Johnston	b: 1895
1.4476) Lottie Johnston	b: 1897

1.4471) David Johnston was a miner. He married Lottie Clyburn (1.14458), widow of Moody Clyburn, (daughter of Stephen and Lucinda Fenton) in April, 1908. Their children included a daughter and sons, Howard and George.

1.4473) Samuel Johnson married Hilda Silver, daughter of Charles and Henrietta Silver of Goldboro, on Apr. 22, 1916.

1.4474) Elgrada Johnston married _____ Fox. They lived in the Toronto, Ontario area.

--

1.448) Rebecca Cook was brought up by James and Eliza (Cook) Langley. She married Marcus Keizer, son of John and Nancy Keizer [CR1.448] at Port Bickerton, on Aug. 20/1883. Mark died as the result of an accident in 1947, at age 83. **Note:** *Within the same family, the Kaiser name is spelled various ways.*
Children:

1.4481) Walter A. Kaiser	b: May 19/1882
1.4482) Byron A. Kaiser	b: May 21/1887
1.4483) Forrest Horatio Kaiser	b: Sept. 20/1892
1.4484) Emma Kate Kaiser	b: June 11/1893
1.4485) Sophia Kaiser	b: May 24/1895 No further info.

1.4481) Walter A. Kaiser married Edna Alice Cook (#1.4444).

1.4482) Byron A. Keizer married Laura Johnston, daughter of Campbell Johnston, (CR1.4482) and Mary Jane (Mason) Johnston #1.4512), on Sept. 18, 1908, at Port Bickerton. Their 35 year old daughter, Emma Matilda, died at Trenton, in 1945. **Note:** *The cross at her cemetery plot at Isaac's Harbour gives her name as Emma Jane.*
1.4483) Forrest Kaiser married Winona Corkum, daughter of Ira and Agnes (Kirk) Corkum.

1.4484) Emma K. Kaiser married Howard Harpell, son of Jeremiah and Louisa (Hurst) Harpell in 1912.

--

1.449) Elias Cook married Emma J. Mosher, daughter of Elisha P. and Margaret (Hurley) Mosher, on Dec. 4/1895, at Sherbrooke. **Daughter**: Minnie Rose Cooke. She married Rhueben Bingley, son of John and Mina (Hynds) Bingley, in 1924. They had **children**: Florence Viola (m: John Douglas O'Hara), Garnet Bingley (m: Doris), Winnifred (m: Earl MacPherson), Burnham Bingley; Mary (m: Bray), Lillian (m: Walter Helin & had 16 children, including 2 sets of twins).

~

1.45) Lydia Cook married George Mason, son of William and Mary (Rogers) Mason, on Jan. 13/1830, at Country Harbour, by Rev. Lewis. Lydia died Nov. 14/1866 at Fisherman's Harbour, of paralysis.
Children:
1.451) William Francis Mason	b: May 20/1831
1.452) Wintrop Cook Mason	b: June 27/1837
1.453) Ann Mason	b: Jan. 17/1845
1.454) Daniel/Donald Mason	b: June 11/1849
1.455) Demas Mason	b: @1844 d: Mar. 12/1895
1.456) Henry Mason	b: ?

1.451) William F. Mason was a carpenter. He married **1ˢᵗ)** Mary Hannah Taylor.
Children:
1.4511) Matilda Mason	b: June/1862
1.4512) Mary Jane Mason	b: 1858
1.4513) George Mason	b: 1860
1.4514) Wentworth Mason	b: Jan. 1/1861
1.4515) William Alexander Mason (twin)	b: Aug. 26/1865
1.4516) Lydia Mason (twin)	b: Aug. 26/1865
1.4517) James Henry Mason	b: Oct. 12/1867
1.4518) Thomas Abner Mason	b: June 2/1871

Mary (Taylor) Mason died, and the younger children were placed in various homes in the area. Lydia, Henry and George were placed at the home of John and Agnes Sutherland at Goshen, and William was with the family of David and Hannah Suttis, Indian Harbour Lake.

William F. Mason married **2nd**) Martha Bell (or Arabella) *(See CR1.4414 for notes)*

Children:

1.4519) Charles Francis Mason	b: Aug. 18, 1885
1.451 10) Edward T. Mason	b: July 9, 1887 No further info.
1.451 11) Ira Louis Mason	b: June 10, 1889

There was another child on the 1891 census, Borden Mason, (b: @ 1891), age 1 mo. He is not shown on subsequent census' - probably died by 1901.

1.451 12) William Marple Mason	b: Nov. 20, 1893
1.451 13) Lillian Queen Mason	b: Nov. 6, 1895
1.451 14) Elizabeth Pearl Mason	b: May 17, 1899

William F. and Martha Mason lived in the area of "The Forks" (Glenelg today) and they and their children are shown on the 1901 census.

1.4511) Matilda Mason married Simon Clyburn, son of Ephraim and Hannah (Hallett) Clyburn. **Children**: Mary Emma Clyburn (m: William H. Myers, widower); Drucilla Clyburn (m: Willoughby Silver as his first wife); Simon S. Clyburn (m: Emma May Myers); Alice E. Clyburn (m: Bruce Cook #1.4199); Esther May Clyburn (m: Howard Holley).

1.4512) Mary Jane Mason married Campbell Johnston, son of Benjamin and Eliza (Pringle) Johnston, in 1879. **Children**: Herman W. Johnston, Alfred Johnston, Dellis Johnston (m: Leonard Hudson), Trueman Johnston, Edith Johnston (m: Willoughby Silver as his second wife), Laura Johnston (m: Byron Kaiser), Alberta Johnston (m: James Costello).

1.4513) George Mason, sailor, age 29, married Maggie A. Fenton (1.4452), daughter of Stephen and Lucinda Fenton, in 1891. Their son, George W. Mason, born @ 1900, died at age 36 at Addington Forks, Antigonish County. His wife was Lena Langley, who had been divorced from Tremaine Cook.

1.4514) Wentworth Mason, seaman, age 23, married Louisa Caroline Cook, daughter of Elias and Priscilla Cook (#1.4172) . See information on children under that number.

1.4515) William Alexander Mason migrated to Cambridge, Mass. He married Alma Persjy (b: Sweden), on July 10, 1897. **Children:** Arvid Mason, Clarence Mason, Arthur Mason, Cora Mason, Hilma May Mason, William A. Mason, Eleanor Mason.

1.4516) Lydia Mason married Alexander Hattie, son of William and Christina (Robertson) Hattie, in 1888. **Children**: Harriet Hattie, Henry Hattie (married Love Maud Fenton #1.445 11), Alexander George Hattie, William Anthony Hattie (married Sarah Jordan), more?

1.4517) James Henry Mason died, aged 83 years, 5 months, 19 days at Marshy Hope, Pictou County, on March 26, 1951. He had a daughter, Stella Mae, who married William Baxter of Marshy Hope.

1.4518) Thomas Abner Mason - No further information.

1.4519) Charles Francis Mason was a teamster. He was a veteran of WWI. He married Agnes J. McDonald, who was born in Antigonish. They were married at New Glasgow on June 12, 1907. Witnesses were John N. and Mrs. John N. Mason. They lived in Springhill in 1911 and had **children:** Edward B. (b: May 1908), Christine B. (b: Oct. 1909), Charles S. (b: May 1911). At the time of the 1911 Census, brother William Mason was living with this family. In 1954, Charles was living in Burketon, Ontario.

1.451 11) Ira Louis Mason was a machinist. He was a veteran of WWI. He married Helen Rankin. They had a son, Ira Louis born Dec. 1910, a son Robert, of Trenton, and a daughter Ivy, who married Cornelius Hogan, a miner from New Waterford in 1928. Helen Rankin Mason died on Sept. 7, 1953 and is buried in Auburn Cemetery, Westville, NS. A granddaughter's name is listed - Nellie Douthwright, of Fox Brook Road.

1.451 12) William M. or F. Mason: Went by William Marple Mason and also William Francis Mason. William used the middle name Marple on the Attestation papers prior to WWI. The birth date is given as Nov. 20, 1894. His mother is given as Next of Kin: Martha B. Mason, living in Joggins Mines. In August 1915 she was getting a Separation Allowance paid to her. Then she moved to Stellarton. In 1918, she was widowed, living in Westville. William married in England and lived there for a long time, finally returning to Canada in the 1940's. *His granddaughter Jennifer Rishworth of England, has been searching for information on William for many years, but he seems to have disappeared without a trace. Surely someone knows what happened to William Mason.*

1.451 13) Lillian Queen Mason married Joseph Walsh, miner, son of John and Cassie Walsh of St. Mary's, on June 26, 1909. They lived in Springhill at the time of the 1911 Census, and the family is shown with daughter Bessie Belle, (born Dec. 1910) living with the family of Ira Louis and Helen Mason. Joseph died in 1918 of Spanish Influenza, at Pictou. She remarried Herbert Canning, widower of her sister, Pearl.

1.451 14) Pearl Mason married Herbert Canning on Oct. 6, 1917, at Westville. The marriage was witnessed by Charles Francis Mason and Helen R. Mason (Ira's wife). Pearl died in 1918 of Spanish Influenza. Herbert Canning remarried, in 1919, Lillian Queen Walsh, Pearl's sister.

--

1.452) Wintrop Mason married Louisa Caroline Cook (#1.4172) See information on children under that number.

--

1.455) Demas Mason was a seaman. He migrated first to Prince Edward Island and was living in the Georgetown area in 1870. He married Elizabeth Murphy, daughter of William Murphy, of Prince Edward Island and they migrated to the USA. He died in Newburyport, Mass., of gastritis, age 51, in 1895. (His parents names are given as *William* and Lydia {Cook} Mason). They had **children:**

1.4551) John Mason   b: 1861   Listed as a potter on the 1881 PEI census
1.4552) Mary Jane Mason   b: 1873   d: TB in 1913 in Newburyport
Elizabeth stated on the 1900 US census that she was the mother of 10 children, but only 2 were living at that time.
At the time of the US 1900 Census, John was a Conductor for the Electric Railroad. In 1910, he was a Shoe inspector.

1.4551) John Mason married Sarah M. O'Grady in 1891, at Newburyport. Mass. **Children**:
1.45511) Honora Mason   b: May/1892
1.45512) Elizabeth M. Mason b: May/1895
Neither one were married at the time of the US 1930 census.

~

1.46) John Cook was a cooper. He married Maria Jane Hallett, daughter of John and Sarah (Chalk) Hallett, (CR1.46) on Apr. 30/1835. They lived on the West Side of Country Harbour approx. 5 miles below the head of the tide, then migrated to Shelburne County. They lived in the Ragged Islands area in the late 1800's.
Children:
1.461) John Francis Cook   b: Jan. 30/1836
1.462) Stephen Cook   b Apr. 7/1843
1.463) Sarah Maria Cook   b: May 15/1845   No further info.
1.464) ? (son) Cook   b: Oct. 27/1847   No further info.
1.465) Lucretia Cook   b: @ 1848
1.466) Anna (Annie) Cook   b: Aug. 13/1850
1.467) Lydia Cook   b: Aug.6/1852
1.468) Edward Cook   b: @1855

1.469) Margaret (Maggie) J. Cook   b: @1860

1.461) John Cook, Jr. was a Master Mariner. He married Margaret <u>Matilda</u>
_____. They had **children**:
1.4611) Ella May Cook   b: @ 1866
1.4612) James <u>William</u> Cook   b: @ 1867
1.4613) John Cook   b: Oct. 2/1868
1.4614) Lindsay Cook   b: Jan./1871

--

1.462) Stephen Cook migrated to Shelburne County. He married **1st)**, aged
21, Rebecca Walls, aged 38, on Jan. 17, 1867, at Ragged Islands. He
married **2nd)** Elizabeth Atkins in 1883, at Green Harbour. **Child**:
1.4621) Clara Cook   b: 1871

--

1.465) Lucretia Cook   married **1st)** John Alexander Young, a seaman, son of
John and Barbara Young, in Dec., 1871. They lived in Brighton. She was a
widow by 1881, with two **children**:
1.4651) Florence Olivia Young   b: Nov. 7/1873   d: 1949
1.4652) Laura Louisa Young   b: Feb./1876
Lucretia married **2nd)** William Ennis in 1882. He was a seaman, born in New
York to Edward and Mary Ennis. He died before 1901. **Children**:
1.4653) Frederick Ennis   b: 1882
1.4654) Gertrude May Ennis   b: 1898 d: 1918

1.4651) Florence   Young married James Holland, son of John and Bridget
Holland, at Shelburne, in 1904. Children: Laura May Holland, Annie Bell
Holland, Alexander Holland.

1.4653) Frederick Ennis married Clara Burke, daughter of Robert and Hannah
(Huskins) Burke, from Green Harbour, in 1907. **Children**: William Ennis,
Gladys Ennis, Arthur Ennis.

1.4654) Gertrude Ennis married Frank I. Townsend of East Green Harbour in
1915.

--

1.466) Anna Cook married **1st)** Charles Jones, a mariner who was born in
London, England, on May 1, 1875. He died at sea on Dec. 27, 1875. She
married **2nd)** William Gause, mariner, who was the son of William and
Catherine Gause, of Southampton, England, at Lockeport, in 1880. She
married **3rd)** William H. Allen, a farmer of Brooklyn, Yarmouth County, in 1904.
She married **4th)** Coleman Killam, of Yarmouth, in 1919. She died on Aug. 20,
1930 at Yarmouth.

--

1.467) Lydia Cook died from burns, single, on Nov. 26, 1869, at Ragged Islands, Shelburne County. *The newspaper article from the Presbyterian Witness stated .....as a result of being terribly burned, a young servant girl living with Colin Locke family.*

--

1.468) Edward Cook was a mariner. He married Eliza Jane Corkum, daughter of William and Lucy Corkum, Bridgewater in 1879.

--

1.469) Margaret (Maggie) Cook, age 16, married **1st)** Jeremiah Allen, age 22, at Osborne. on March 24, 1876. **Children**:

1.4691) Maggie Allen   b: 1877
1.4692) Louise Mary Allen   b: 1878   d: Nov. 9/1948   m: Wilson Cook

She married **2nd)** Charles Flinn, a seaman, in 1880 at Shelburne. The two children were raised by her sister, Anna.

~

1.47) Wintrop Cook was a cooper and a fisherman. He married Sarah Ann Beiswanger @ 1846. She was born July 25/1820, and died aged 99 years on Nov. 4/1919. She was known as *Aunt Sally*, and was a familiar sight as she walked from Stormont to the stores at Isaac's Harbour each week. She kept a ball of yarn in the pocket of her apron, and knitted as she walked. On the 1901 census she is listed as a "weaver". Wintrop's brother, James Cook, married her sister Charlotte Eve Beiswanger. (CR1.47W) Wintrop Cook died, aged 77, on July 26/1891. **Children:**

1.471) George Wintrop Cook	b: Mar. 23/1847
1.472) William Charles Cook	b: Sept. 2/1850
1.473) Abraham Jorden Cook	b: Nov. 4/1852
1.474) Charlotte Ann Cook	b: July 26/1855
1.475) John Cook	b: Apr. 23/1859 d: a baby
1.476) Sarah Adalaide Cook	b: Aug. 5/1861
1.477) Eliza Jane Cook	b: @ 1865

1.471) George Cook married Bethia Stewart (b: Apr. 10, 1857), daughter of John and Elizabeth Stewart, Miller, of Stormont. They were married on Dec. 17, 1873, at New Glasgow. He was a mariner, residing at that time at Stillwater, and became a miner for a while. Later, they migrated to Prince Edward Island. **Children:**

1.4711) Henry (Harry) W. Cook	b: July 1, 1876	Mount Uniacke
1.4712) Ernest Cook	b: Mar. 5, 1878	
1.4713) Clarence Cook	b: Aug. 26, 1881	d:June/1968

1.4712) Ernest Cook married Margaret McLean. This family migrated to Massachusetts, USA, and were living there by the time of the 1930 census. All the children were born in Canada (PEI). [CR 1.4712] **Children:**

1.47121) George Wilfred Cook	b: Apr. 17/1903
1.47122) Paul Hubert/Herbert Cook	b: Sept. 2/1904
1.47123) Bertha Cook	b: June 2/1906
1.47124) Mary Adratta Cook	b: Sept. 16/1907
1.47125) Stephen Cook	b: Feb./1909
1.47126) Margaret Viola Cook	b: Oct. 24/1911
1.47127) Olive Mary Cook	b: Sept. 3/1914
1.47128) Ernest Aeneas Cook	b: Jan. 1/1917
1.47129) Mary Alvina Cook	b: Mar. 18/1919
1.4712 10) Amba ? Cook	b: 1923 m: Lionel A. LaPointe

1.4713) Clarence Cook migrated to Boston, where he worked for the Electrical Railway. He never married.

--

1.472) William C. Cook married Hattie A. Fraser from New Brunswick, on March 11/1895. She was born Nov. 10, 1874, and died Nov. 10/1919 of dropsy. William C. Cook was a well-known carpenter and worked for a time in Philadelphia, where he built bridges. He built his own house and some of the furniture in it, including the dining-room table. He taught his son, Charlie, the carpenter trade. When he returned from Philadelphia, William brought back a lime tree and planted it near the end of his driveway at Stormont. It never bears fruit, but it flowers every seven years. William died on Feb. 3/1938.

Child:
1.4721) Charles Albion Cook
b: Jan. 21/1896   d:Sept. 14/1973
He married **1st)** Viola Ann Hayne (b: Mar. 2/1902, d: May 11/1954), daughter of James and Eva (McDonald) Hayne. They had no children. Many years later, he married **2nd)** Alberta (Kirby) Cooke, the widow of Hal Cooke, Isaac's Harbour (#1.41812).

Charlie Cook

--

1.473) Abraham Cook married Sabrina Esther Smith, Melrose, on June 6/1876. They moved to Minnesota. He was lost at Rainy Lake of Lake Superior.

--

67

1.474) Charlotte Ann Cook was a dressmaker. She married Charles A. Musgrave, a widower who was a jeweler. **Children:**
1.4741) Gertrude Musgrave   Married Fred Horley.
      Two children, Charles and Alice.
1.4742) Jennie Musgrave
      Married **1ˢᵗ)** Rudolph Cummings.
      Married **2ⁿᵈ)** Louis Wood. There were no children
      from either of these marriages.

--

1.476) Adalaide Cook married Captain William L. Ross, son of Thomas and Nancy (Nickerson) Ross. She was the second of his four wives; he outlived all of them and died in 1941 of prostate cancer. Addie died while her children were young, and her mother raised her son; her daughter was raised by her Ross grandparents in Shelburne County. Capt. Ross lived in the Cape Negro, Shelburne County area. **Children:**

1.4761) Jairus John Ross	b: Oct. 7/1884	d: 1963
1.4762) Leah Adelaide Ross	b: July 22/1886	

Both children were born in Port LaTour, Shelburne County.

1.4761) Jairus Ross married Margaret Hayne, daughter of William and Viola (McNeil) Hayne. **Child**: 1.47611) Harold Ross   b: & d: 1912

1.4762) Leah Ross married **1ˢᵗ)** Samuel Swain in 1904.
Child: 1.47621) Lottie May Swain   b: 1904 (Married a Thomas)
Leah married **2ⁿᵈ)** Reuben A. Smith, Cape Negro, N.S., in 1909.
Child: 1.47622) Ruby Smith (Married ___ Perry).

~

1.48) James Cook was a cooper. He married Charlotte <u>Eve</u> Beiswanger on April 9/1845. She was born @ 1826. They migrated to Lockeport, Shelburne County, and some of their children also moved there.
Children:

1.481) Guyon Cook	b: Nov. 11/1844	
1.482) Edward James Cook	b: Oct. 19/1846	d: June 8/1901
1.483) Gideon Cook	b: Mar. 24/1848	
1.484) Sarah Ann Cook	b: Mar. 5/1851	d: Mar. 31/1889
1.485) Shadrack Cook	b: Sept. 16/1853	No further info.
1.486) Lucy Oridge Cook	b: May 18/1856	
1.487) Emily Cook	b: Jan. 24/1859	
1.488) John Adam Cook	b: Oct. 19/1861	
1.489) Louisa Laurinda Cook	b: July 29/1864	
1.48 <u>10</u>) Elisha E. Cook	b: Sept. 6/1866	d: Feb. 2/1950
1.48 <u>11</u>) William Malachi Cook	b: Sept. 18/1871	d: young

1.481) Guyon Cook was a Master Mariner. He married Martha McDonald, daughter of Alexander and Olivia McDonald, at Port Jolie in 1870. They lived in Lockeport. In 1904, this family migrated to the USA, living in Boston city at the time of the 1910 census. **Children**:

1.4811) Frank Cook	b: Sept.25/1872
1.4812) James Cook	b: Aug. 26/1874
1.4813) Alexander Cook	b: Dec. 4/1876
1.4814) William H. Cook	b: May 5/1879
1.4815) Ida May Cook	b: @1882
1.4816) Harry L. Cook	b: June 10/1884
1.4817) Grace Cook	b: Apr. 21/1887
1.4818) Alma Ruth Cook	b: Jan. 14/1889
1.4819) Minnie L. Cook	b: Dec. 9/1892

1.481 10) Unknown, but Martha stated on the 1910 census that she had 10 children, and at that time, only 6 were still living. Guyon was a Watchman at a fish wharf. William, Harry, Grace, Alma and Minnie were still at home. One of the sons married a McCoy in 1914, in Mass., USA.

1.4815) Ida Cook married Harry M. Cole, son of Albert and Angenette (Ewell) Cole, at Boston, on Oct. 14/1901.

1.4818) Alma Cook married Wallace C. Wright at Malden, Mass., in 1911.

--

1.482) Edward Cook married Margaret Fenton (b: Nov. 11/1848, d: June 1/1940) on Dec. 5/1871. She was a daughter of Charles and Hannah (Hines) Fenton, and a granddaughter of Benjamin and Amy (Pride) Hines. This family stayed in Stormont/Country Harbour. **Children:**

1.4821) Effie Jane Cook	b: Nov. 4/1872
1.4822) Archibald Fenton Cook	b: July 18/1875
1.4823) Maggie Bell Cook	b: May 3/1877
1.4824) Delilah Bessie Cook	b: Dec. 17/1879
1.4825) Edward Mardon Cook	b: Jan. 15/1883
1.4826) Eva Hannah Cook	b: Aug. 31/1886
1.4827) Charles Gordon Cook	b: July 31/1889 d: 1974

1.4821) Effie Cook lived to be 97 years old. Her daughter, Alma, married ___Burton and had two children.

1.4822) Archibald Cook was a boat builder, and one schooner of 50 tons was built at Stormont near his home. He died, unmarried, aged 26 on May 20/1901, of consumption (T.B.), at the VG Hospital, Halifax.

1.4823) Maggie Bell Cook married George Wilson Hallet, son of John and Marjorie (Johnstone) Hallet, on Sept. 12/1895. She died of T.B. when her children were still young and her three sons were raised by their Hallet

grandparents. He remarried, to Ada B. Hodgson, daughter of Benjamin and Margaret (Hudson) Hodgson and had more children. **Children:**
1.48231) George Hallett   b: Dec./1896
1.48232) Lawrence Archibald Hallet   b: Feb. 20/1898   d: Mar. 2/1967
          (m: Lillian Fenton {1908-1985}; 2 daughters: Alma and Maxine)
1.48233) Wilson Hallet   b: Aug./1902

1.4824) Bessie Delilah Cook married John Campbell Fenton (1861-1953), widower, son of James and Charlotte (Banks) Fenton, on Oct. 31/1900. He had previously been married to Margaret McBain of East River St. Mary's.
Child:
1.48241) Edward Clarence Fenton   b: Apr. 4/1903
          (Married Alice E. Hudson & had 6 children).

--

1.4825) Mardon Cook died on Aug. 16/1914, of tuberculosis.

1.4826) Eva Cook died at age 16, May/1903, of tuberculosis.

1.4827) Gordon Cook married Phoebe Florence Jack, daughter of Alfred and Esther Jane (Mailman) Jack from Gegoggin (now Liscomb), on March 18, 1912. She was born Jan. 8, 1889, and died in 1979. Before her marriage, she worked for the S. R. Giffin family in Goldboro.
They had five **children:** Eva (m: Elijah Clyburne); Arch (m: Marguerite Smith; Greta (m: **1st**) Harry Silver, **2nd**) George Ball; Phyllis (m: Malcolm Martin; Vincent (m: Vina Jackson).

Gordon Cook

--

1.483) Gideon Cook married Margaret Holley, daughter of James and Elizabeth (McMillan) Holley from Isaac's Harbour, in 1870. This family moved to the Lockport, N.S. area, then Yarmouth, N.S., then to Boston, Mass., where he was a cooper in a slaughterhouse in 1910. Margaret died in 1912, in Boston.
Children:
1.4831) Arthur Wilson Cook   b: Apr. 4/1870   d: 1952
1.4832) Edith Cook   b: @ 1873 No further information

1.4833) Bessie Ernestine Cook	b: Feb. 1/1875	
1.4834) Henry Roland Cook	b: Apr. 5/1877	d: 1936
1.4835) William W. Cook	b: @ 1883	

1.4831) Wilson Cook was born at Drum Head, Guysborough County, where his father was a cooper. He married Mary Louise Allen, daughter of Jeremiah and Margaret Allen (#1.469) of Lockeport, on Nov. 2, 1900, at Yarmouth. Wilson narrowly escaped drowning when the *City of Monticello* sank. [CR1.4831]
Children:
1.48311) Arthur Wilson Cook   b: 1901
          Married Elizabeth May Nickerson in 1920.
1.48312) Cecil Leroy Cook   b: 1903
1.48313) George Wilbert Cook   b: 1910
          Married Dorothy Margaret Cann in 1931.

1.4833) Bessie E. Cook married Joseph H. Crowell, a lumberman from Kemptville, in 1896. **Children**:
1.48331) Everett Crowell   b: 1897
1.48332) Margaret Crowell   b: 1906

1.4834) Roland Cook married Carrie ?__. He migrated to Yarmouth area, and worked at the C.N.R. station there. They had a **daughter**:
1.48341) Emily Cook

1.4835) William W. Cook migrated to Massachusetts, where he was a sheet metal worker. He married Etta M. Pitman, daughter of Andrew and Louise (Nickerson) Pitman of Yarmouth. **Children**:
1.48351) Eva Cook   b: 1909
1.48352) W. Wallace Cook   b: 1910   d: 1 yr. of pneumonia
          following an operation for harelip & straightening of the nose.
1.48353) Eleanor Cook   b: 1914

--

1.484) Sarah Ann Cook married James MacDonald, shoemaker, of Isaac's Harbour. (He was born at St. Mary's, a son of Duncan and Mary A. McDonald.) They were married on Dec. 28/1870.
Children:
1.4841) Mary Eva MacDonald   (Married James Hayne, butcher. They were the parents of Viola Hayne, who married Charlie Cook #1.4721. Their other children were: Levi R. Hayne (m: Marion {MacArthur} Taker, Margaret W.

Hayne, George Rufus Hayne {m: Marjorie Hodgson}).
1.4842) Ellsworth MacDonald (daughter).

--

1.486) Lucy Oridge Cook married **1st)** Henry Seaboyer, a teamster, of Jordan River. **Children**:
1.4861) Robert Seaboyer   b: @1880
1.4862) Lucy Seaboyer   b: @ 1885
Lucy worked as a servant at a hotel run by the Quinlan family in Shelburne in 1891. Her daughter Lucy lived with her grandmother Eve Cook. She maried **2nd)** John Campbell Bethune, a widower, who was born in Scotland. They married in 1893. He was a surveyor of lumber at the time, later becoming a fisherman. **Child**:
1.4863) Emily Cooke Bethune   b: 1899 East Jordan
John Campbell Bethune died on April 21, 1914, found dead in his boat. *"Supposed heart disease"*.

--

1.487) Emily Cook married Thomas Rawlings, a mariner who was born in London. He became a barber at Lockeport. He was a son of Thomas and Caroline (Copeland) Rawlings. They married at Lockeport in 1878.
Children:
1.4871) Robert Henry Rawlings   b: Oct. 23/1879 He was a veteran of
       WWI. He married Mary Fox & had a **daughter**   Ruby Mae Rawlings.
1.4872) Adina Rawlings   b: Jan. 7/1885
1.4873) Eva Rawlings   b: Jan. 17/1889
1.4874) Raymond Clifford Rawlings   b: Jan. 25/1890   d: 1937
       He also was a barber at Lockeport. He married Artie Arista Moore,
       and they had a son, Douglas
1.4875) Isabel Archer Rawlings   b: Aug. 28/1894

--

1.488) John Adam Cook migrated to Shelburne County, where he married Lenora Bell Fenton, [CR1.487] then they returned to live at Isaac's Harbour. There was a daughter listed on the 1911 census, Belle, born June 1898, but I have not been able to trace her further. Lenora died on Oct. 1, 1912, aged 43. Her death record states, "This death was caused by the woman falling into her own well".

John Adam Cook [CR1.488]

--

1.489) Louisa Cook married Ebenezer Shupe, a lumberman from Jordan River, in 1882. He was born in Charleston.
Children:

1.4891) Aubrey Chester Shupe	b: 1884
1.4892) Nora Blanche Shupe	b: July 14/1885
1.4893) Ernest Shupe	b: 1887
1.4894) Tingley L. Shupe	b: 1889 drowned 1914
1.4895) Daughter (Janthie?)Shupe	b: Oct. 21/1891
1.4896) Norman Shupe	b: Sept. 29/1893
1.4897) Hibbert Shupe	b: Jan. 23/1896
1.4895) Greta Helen Shupe	b: Jan. 14/1898
1.4896) Jessie Beatrice Shupe	b: 1901

Later, Eben and Louisa migrated to Worcester, Mass., and were living there in 1929, where he worked as a salesman. City directories show this couple in Worcester as late as 1944.

--

1.48 10) Elisha Cook lived at Lockeport, N.S. He was a carpenter by trade. He married Priscilla Hann, originally from Newfoundland, in 1891. He was a member of the Masonic Taylor Lodge, an elder and trustee of the United Church, and the Superintendent of the United Church Sunday School. He died at age 83.

1.49) Francis (Frank) Cook (CR1.49) married Sarah Ann Hallet, daughter of John and Sarah (Chalk) Hallet (CR1.46). Some of their children were born in Halifax.

Children:

1.491) Eliza Jane Cook	b: Oct. 13/1844	d: Feb.28/1925
1.492) William Francis Cook	b: Dec. 4/1845	d: May 28/1867
1.493) Annie Maria Cook	b: Jan. 17/1848	d: Oct. 14, 1925
1.494) Thomas David Cook	b: June 20/1852	d: Apr. 23/1922
1.495) Howard Elijah Cook	b: July 31/1853	d: Sept. 1941
1.496) Olivia Bethia Cook	b: Nov. 26/1863	d: 1939

1.491) Eliza Jane Cook married James Langley, Shipwright, on Dec. 14/1866, at Halifax, N.S.

Children: *There were eleven children in this family.*

1.4911) Alma Langley	b: @ 1867
1.4912) Abner James Langley	b: @ 1868
1.4913) William Everett Langley	b: Mar. 19/1870
1.4914) Arthur H. Langley	b: Dec. 22/1871
1.4915) Orris Belle Langley	b: Mar. 25/1874
1.4916) Elijah M. Langley	b: Mar. 25/1876

1.4914) Arthur Langley, butcher, married Bertha A. Davidson, (b: 1873, d: 1957), daughter of James and Mary Davidson, on Feb. 27/1895, at Isaac's Harbour.

Children:

1.49141) Lena Mae Langley	b: May 30/1895	d: May 18/1966
1.49142) Hilda Lee Langley	b: Oct. 12/1904	
1.49143) Freda B. Langley	b: 1900	d: 1969
1.49144) Inez Langley	b: 1911	d: July 7/1992
1.49145) Hetty Langley	b: Sept. 8/1903	d: 1978
1.49146) Grace Langley	b: Aug. 20/1908	d: Oct. 24/1972
1.49147) Chester Langley	b: June 3/1902	d: Dec. 18/1968
1.49148) Edith Langley	b: Oct. 8/1915	

1.4912) Abner Langley was lost at sea in 1890. (CR1.4912)

1.4915) Belle Langley married Aaron Hodgson. They lived at Isaac's Harbour North, where they ran the post office from their home. In later years, Belle operated a small clothing store also from her home. She had a wonderful flower garden, and had tea parties there in the summer months.

Child:

1.49151) Louie Mae Roberts (adopted)	d: June/1992

--

1.492) William F. Cook was drowned on May 28/1867, at Isaac's Harbour. He was unmarried.

--

1.493) Annie Maria Cook married Elijah Richardson, son of James & Eunice Richardson, Jeddore, on Nov. 29, 1869. She is buried in Camp Hill Cemetery, Halifax.
Children:
1.4931) Violet Richardson, who married Capt. T. H. Giffin in 1919
1.4932) Frank Richardson (moved to Alberta)

--

1.494) Thomas D. Cook was first a Master Mariner, then a captain of vessels that sailed to the West Indies. He became a merchant with a large warehouse (dry goods and fish), and wharf at Isaac's Harbour. He married **1st)** Elizabeth B. Giffin (b:1854, d: 1905) on Apr. 26/1878.
Children:

1.4941) Walter Seymour Cook	b: Nov. 22, 1878	
1.4942) Lotty <u>Odessa</u> Cook (Dessie)	b: 1881	
1.4943) Ella Bessie Cook	b: 1883	d: Jan. 26/1954
1.4944) Truman Bishop Cook	b: 1885	d: Oct. 29/1960
1.4945) Lida Mabel Cook	b: Nov. 27/1887	
1.4946) Price Giffin Cook (adopted)	b: ?	

Thomas D. Cook married **2nd)** Annie Catherine (MacMillan) Sinclair of Peabody, Mass., U.S.A. on Nov. 1/1910. She was born in Antigonish, a daughter of Hugh and Barbara MacMillan.

1.4941) Walter Cook married **1st)** Bessie B. Silver @ 1902. Had son Deane Alva Cooke, b: 1904, at Goldboro.
He married **2nd)** Ruby ?

1.4942) Dessie Cook never married. She died at Tatamagouche, N.S. In 1956.

1.4943) Ella B. Cook married William D. Giffin @ 1906.

1.4944) Truman B. Cook married Lena Margaret Fraser in 1908 at Stellarton, N.S. They had **children:** Clarence Fraser Cook b: Oct. 27/1908, and Fraser Giffin Cooke b: Sept. 6/1910.

1.4945) Lida Cook married James Clish Ross, son of Daniel and Margaret (Clish) Ross. on Dec. 12/1911. They lived at Stellarton, N.S.

--

1.495) Howard Elijah Cooke was a sea captain at the age of 19 years, then became a Minister. He married Annie Miller in Halifax, on June 19, 1882. He lived and preached at Burtt's Corner, New Brunswick for over 30 years. (CR1.495)They had a **daughter**, Violet May Cook, born Oct. 14, 1882.

--

1.496) Olivia Bethia Cook married John William Rhude, son of Simeon and Mary Ann Rhude from Indian Harbour in 1875. He became a sea Captain, as his father also was.
Children:

1.4961) Maude Estella Rhude	b: @1879	d: age 15
1.4962) Bertha Rhude	b: @1880	m: Neil McGinnis
1.4963) Grace Lillian Rhude	b: @1886	m: David J. Keeler
1.4964) Herman Harry Rhude	b: Jan. 11/1890	d: 1949

This ends the section on the
Isaac's Harbour/Country Harbour Cookes

1.5) Ambrose Cook was a tailor. He married Eleanor Bigsby [CR1.5] on May 29/ 1802, at St. Matthew's Presbyterian Church, Halifax. They lived at Cook's Cove. **Children:**

1.51) Harriet Cook	b: Mar. 26/1803
1.52) Eleanor/Ellen Cook	b: Oct. 5/1805
1.53) Mary Charlotte Cook	b: Nov.7/1808
1.54) Ann Cook	b: June 4/1811 No further info.
1.55) Deborah Godfrey Cook	b: Oct. 28/1814
1.56) Sarah Cook	b: @1819

1.51) Harriet Cook never married.

--

1.52) Eleanor Cook married William Edward Cook (#2.6) on Jan. 3/1826.

--

1.53) Mary C. Cook married Thomas Horton (# 1. 2 11) **Children:**
1.531) Charity Horton - Married Elias Spanks on Dec. 30/1858
1.532) Esther Marshall Horton - Married George Washington Horton *(Their daughter, Armenia Cooke Horton married Robert Mason, Country Harbour. Another daughter, Victoria Horton, married Albert Mason, Country Harbour.)*
1.533) Elizabeth Horton
1.534) Eleanor Horton

--

1.55) Deborah Cook married John G. Gratto from River John, Pictou Co., on July 7/1840.

--

1.56) Sarah Cook married John Godfrey Peart Cook (#1.1061) on Oct. 12/1841. Her marriage, as noted in the Acadian Recorder, referred to her as the fourth daughter of Ambrose Cook, although there is record of five older sisters.

~

1.6) Edmund Cook married Elizabeth Hooten/Whooten.   They lived at Cook's Cove. The 1817 census showed a total of six in this family: 3 boys and 1 girl plus Edmund and wife. 1 "American" and 5 "Acadians" - Edmund was born in the U.S. In the 1840's most of this family had migrated to Georgetown, Maine. **Children:**

1.61) Edmund Cook	bapt. June 5/1814	
1.62) Robert Cook	b: @ 1818	d: 1897
1.63) Sarah Demas Cook	b: Jan. 19/1819	
1.64) William Owen Heffernan Cook	b: Aug. 19/1827	
1.65) Demas Samuel Cook	b: Nov. 23/1829	
1.66) Joseph M. Cook	b: @1833	
1.67) Gideon S. Cook	b: @1836	

1.61) Edmund Cook married Lucy Elizabeth Allen, daughter of James T. Allen and Lucy (Blatchford) Allen, on Jan. 3, 1842, at Gloucester. **Children:**

1.611) Julia Ann Cook	b: @ 1844
1.612) Edmund Cook, Jr.	b: Sept. 22/1845
1.613) Caroline Cook	b: Mar. 22/1848
1.614) Lemuel Cook	b: @1850
1.615) William Cook	b: Apr. 17/1852

Edmund Cook drowned on Mar. 10, 1852. [CR1.61] His widow, age 30, married Watson Middleton in 1857. It was his second marriage as well; both had small children.

1.611) Julia Cook married William Calvin Herrick, at Gloucester. She died of heart disease at age 35. **Children**:

1.6111) Amos Watson Herrick	b: 1863
1.6112) Carrie Herrick	b: @

1.612) Edmund Cook, Jr. married Lizzie M. Day, daughter of Joseph and Elizabeth (Chard) Day, at Gloucester, in 1870.

1.613) Caroline Cook married Henry A. Howard, of Beverly, Mass. A niece, Carrie Herrick, lived with them.

--

1.62) Robert Cook married **1st)** Rhoda Witham, on Jan. 6, 1842, at Gloucester. She died in 1863. **Children:**

1.621) Rhoda E. Cook	b: @ 1843	d: 1846
1.622) George H. Cook	b: @ 1844	Married Amelia F. Emery
1.623) Samuel/Lemuel E. Cook	b: @ 1845	d: 1846 Scarlet fever
1.624) Mary Eliza (May)	b: @ 1847	Married Horace C. Kelly
1.625) Anna E. Cook	b: @ 1856	

He married **2nd)** Sophia E. McKenzie, at Gloucester, in 1864.
Child:
1.626) Ella F. Cook (Married Charles H. Kendall, Jr. in 1869).

--

1.64) William O. Cook was a ship carpenter. He migrated first to Georgetown, Maine, then to Gloucester, Mass., and became naturalized in 1856. He married Caroline Allen, daughter of James T. Allen and Lucy (Blatchford) Allen. (She was a sister to his brother Edmund's wife.) William died in 1909, at the Oddfellows Home, Worcester, Mass. **Children**:

1.641) Frank D. Cook	b: 1852 (was a painter)
1.642) William E. Cook	b: 1855
1.643) Lucy Mary Cook	b: 1862

1.644) Elizabeth (Lizzie) G. Cook (married Arthur W. Hall, a wharf builder in 1888. They had a large family).

--

1.65) Samuel Cook was a sea captain. [CR1.65] He married Sarah (Sally) Snowman, daughter of Oliver and Charlotte (Saddler) Snowman. He lived to be 90 years old and spent his last days at a Home for the Aged in Bath, where he died in 1920.

Children:

1.651) Dorinda F. Cook	b: @ 1852 (Married Nichols Blaisdell)
1.652) Albertine Cook	b: @ 1850 (Married Edward Rowe)
1.653) Martha E. Cook	b: @ 1851
1.654) Edward E. Cook	b: @ 1850
1.655) Charles F. Cook	b: @ 1853

--

1.66) Joseph Cook married Sarah B. Williams. **Child:**
1.661) Gideon F. Cook   b: @ 1856 He married Julia A. (Oates) Hadley, daughter of William A. and Julia A (Sayward) Oates, at Gloucester, in 1882.

--

1.67) Gideon Cook married Cordelia Campbell, daughter of Alexander and Nancy Campbell of Georgetown, Maine. They migrated to Chelsea, Mass.

Children:

1.671) Mary E. Cook	b: @ 1854
1.672) Edward Cook	b: @ 1859
1.673) Alexander Cook	b: @ 1862
1.674) George A. Cook	b: @ 1864
1.675) Winfield Cook	b: @ 1868
1.676) Thomas Cook	b: @ 1870
1.677) Fred Cook	b: @ 1873

1.674) George A. Cook was a butcher. He married Lena M. Card (b: Vermont to James and Emma Card). **Child**:
1.6741) Alexander Gideon Cook   b: @ 1899 W W 2 Veteran & a Mason

1.675) Winfield Cook was a Type Inspector. He married Elizabeth J. McKenzie (b: Dartmouth, NS, to William and Elizabeth J. McKenzie). They lived in Chelsea, Mass.

1.676) Thomas Cook was a Saw Filer. He married Elizabeth C. Totten.

~

1.7) Samuel Cook ? No further information. He was not mentioned on the estate papers dealing with his father's death @ 1837, so he probably died before that time.

~

1.8) Ann Cook married Matthew Hutcheson, cooper, on April 17/1806 and migrated to Cape Canso. She died Jan. 28 /1868. Matthew, along with his sons Matthew, Elias and John, can be found holding various positions within the town of Canso (Wilmot). They were Inspector of Barrels, Staves & Hoops, Hogreaves, Fence Viewers, Overseers of the Poor, etc. in the 1820's and 1830's.

Children:

1.81) Matthew Hutcheson	b: Mar. 6/1807	d: 1843
1.82) John Hutcheson	b: @ 1810	d: Feb. 14/1891
1.83) William Archibald Hutcheson	b: Sept. 7/1815	
1.84) Isaiah Hutcheson	b: @ 1817	
1.85) Francis Hutcheson	b: @ 1818	
1.86) Lydia Hutcheson	b: July 22/1822	
1.87) Demus Cook Hutcheson	b: Oct. 3/1823	
1.88) Archibald Hutcheson	b: @ 1826 bapt. June 30, 1831 at St. John's Anglican Church, Arichat	
1.89) Janet (or Jane) Hutcheson	b: July 12/1830	
1.8 10) Elias Hutcheson	b: Feb. 14, 1810 at P.E.I.	d: Jan. 19, 1893

1.81) Matthew Hutcheson married Mary Eleanor (Harty) Foster on Aug. 24, 1836. She was the widow of James Foster (#1.96).

--

1.82) John Hutcheson married Sarah J. Scott (b: 1819, d: May 9, 1872). She was a daughter of Abijah Scott. John Hutcheson was appointed a Petit Constable around 1830, in Canso. This family moved back to Guysborough, where he was a merchant. On other documents he is listed as a sea captain.

Children:

1.821) Joseph Hart Hutcheson	b: 1858	d: Oct. 8/1873 age 15, of consumption
1.822) Ruth Maria Hutcheson	b: 1846	d: Oct. 24/1847
1.823) John R. Hutcheson	b: @1852	
1.824) William Scott Hutcheson	b: @1841	d: Nov. 30/1916
1.825) Lucinda A. Hutcheson	b: Sept. 23/1853	d:Nov. 26/ 1929

1.823) John R. Hutcheson married Alice M. Peebles, daughter of James and Maria Peebles, of Port Mulgrave, on Jan. 31, 1882.

1.824) William Scott Hutcheson married **1ˢᵗ)** Elizabeth Grant on Jan. 4, 1866, at Guysborough. The marriage record has conflicting information: in the margin it is written Elizabeth Grant, but the bride's name is Lizzie Morrison, age 22, born at New Harbour, daughter of Andrew Sangster. The Hutcheson family moved to Halifax, where he was a merchant (Some records say Wholesale merchant).

He married **2nd)** Rebecca Brownell, daughter of Edward and Margaret Brownell of Amherst Shore, on Feb. 6, 1895. He is buried in Pine Grove Cemetery, Oxford, where the family moved in the late 1800's.

Children:

1.8241) Lillian Isabell Hutcheson	b: Mar. 13, 1867	
(m: **1st)** James O'Bryan, **2nd)** Whitman)		
1.8242) Bessie Maud Hutcheson	b: Apr. 28, 1869	

Never married. She was a Milliner. She died of cancer of the gall bladder, age 72, on Dec. 16, 1940.)

1.8243) Cora Estel Hutcheson	b: Apr. 13, 1871
1.8244) Charles Edward Hutcheson	b: Feb. 13, 1884
1.8245) Pearl Hutcheson	b: 1886
1.8246) Daisy Hutcheson	b: 1889

Married Charles E. Bryant on June 3, 1909 at Newport Landing, Hants Co., NS.

1.8247) Florence Edith Hutcheson   b: Jan. 30, 1899

1.8248) Baby stillborn, 1896. Buried at Camp Hill Cemetery, Halifax

1.8249) Baby boy who died at 7 days old in 1896, buried at Camp Hill Cemetery, Halifax.

1.825) Lucinda A. Hutcheson married Lewis E. Hart, on Dec. 14, 1881. He was a Merchant, son of William and Letitia Hart.

Children:

1.8251) Vernon Noble Hart	b: Nov. 20, 1882	
1.8252) William Hart	b: May/1884	d: 1917
1.8253) Norman Hart	b: 1888	
1.8254) Marion Louise Hart	b: Mar. 1895	

--

1.83) William Archibald Hutcheson was a Master Shipbuilder at Canso. He married **1st)** Mary ? (born Indian Harbour). She drowned at sea during the August Gale, 1873. He married **2nd)** Sarah Jane O'Hara, daughter of Capt. James and Jennie O'Hara, on Dec. 16, 1874, at Canso. He d. Kennebunkport, Me., May 7, 1892   **Child:**

1.831) William James Hutcheson   b: Oct. 6, 1876

He married Harriet Hannah Pierce on July 19, 1905 at Somerville, Mass. He was a writer for a newspaper. Their daughter, Minna S. Hutcheson was b: 1908.

--

1.86) Lydia Hutcheson [C105] married Benamin N. Pentz about 1845.
Children:

1.861) Rhoda Maria Pentz	b: Feb 13, 1850 at Canso
1.862) Archibald Francis Pentz	b: June 9, 1851
1.863) John Wesley Pentz	b: June 7, 1854
1.864) Eurma Sarah Harrington Pentz	b: Feb 18, 1857
1.865) William H. Pentz	b: 1859
1.867) Annie Elizabeth Pentz	b: 1862
	died 1910, Newtonville, Mass.

1.861) Rhoda Maria Pentz married Leonard P. Morris (b: abt 1850, adopted) and they had at least one **daughter:** 1.8611) Wilna Margaret Morris b: 1881. She married Allen Edwy Davis b: April 18, 1884.

--

1.87) Demas Hutcheson married Caroline Lyle from Melford. They were married at Mulgrave on Dec. 29, 1845. They had children, including a son, Henry T. Hutcheson.

--

1.8 10) Elias Hutcheson married 1st) Ann Stewart 2nd) Ann Foster Cummings, daughter of James and Mary (Foster) Cummings (#1.91) . He migrated to Prince Edward Island and had **children:** Elizabeth Ann Hutcheson (b: 1838), John Francis Hutcheson (b: 1840), Isabel Hutcheson (b: 1849), William A. Hutcheson (b: 1850).

~

1.9) Mary Cook married William Foster on Jan. 6/1791. He was one of the tavern-keepers at Guysborough, and in 1802 was granted a free license for the sale of intoxicating liquors. Mary died in August, 1825, and her death was reported in the Acadian Recorder: "Died at Guysborough, Mrs. Mary Foster. Left husband, large family". William died at age 85, in January, 1833. Some of their **Children:**

1.91) Mary Foster	bapt. June 3/1792	
1.92) John Foster	b: @ 1793	d: Jan. 1845
1.93) Ann Foster	b: Oct. 9/1797	d: Jan. 1893
1.94) Elizabeth Foster	b: Nov. 15/1799	
1.95) William Nixon Foster	b: Apr. 28/1803	
1.96) Elias Foster	b: Sept.11/1805	
1.97) James Foster	b: Dec. 5/1807	d: Dec.25/1833
1.98) Thomas Foster	b: May 13/1810	d: Mar. 27/1873 of Consumption

1.91) Mary Foster married James Cummings. They had 8 **children**, of which one daughter, Ann Foster Cummings, married Elias Hutcheson (# 1.8 10)on June 27, 1836.

--

1.93) Ann Foster married Moses Cook (#4.2).

--

1.96) Elias Foster married Elizabeth Sarah Hughes on Feb. 15, 1831.She was a daughter of Thomas and Sarah (Aikens) Hughes.
Children:

1.961) William Thomas Foster	b: Dec. 12/1831	d: Oct. 3, 1875
1.962) Mary Jane Foster	b: Apr. 7/1834	
1.963) Elias Foster	b: July 7/1836	d: Sept./1860
1.964) James Francis Foster	b: July 29/1840	
1.965) Ann Cook Foster	b: Nov. 12/1842	d: Aug./1855
1.966) Charles Shreve Foster	b: July 16/1846	

> *Charles Foster, of Guysborough, N.S. was lost from the Schooner Florence Reed, out of Gloucester, Mass., on Nov. 10/1868.*

1.967) Moses Cook Foster   b: Jan. 6/1850

1.961) William Thomas Foster married Lydia M. Henderson, daughter of Alexander and Isabel Henderson on Feb. 27, 1856, at Manchester. (The date of Feb. 27 should be accurate - on 6 of his children's birth records, that is the date given of their marriage, however the year varies from 1836, 1846, 1855, 1856. This family migrated to Isaac's Harbour, where he was a merchant, among other things. He became the Lightkeeper at Green Island, (as was his son, James Alexander Foster). After he died of consumption, Lydia married Rufus Hale, a Merchant, on Jan. 2, 1885. They lived in Antigonish.
Children:
1.9611) William Thomas Foster   b: Apr. 27/1857
        Drowned Feb. 25, 1873, Goose Island (off Marie Joseph)
1.9612) James Alexander Foster   b: Dec. 17/1858
        Lightkeeper of Green Island (off Country Harbour). Married Louisa A. Crooks, Jan. 31, 1882, daughter of Charles and Susan Crooks of Seal Harbour.
1.9613) Maria Nixon Foster   b: Mar. 7/1862 Married John J. Langley, a fisherman of Seal Harbour, son of Edward and Elizabeth Langley, at Isaac's Harbour, on Nov. 27, 1883.
1.9614) Maud Isabella Foster   b: July 25/1865 Married Albert W. Kennie, Dentist, of Antigonish. He was born in Albert County. They married on Aug. 6, 1888.
1.9615) Elizabeth Foster   b: at Isaac's Harbour, July 8, 1868.

1.9616) Emma Elizabeth Foster   b: at Isaac's Harbour. Married James
        Henry McDougall, who was a Marble Cutter. He was born at New
        Glasgow, son of Donald and Susan McDougall. They married on
        Sept. 26, 1898, at Antigonish.
1.9617) Annie May Foster   b: @1876 at Isaac's Harbour. She
        married Frederick H. Randall, a widower, who was a Trader. He was
        born at Boston, USA (but his father had been born at Antigonish).
        They were married at Antigonish, at her brother Tupper Foster's home,
        on Hawthorne Street, on Mar. 30, 1921.
1.9618) Elias Tupper Foster   b: Oct. 22, 1866. He became a
        druggist at Antigonish, where he owned a drugstore. He married
        Laura Stephens, who was born in Hants County. They had children:
        Katherine Stephens Foster b: Oct. 5, 1902, at Antigonish, and William
        Gordon Foster, b: Aug. 5, 1907, at Antigonish (He migrated to P.E.I.
        and then to Halifax.) Tupper died on Sept. 19, 1940 of T.B., at St.
        Martha's Hospital, Antigonish.
1.9619) Lydia Letitia Foster   b: July 4, 1872 at Isaac's Harbour.
1.961 10) William Thomas Foster   b: July 10, 1875 at Isaac's Harbour.
        He became a druggist, along with his uncle Tupper Foster, at
        Antigonish. He married Alice Louise Henry, a nurse, daughter of R. N.
        and Laura Henry of Antigonish. They had a son: Courtney Henry
        Foster b: Aug. 9, 1899, at Antigonish. Alice died "abroad" in 1919, of
        poisoning from an overdose of medicine.

--

1.967) Moses Cook Foster was a carriage maker. He married Ida Mary
Nieforth.
Children:
1.9671) William Herbert Foster   b: July 2/1912
1.9672) Helen Maud Foster   b: Sept. 17/1899
1.9673) Arthur James Foster   b: Aug. 12, 1902
1.9674) Lillian Clemence   b: Apr. 7, 1908

--

1.97) James Foster married Mary Eleanor Harty.
Child:
1.971) Michael Harty Foster   b: Dec. 7/1833
James Foster died Dec. 25, 1833. His widow married Matthew Hutcheson (#
1.81) on Aug. 24, 1836.

--

1.98) Thomas Foster married Mary Patterson Peart on May 25, 1854. She was
a daughter of John Godfrey and Maria (Nixon) Peart.

--

1. <u>10</u>) John Cook married Elizabeth Callahan on May 22/1801. She was born @ 1782 and died Oct. 2/1843. They lived in the area of Bantry, or, as it was called on school records, Salmon River Bridge. In later years John migrated with some of his grown children to Minnesota.

Children:
1. <u>10</u> 1) William Edward Cook   b: June 12/1802
1. <u>10</u> 2) Lydia Cook   b: Feb. 8/1804
1. <u>10</u> 3) Ruth Cook   b: @ 1805
1. <u>10</u> 4) Diana Cook   b: Apr. 14/1809
1. <u>10</u> 5) Susannah Horton Cook   b: Dec. 14/1811
1. <u>10</u> 6) John Godfrey Peart Cook   b: July 11/1818
1. <u>10</u> 7) Francis Cook   b: @ 1821

1. <u>10</u> 1) William <u>Edward</u> Cook was a farmer. He married Eleanor Cook ^(CR1.10 1) (#1.52) on Jan. 3/1826.

Children:

	b:	d:
1. <u>10</u> 11) Moses Cook	b: Oct. 22/1826	d: 1900
1. <u>10</u> 12) George Cook	b: @ 1828	
1. <u>10</u> 13) Lydia Cook	b:	
1. <u>10</u> 14) Maria Cook	b:	
1. <u>10</u> 15) Frank Cook	b:	d: 19 years
1. <u>10</u> 16) William Cook	b:	d: young
1. <u>10</u> 17) Amelia Cook	b:	
1. <u>10</u> 18) Sarah E. Cook	b: @ 1842	
1. <u>10</u> 19) John C. Cook	b: Mar. 22/1844	d: May/1922

They also brought up Dora Horton, (b: @ 1860), daughter of Lydia Horton. Dora married Robert Cook (#4.133).

1. <u>10</u> 11) Moses Cook married Mary <u>Jane</u> McIntyre in Essex, Mass., where he was a shoe manufacturer, on July 5, 1854.

Children:
1. <u>10</u> 111) Clarence E. Cook   b: 1857
1. <u>10</u> 112) Loring C. Cook   b: 1858
1. <u>10</u> 113) Frank A. Cook   b: 1864
1. <u>10</u> 114) Carrie F. Cook   b: 1866
1. <u>10</u> 115) Grace E. Cook   b: 1868
1. <u>10</u> 116) Lottie G. Cook   b: 1873

1. <u>10</u> 112) Loring C. Cook married Lucy S. _____ and had children: Loring A. Cook, Horace S. Cook, Mason B. Cook and Lucy H. Cook.

1. <u>10</u> 12) George Cook married ? They lived in U.S.A. **Child:**
1. <u>10</u> 121) John Cook   - No further information

1. <u>10</u> 13) Lydia Cook married Fritz Harvey, a blacksmith at Gloucester, son of Joseph and Charlotte Harvey.

1. <u>10</u> 14) Maria Cook married Nathanial Witham. They had two children: Nathanial (b: 1855) and Ella (b: 1859). At the time of the 1860 census, Nathaniel was a farm worker in Gloucester, Mass. Their parents are not found on the 1870 census, but the two children lived with her sister Sarah's family.

1. <u>10</u> 17) Amelia Cook married Michael Harty, a carpenter from Gloucester, Mass., on Jan. 4/1860. They lived with her sister Maria at the time the US census was taken in 1860. She had a son, George E. Harty (b: 1863), who died of consumption, as she did, both of them in 1864.

1. <u>10</u> 18) Sarah Cook married John S. Coffin. They had children: Edward, John and Sarah E. and lived in Gloucester, Mass. At the time of the US 1870 census, also living with this family were Nathanial Witham, age 15, fisherman, and Ella Witham, age 11, attending school. These were her sister Maria's children.

1. <u>10</u> 19) John C. Cook, shoemaker, married Amelia Edson Cook (#4.137), on March 21/1878. This family lived at Roachvale. John C. Cook died on May 10/1922.
Children:
1. <u>10</u> 191) Florence Nightingale Cook   b: @ 1879
1. <u>10</u> 192) Cordelia Cook   b: Jan. 1/1881
1. <u>10</u> 193) Lorne Cook   b: Mar. 24/1883
1. <u>10</u> 194) Victoria Cook   b: Apr. 1/1886

1. <u>10</u> 191) Florence Cook migrated to Mass. as a young girl,where she trained to be a nurse. She married William Burton Grant, on Nov. 22/1899. (Her sister Vicky married her brother-in-law, George Grant, and Florence and Will brought up their two youngest children, after George was killed by a falling tree, while working in the woods).
Children:
1. <u>10</u> 1911) Florence Nightingale Grant   b: Apr. 25/1909
1. <u>10</u> 1912) Victor Grant
1. <u>10</u> 1913) Marion Grant. Married ___Butt.

1. <u>10</u> 1911) Florence Grant was a teacher. She was engaged to be married when she died of "consumption" and was buried in her wedding dress.

1. <u>10</u> 193) Lorne Cook was an architect as well as a house carpenter. He never married.

1. <u>10</u> 194) Victoria Cook married George Wallace Grant, son of Joseph and

Janet Grant of Roachvale, on Sept. 21, 1910.
Children:
1. 10 1941) Wesley Grant   b: Jan. 2/1915   d: Jan. 3/1915
1. 10 1942) Cordelia Jenetta Grant   b: Jan. 23/1916
1. 10 1943) Milton Wallace Grant   b: Mar. 31/1919

--

1. 10 2) Lydia Cook married John Mason, son of William and Mary (Rogers) Mason (***See Mason family notes in back of book***), of Country Harbour. He was a carpenter. He died before the 1881 census, where Lydia is shown in the household of her son Moses Mason and family.
Children:
1. 10 21) John <u>Godfrey</u> Mason   b: @ 1839
1. 10 22) Sarah Mason   b: @ 1840
1. 10 23) Moses Mason   b: @ 1841
1. 10 24) Daniel/Donald Mason   b: @ 1845
1. 10 25) Mary Mason   b: @ 1846
1. 10 26) Emma Mason   b: @ 1856
(Probably more children.)

1. 10 21) John <u>Godfrey</u> Mason married **1ˢᵗ)** Eliza Jane (or Elizabeth) Glencross of St. Mary's. She died on March 8, 1875. He married **2ⁿᵈ)** Caroline (Glencross) Fenton, widow, in 1878.
Children:
1. 10 211) Joseph Charles Mason   b: @1864
1. 10 212) John George Mason   b: @1866
1. 10 213) Mary Ann Mason   b: @1870
1. 10 214) James Arthur Mason   b: @1872

1. 10 22) Sarah Mason married **1ˢᵗ)** Charles DeW. Laurilliard, a tailor, son of Henry and Matilda (Rogers) Laurilliard; **2ⁿᵈ)** Aubrey Bennett in 1912.

1. 10 23) Moses Mason married Rebecca Taylor.
Children:
1. 10 231) Emma Mason
1. 10 232) Catherine Mason
1. 10 233) Margaret (Maggie) J. Mason (m: George E. Mason, son of Edward H. and Janet Mason)
1. 10 234) Elizabeth A. Mason
1. 10 235) John Francis (Frank) Mason
1. 10 236) Lydia <u>Abigail</u> Mason   b: 1875   d: 1892
1. 10 237) Eliza B. Mason
1. 10 238) Mary Edith Mason

1. 10 24) Daniel/Donald Mason married Catherine Walsh, daughter of John and Mary Walsh (**See Walsh family notes in back of book**).

1. 10 25) Mary Mason married **1st)** John Taylor, a widower of St. Mary's in 1872. He was a boot maker. She married **2nd)** Charles Chadwick, a mechanic from Sackville, N.B. in 1898.

1. 10 26) Emma Mason married Henry Mason, son of James A. and Maria Mason. He was a carpenter. They had children: Eliza Blanch Mason, Henry Havelock Mason, Nora? Mason, Stanley Brown Mason (m: Tressa Worth), William Herman Mason (m: Aravella Angeline Mason, daughter of Robert and Minnie {Horton} Mason), Sarah Jane Mason (m: Henry Edward Worth, son of Joseph and Annie Worth), Gardiner Everett Mason.

---

1. 10 3) Ruth Cook married Daniel Lawlor, who was born @ 1795 in Carlow, Ireland. (One document states Waterford as his birthplace). He died on Feb. 3, 1877, age 82. They lived in the Salmon River area. There were more children than what is shown below; the 1838 Census shows 8 children by that year, although some may have died young.
Children:

1. 10 31) John William Lawlor	b: 1825	
1. 10 32) Winneford Lawlor	b: 1829	
1. 10 33) Daniel Lawlor	b: May 24, 1831	d: Jan. 11, 1924
1. 10 34) Patrick Lawlor	b: @ 1844	
1. 10 35) Henry Lawlor	b: @ 1846	d: Oct. 11, 1924
1. 10 36) James Godfrey Lawlor	b: Mar. 27, 1849	

1. 10 31) John Lawlor married Mary E. O'Neil, at Mulgrave in 1860. They lived in Ogden. Their **children** were: Daniel Lawlor (m: Annie __); John Lawlor; Eleanor Lawlor (m: William Fraser); Susanna Lawlor (m: John Rogers); William H. Lawlor; Mary Ann Lawlor; Margaret Lawlor (m: John O'Connor).

1. 10 32) Winneford Lawlor married Charles Kenney, who owned the first sawmill in the Salmon River/Ogden area. (CR1.10 32) They had a large **family**: Robert Kenney (m: **1st)** Anne Doyle, m: **2nd)** Jessie McPherson); Ruth Kenney (m: Patrick Connolly, widower); Agnes Kenney (m: Richard White); Mary Kenney (m: Edward Farrell); Hugh F. Kenney (m: Margaret MacDonald); Charles J. Kenney (m: Elizabeth Farrell & they had a daughter Winneford); Winneford Ann Lawlor Kenney; Elizabeth Ann Kenney (never married).

1. 10 33) Daniel Lawlor married Margaret Kennedy. They had **children**:

Bridget Lawlor; William Albert Lawlor; Daniel Lawlor (m: Monica O'Connor); Mary Ann Lawlor (never married); Annie Lawlor (m: Edward Sullivan); Joseph Henry Lawlor (Johannah Walsh); Vincent Lawlor (m: Isabel Dunphy).

1. <u>10</u> 34) Patrick Lawlor became a miner. He married **1st**) Mary Gerroir in 1871. She was born at Tracadie. They had **children**: Ruth Lawlor (not married, became an R.N.); Mary E. Lawlor; John Daniel Lawlor (m: Addie Mae Evans, lived in Londonderry, Col. Co.); Winnifred Ann Lawlor; James W. Lawlor; Catherine Jane Lawlor. He married **2nd**) Olive Hodgson, daughter of Benjamin and Margaret Hodgson of Country Harbour, in 1894.

1. <u>10</u> 35) Henry Lawlor was a farmer and Postmaster at Salmon River. He married Annie Chisholm, from Monk's Head, Antigonish County, and had **children**: Daniel Christopher Lawlor ("Dan C", who m: Elizabeth McAllister); Collin Francis Lawlor (m: Catherine Kenny); Jessie Ann Lawlor.

1. <u>10</u> 36) James Lawlor became a miner at Goldenville. He married Bridget Kennedy (b: 1849, d: 1919), daughter of James and Ann (Fitzgerald) Kennedy, on Sept. 30, 1872. They had **children:** Mary E. Lawlor died at 3 months old, at Goldenville; David Lawlor (d: at age 3 of Scarlatina in 1876; Ann Laura Lawlor (m: John Edmund Cohoon, a Tel. Lineman from Canso); David James Lawlor (never married and died of TB, aged 51); Patrick Bernard Lawlor (a miner, migrated to the mines in northern Ontario He contracted "Miners Consumption" and died age 43, in 1928. He never married); Margaret H. Lawlor (m: Samuel Durkee at Lynn, Mass.); Mary Lawlor.
There are more records available for the Lawlor family, but are difficult to sort out without personal knowledge of the family groups. For instance, at one time, there were three Daniel Lawlors living in the same area, all married with children who had similar names. Also, there may have been 2nd marriages following the death of a wife but it is very difficult to determine without documentation. Lawlors married into most of the prominent families of the Salmon River area, including Sullivan, McAllister, McDonald, White, Walsh, Rogers, O'Neill, Kennedy.

--

1. <u>10</u> 4) Diana Cook married James O'Gorman. He was born in Ireland, and became the school teacher at Salmon River Bridge from 1831 to at least 1839. The school was supported by voluntary subscription. The amount raised in 1831 for the teacher's salary was 17.50 lbs. for teaching 34 children. In 1846, he is found as a teacher at Manchester. By 1850, his name is not found on the roster of teachers in Guysborough County. By the mid to late 1800's this family dropped the O' from their surname, becoming Gorman.
Children:

1. <u>10</u> 41) Richard O'Gorman   b: 1826
1. <u>10</u> 42) Margaret O'Gorman   b: 1828
1. <u>10</u> 43) James O'Gorman   b: 1835
1. <u>10</u> 44) Joanna C. Gorman   b: ?
1. <u>10</u> 45) John Gorman   b: 1839
1. <u>10</u> 46) Frances Gorman   b: @1840   d:1917 Port Shoreham
1. <u>10</u> 47) David Gorman   b: @ 1844
1. <u>10</u> 48) Susan M. Gorman   b: @ 1851
1. <u>10</u> 49) Joseph G. Gorman   b: @ 1853   d: Apr. 16/1912

1. <u>10</u> 41) Richard O'Gorman married Elizabeth ? They had **children:** Martha Ellen O'Gorman (m: Michael Coady), Agnes O'Gorman (m: James Nichols from Bayfield - This marriage was witnessed by Samuel O'Gorman - probably her brother), Sarah M. Gorman (m: Thomas W. Taylor of Little River, Ant. County - she died and Thomas Taylor remarried in 1884).

1. <u>10</u> 43) James O'Gorman was a farmer at Clam Harbour. He married Catherine Purcell in 1866. She was born on Prince Edward Island, daughter of William and Ann Purcell. They had a **son** (b: 1867 at Manchester).

1. <u>10</u> 44) Joanna C. Gorman married Alexander George McKay of Ragged Head. They married at Clam Harbour on Aug. 25, 1864. No parents names are given on the marriage record. Joanna and George McKay had **children:** Joseph J. McKay (m: Irene Leet in 1916), Esther Ann (m: Edmond Francis Grant in 1904), Wallace McKay, who never married and died of a self-inflicted gunshot wound in 1932 at Manassette Lake, George Clement McKay (m: Jane Nora Carter in 1902, at Boylston).

1. <u>10</u> 45) John Gorman was a fisherman,and at times, working in the shoe industry in Massachusetts. He married Catherine McNeil, daughter of Peter and Jane McNeil, of Port Hood, at Gloucester, in 1863. They had **children**: William N. (Willie) Gorman, John Gorman, Adelia Gorman, Plandela Gorman, Joseph H. Gorman. John died of typhoid fever at age 44.

1. <u>10</u> 46) Frances Gorman married James Alexander (or James William) McKay. They had **children**: Fred McKay (b: 1873, d: 1923, never married), Harriet Louisa McKay (m: Philip Fitzgerald, lived in Mass., USA), Capt. John Henry McKay (b: 1862 - married twice: **1**^{st)} Mary ?, **2**nd) Lizzie Lucy Long at Canso, in 1908), Annie McKay (b: 1864 - m: Chamberlain, lived in Lynn, Mass.)

1. <u>10</u> 47) David Gorman married Alice M. White on June 21, 1874, at Gloucester. She was the daughter of Thomas and Mary Ann White of Guysborough area. **Children**: David S. Gorman, Thomas A. Gorman. David

drowned while fishing out of Gloucester in the November gales of 1879
(CR1. <u>10</u> 47)

1. <u>10</u> 48) Susan Gorman married Alexander Harris, a mariner born at Richibucto, N.B. to John and Edith "Childe" Harris, on Mar. 23, 1874, at Gloucester.

1. <u>10</u> 49) Joseph Gorman migrated to Gloucester, where he was a teamster. He married **1st)** Emma F. Merchant, daughter of James R. and Mary Ann Merchant, on June 25, 1875. She died in 1882. **Children:** Mabel C. Gorman, Joseph E. Gorman, Walter Gorman. He married **2nd)** Henrietta (Aikins) McIsaac, daughter of George Aikins and Mary N. (Rogers). **Children:** Alfred N. Gorman, Ella O. Gorman, Esther Maud Gorman, Hazel Dell Gorman, Lottie May Gorman. Henrietta died in 1894, Joseph in 1912.

--

1. <u>10</u> 5) Susannah Horton Cook married William McAllister, who was born in Ireland to John and Grace McAllister. After his death in 1867 from cancer, she migrated to Lynn, Mass. and was living there at the time of the US 1880 census. She died at Lynn, age 84 in 1895.
Children:

1. <u>10</u> 51) Sarah <u>Esther</u> McAllister	b: Sept. 24/1824	bapt. Jan. 14/1827
1. <u>10</u> 52) Elizabeth Cook McAllister	b: Dec. 17/1828	d: Nov. 16/1910
1. <u>10</u> 53) Grace McAllister	b: 1832	No further info.
1. <u>10</u> 54) Maria McAllister	b: 1835	
1. <u>10</u> 55) William McAllister	b: @1836	
1. <u>10</u> 56) John McAllister	b: Dec. 24/1844	
1. <u>10</u> 57) Mary A. McAllister	b: Mar. 2/1848	d: May 17/1915
1. <u>10</u> 58) Frances E. McAllister	b: 1850	d: Apr. 19/1914

1. <u>10</u> 51) Esther McAllister married William Cameron Cook (See children under #4.8).

1. <u>10</u> 52) Elizabeth McAllister married James Jones, carpenter, son of Dow and Elizabeth Jones of Nova Scotia, at Lynn, Mass. **Child:**
1. <u>10</u> 521) Lizzie M. Jones   b: 1868 (m: Albert L. Brackett)

1. <u>10</u> 54) Maria McAllister married George W. Herrick (his 3rd wife) , son of John and Mary Herrick of Beverly, Mass, at Lynn, in 1859. Maria died on Jan. 5/1877, age 43. **Children:**

1. <u>10</u> 541) Frederick Herrick	b: 1860
1. <u>10</u> 542) Susan M. Herrick	b: 1862
1. <u>10</u> 543) Mabel Florence Herrick	b: 1875

1. <u>10</u> 55) William McAllister married Sarah (Sally) McLean, daughter of John and Annie (McPherson) McLean. **Children:**
1. <u>10</u> 551) John McAllister (b: 1872, d: 1872)
1. <u>10</u> 552) Mary McAllister (m: Patrick Murphy)
1. <u>10</u> 553) Sarah McAllister (d: age 18 mos.)
1. <u>10</u> 554) Susan M. McAllister (m: Patrick Shea)
1. <u>10</u> 555) William A. McAllister
1. <u>10</u> 556) Annie Catherine McAllister (Not married)
1. <u>10</u> 557) John Henry McAllister

1. <u>10</u> 56) John McAllister married Janet McPherson and had a large family, including James, Janet Isabella, Mary (m: Clayton Buckley), Maria (m: Charles Hogan), Donald, James Alfred.

1. <u>10</u> 57) Mary A. McAllister married William A. Cotton, who worked in a Shoe Factory in Lynn, Mass. **Children**:
1. <u>10</u> 571) Emma F. Cotton
1. <u>10</u> 572) Ralph W. Cotton
1. <u>10</u> 573) George D. Cotton

1. <u>10</u> 58) Frances E. McAllister married **1**[st)] John McPherson (b: NS).
Child:
1. <u>10</u> 581) John H. McPherson b: @1867.

She married **2**[nd)] Alvin A. Pitman, a shoemaker, born in New Hampshire to Samuel J. & Mary A. Pitman, at Lynn, Mass., in 1878.

--

1. <u>10</u> 6) John Godfrey Peart Cook married Sarah Cook (#1.56) on Oct. 12/1841. They migrated to western USA in 1849, first living in Spring Grove, Minnesota, then settling in Cedar Falls, Iowa, where some of their cousins also settled, and whom may have migrated west at the same time. After many years in the west, John and Sarah went to New York state, and spent their remaining years in a Methodist retirement home in Gerry. They both died there in 1892.
Child:
1. <u>10</u> 61) Mary Ann Cook   b: Jan. 21/1843   d: Jan./1932, Orange Co., California, USA. Married Amos E. Glanville, a cattle farmer who was born in England on Apr. 22, 1860. They migrated to Kansas, where Amos died in Leoti on Sept. 30, 1916.
Children:

1. <u>10</u> 611) Benjamin Glanville   b: Nov. 29/1861
        Married Maude Evelyn Taylor
1. <u>10</u> 612) Sarah Maria Glanville   b: June 10/1863 d: Oct 20/1941
1. <u>10</u> 613) Mary E. Glanville   b: June 18/1866
1. <u>10</u> 614) Elizabeth O. Glanville   b: Oct. 21/1867
1. <u>10</u> 615) Amos E. Glanville   b: Sept. 12/1870
1. <u>10</u> 616) Charlotte C. Glanville   b: Mar. 31/1876
1. <u>10</u> 617) John G. Glanville   b: Jan. 29/1872
1. <u>10</u> 618) Perlina M. Glanville   b: Oct. 1/1885

1. <u>10</u> 612) Sarah Maria Glanville married John Galen Dixon on March 12, 1893. **Children:**
1. <u>10</u> 6121) Mary Gladys Dixon   b: Mar. 28/1894 d: Oct. 9/1943
1. <u>10</u> 6122) John Glanville Dixon   b: Mar. 11/1896
1. <u>10</u> 6123) Galen Dixon   b: Mar. 28/1894 d: Mar. 29/1894
1. <u>10</u> 6124) Charlotte Dixon   b: Aug. 31/1901 d:Aug 24/1904

1. <u>10</u> 6121) Mary Gladys Dixon married Francis Nelson Banta, on June 7, 1923: **Children:**
1. <u>10</u> 61211) Frances Jean Banta
1. <u>10</u> 61212) Roger Wade Banta*   b. Jan. 12/1929
                        Married Janice Law on Dec. 27/1951
*Roger Banta travelled from California to Guysborough, NS, hoping to find family. He stopped in at a coffee shop and mentioned that he was looking for Cook family relatives. Chris Cook was phoned; with genealogical notes in hand, met with Roger and, although Roger's ancestors had been gone from the area for over 160 years, within minutes established the connection to our family.

This ends the section on Elias (4ᵗʰ).

2) John Cook married Elizabeth Tobey, daughter of Nathaniel and Elizabeth (Hopkins) (Godfrey)Tobey*. The Tobeys were also pre-loyalist settlers at Cook's Cove.

Children:

2.1) Sarah Cook	b: June 22/1786
2.2) Elisha <u>Godfrey</u> Cook	b: 1782
2.3) John Cook	b: Jan. 8/1789 d: Feb. 5/1875
2.4) Nathaniel Tobin (Tobey?) Cook	b: May 15/1796 twin
2.5) Mary Maria Cook	b: May 15/1796 twin
2.6) Edward Cook	b: June/1798

*Note : Elizabeth Hopkins Godfrey was a descendant of Stephen Hopkins of the Mayflower, and the widow of Benjamin Godfrey. Her parents were Elisha Hopkins, M.D., and Experience (Scudder) Hopkins. Elisha Hopkins was a son of Joshua Hopkins, who was a son of Giles Hopkins, who was a son of Stephen Hopkins. Giles also had a daughter, Deborah Hopkins, who married Josiah Cooke; their daughter, Deborah Cooke, married Moses Godfrey. Their son was Benjamin Godfrey, who married Elizabeth Hopkins.

Elizabeth Hopkins had two Godfrey children when she married Nathaniel Tobey: Benjamin Godfrey (who married Bethia Atwood - their daughter Deborah Godfrey married Elias Cook [4th] (#1.1), and Gideon Godfrey (who married Sarah Hadley).

Benjamin and Bethia (Atwood) Godfrey had a large family, and another of their daughters, Lucy Godfrey, married Lt. John Cameron and had a daughter, Lucy **Cameron**, whose first husband was Benjamin Cook (#4).

--

2.1) Sarah Cook married **Joseph Atwood Godfrey Cameron** on Dec. 24/1811. (Son of John and Lucy Cameron and sister of both **Lucy Cameron**, who married #4, Benjamin Cook, and **Mary Cameron**, who married Sarah's brother, John #2.3). Joseph and Sarah's son, Joseph Cameron married **2nd)** Ann Cook, daughter of William and Elizabeth Cook, of NS. (His first wife was Harriet Adams).

--

2.2) Godfrey Cook married Amelia Teresa Hopkins, daughter of Elisha Hopkins, Esq. and wife Sarah, Liverpool, N.S. on Dec. 13, 1807.[CR2.2] Apparently Godfrey died at Arichat, as there is record of his burial there in the St. John's Anglican Church records, although it gives his abode as Glasgow Point, which is in Canso. He was buried on April 2, 1852, aged 70.

Children:

2.21) George William Henry Cook	b: May 2/1812
2.22) Nathaniel James Cook	b: Oct. 31/1814
2.23) John <u>Francis</u> Cook	b: June 16/1820
2.24) Edward <u>Freeman</u> Cook	b: Nov. 20/1822
2.25) Child	bap. July 29/1827
2.26) Henry Hopkins Cook	b: Aug. 29/1828

2.22) Nathaniel Cook married Margaret Lindloff. They lived in the St. Peter's area of Cape Breton in 1846, where Margaret died on May 20, 1846, aged 30 years. Nathaniel Cook and Margaret Lindloff appear mainly in River Bourgeois church records. Margaret's father, Hans Lindloff, was a Swede, who moved to St. Peter's area, received a grant of land [CR-2.22a]. He married a local widow, Ann (Harris), widow of Edward Hearn. The Lindloffs lived on what had been Harris land, outside St. Peter's. There is a Cook's Lake in the vicinity. Ann Harris Hearn Lindloff probably inherited the Harris land at River Tillard area.

2.221) Amelia Ann Cook	b: April 12, 1841	
2.222) Sarah Ann Cook	b: Feb. 28, 1843	
2.223) Andrew Cook	b: July 17, 1845	
2.224) Godfrey Cook	b: @ 1842	d: Sept. 4, 1870
2.225) Henry Cook *	b: @ 1852	
2.226) Hans Cook	b: Sept. 26, 1851	

Nathaniel was living in Cape Canso at the time of the 1871 census. He was a widower, with a son, Henry living with him. He died on Feb. 16, 1877 aged 60 years. *Son Henry probably had been mistaken for Hans. There is no further record of Henry Cook.

2.221) Amelia Ann Cook
Child: 2.2211) Lawrence/Laurent Martin Cook   b: Oct. 14, 1863
She married Thomas Taylor, 46 year old widower, who was a miner at Goldenville. He was born at Sherbrooke to William Taylor (saw miller) and Hannah Redden. They were married at Goldenville, Oct. 26, 1868
Children:
2.2212) Godfrey Taylor (b: 1871, m: Mary Druce, Goldboro)
2.2213) George Henry Taylor (b: 1879, m: Bridget Sullivan at Chelsea, Mass.)
2.2214) Matilda A. Taylor (b: 1869)
2.2215) Jane Taylor (b: 1873)
2.2216) Melinda Taylor (b: 1876)
2.2217) Elizabeth Jenette Taylor (b: 1880, m: George MacCutcheon at Somerville, Mass.)

2.224) Godfrey Cook married Marguerite Yvon, who died on April 22, 1870. She was a daughter of Francois Yvon and Victoire Martell, parish of River Bourgeois. There are several records of Godfrey Cook and Freeman Cook, both of NS, fishermen, travelling to Boston for work, in 1865 and 1866. The Freeman Cook would have been born around 1846. He could have been a brother, or cousin. Godfrey was lost at sea on Sept. 4, 1870.

2.226) Hans Cook was a seaman and was listed on the Digby County census of 1881, age 28. From records at Richmond County Deeds Office, Arichat: On July 31, 1886 (registered Feb. 07, 1887), Hans Cook, yeoman of Digby, Nova Scotia, transferred land to William Urquhart, Esq., of Sporting Mountain, land on the north side of the main road along the north side of St. Peter's Bay. On May 25, 1872, William Urquhart agreed to sell land at St. Peter's to Hans Cook and to Nathaniel Cook (father of Hans Cook), and to MacCarron. Nathaniel Cook has since died and Hans Cook now agrees to cancel the agreement with William Urquhart. Hans migrated to USA in 1890, where he worked as a labourer for the B&M Railroad. He married Annie Martell, and had daughters Minnie and Elizabeth. He died in Lawrence, Mass. on March 31, 1905. Daughter Minnie married Alfred Vogt on Sept. 7, 1904, at Lawrence, Mass.

--

2.23) Francis Cook married Ellen Catherine Luce (or Snow) on March 3, 1846 at Arichat. (CR2.23). They had **children**:

2.231) Amelia Theresa Cook	bapt. Sept. 5/1846
2.232) Elisha Cook	bapt. July 6/1851
2.233) John Cook	b: @1852
2.234) James Godfrey Cook	b: Mar. 9/1854
2.235) Levi Cook	b: Oct 20/1857
2.236) George Cook	b: @ 1863
2.237) Ellen Cook	b: April 3/1865

The family lived at various locations as shown by the birthplaces of the children: John and Amelia Theresa at St. Peter's Passage, Elisha William at Janvrin's Island, James Godfrey, Levi and Ellen at Madame Island. Francis died at Madame Island and was buried on June 18, 1868, aged 50 years.

2.233) John Cook married Eliza Greencorn of Phillip's Harbour, daughter of Thomas and Caroline Greencorn, on Dec. 24, 1879. At the time of the marriage, John was a seaman, who resided at Canso. A witness to the marriage was Levi Cook. *Lost from the schooner Lina May, with his brother Levi, in 1887.*

2.235) Levi Cook was captain of A.N. Whitman's schooner *Lina May*, which sailed from Halifax for the West Indies and was never heard from again, in 1887, his brother John was also lost, as was William Snow and a MacDuff, all from Canso. (CR2.235)

--

2.24) Edward Freeman Cook migrated to the U.S.A. The following excerpt was found in a Massachusetts newspaper dated @ 1918-1920, and sent home to her parents, George and Martha Cook, by Flora Cook. It is believed to refer to Edward Freeman Cook.

"CAP" COOK OF QUINCY MARKS 95TH BIRTH DATE

....*Freeman Cook, known as "The Grand Old Man of Germantown", today quietly observed his 95th birthday anniversary at the Sailors' Snug Harbor, which has been his home for almost 20 years.*
.... *"Cap" Cook was born in Guysboro, N.S., and when 12 years old went*

to live in Gloucester. That same year he shipped aboard a fisherman for the Grand Banks, then followed the sea for 65 years.

....Almost every day he strolls through the Germantown section, stopping here and there for chats. It is not unusual to see "Cap" doing chores at the Snug Harbor. He attributes his age to walking. He expresses himself as disgusted with "these young fellows who give up and go to bed at the slightest ache," and says, "when I feel sick I go out for a walk. If I gave up and went to bed, I'd just die".

~

2.3) John Cook married Mary Cameron on Dec. 6/1819.
Children:

2.31) Louisa Cook	b: @1820	
2.32) Edward Cook	b: ?	
2.33) William Cook	b: @1815	d: 1885
2.34) Henry Cook	b: ?	
2.35) Benjamin Cook	b: ?	
2.36) Godfrey Cook	b: ?	
2.37) Eliza Cook	b: ?	

2.31) Louisa Cook married Charles Gosbee on Jan. 28/1845.
Children:

2.311) Mary Elizabeth Gosbee	b: 1849	d:1903
2.312) Charles Archibald Gosbee	b: @ 1848	
2.313) Marshall Gosbee	b: June 4, 1851	
2.314) Alma Louisa Gosbee	b: Mar. 25/1853	
2.315) Caroline Ada Gosbee	b: Jan. 8/1857	
2.316) John C. Gosbee	b: @ 1860	
2.317) Maria (or Eliza M.) Gosbee	b: Apr. 1/1863	

--

2.33) William Cook migrated to Gloucester, Mass., where he was a shoemaker. He never married. He died on Dec. 24, 1885.

~

2.5) Mary Maria Cook married ?? Gerry. She died at Guysborough on Feb. 22/1875 of "inward cancer". She was 82 years old.

~

2.6) Edward Cook married Ellen_____.
Child:
2.61) George H. Cook   b: @ 1829
George married Margaret E. Panton (b: Montreal, Canada), daughter of William and Catherine Panton on July 9, 1856, at Quincy, Mass., where he worked as a Boot Caulker. He died of consumption at age 38 at Ipswich, Mass.
Children:
2.611) John Edward Cook   b: April 30/1858
2.612) Isabella Cook   b: June 16, 1864 d: of disease of the
                                   spine in 1878, at Ipswich.
Mother Margaret and son John migrated to Nebraska, where they farmed at Adams Township. Later in life, John married Eva A. _____, who was born in Pennsylvania. They had no children.

This ends the section on John Cook.

3) Edward Cook   b: @ 1752,   d: Aug. 16/1846
                                                    aged 94 years.

He married Elizabeth ?
Child:
3.1) Elizabeth Ann Cook   b: Feb. 15/1812
She married Patrick Sheehan on Jan. 26/1830.

This ends the section on Edward Cook.

4) Benjamin Cook   b: @ 1766   d: Feb. 18/1833.
     Married **1**st) Philomela Hull, daughter of Moses Hull, on Mar. 4/1787.
She was b: @1769, d: May 16/1809. She died in childbirth, aged 40 years.
The baby must have died at the same time.
Children:

4.1) Elias W. Cook	b: Sept. 8/1788	d: Sept. 5/1870
4.2) Moses Cook	b: July 8/1793	d: Dec. 30/1860
4.3) William <u>Francis</u> Cook	b: Feb. 4/1796	d: Apr. 8/1862
4.4) Mary Elizabeth Cook	b: Jan. 23/1798	
4.5) Sarah <u>Amelia</u> Cook	b: Mar. 4/1803	d: Apr. 18/1870

     Benjamin Cook married **2**nd) Lucy Maria Cameron, on Aug. 31/1810.
She was born in Sydney, Cape Breton, on July 21, 1791, daughter of Lt. John
and Lucy (Godfrey) Cameron. [CR4.0]
Children:

4.6) Benjamin Cook	bap. Jan. 12/1812	
4.7) James Wm. Fred. A.	b: Nov. 20/1812	d: Jan. 22/1884
4.8) William Cameron Cook	b: May 5/1815	d: Sept./1866
4.9) Lucy Maria Cook	b: @ 1816	
4.<u>10</u>) Caroline Elizabeth Cook	b: Aug. 3/1819	d: May 12/1913
4.<u>11</u>) Wentworth Cook	b: ?	No further info.
4.<u>12</u>) Joseph Henry Cook	b: Nov. 11/1829	d: Mar. 7/1921
4.<u>13</u>) Charles Cook	b: ?	No further info.

     * Wentworth (and Joseph) were not on the listing of school children in
1826, but Joseph and *George* Cook were on the 1835 list as children of the
Widow Cook.

     After Benjamin's death, his widow, Lucy Cook, married Elisha
Freeman from Pleasant River, at Brookfield, Queens County, N.S., on Jan.
20/1839, and moved to his home. She took several of the younger children
with her.

4.1) Elias Cook was a farmer and fisherman. He married Anna Horton,
daughter of Isaiah and Zipporah (Hyde) Horton, on Jan. 3/1811. She was born
on April 23/1794, and died at age 101 in 1895. Elias and Anna gave the land
for the Wesleyan Chapel at Cook's Cove @ 1862.
Children:

4.11) John James Hyde Cook	b: May 14/1812
4.12) Philomela Cook	b: Oct./1814
	d: Cal., USA, June 16/ 1895
4.13) Benjamin Cook	b: Dec. 3/1816 d: Sept. 2/1884
4.14) Elias William Cook	b: Aug. 18/1819 d: Oct. 8/1880

4.15) William Francis Cook   b: @ 1822   d: July 1/1864
4.16) Moses Cook   b: Dec. 19/1823   d: 1882
4.17) Zipporah Margaret Cook   b: @ 1826   d: May 7/1910
4.18) Arthur McNutt Cook   b: Jan. 7/1833   No further info.
4.19) Sarah Jane Cook   b: Aug. 10/1834

4.11) John James Hyde Cook went to the U.S.A. as a young man. He returned to Cook's Cove after his father's death and married Maria Cook, widow of his brother William Francis Cook (#4.15). They migrated to California, and settled west of Cacheville (Yolo), where they farmed.

Children:

4.111) John <u>Frank</u> Cook   b: Sept. 24/1876   d: Apr. 8/1946
4.112) Anna <u>Mae</u> Cook   b: Nov. /1879
4.113) James <u>Garfield</u> A. Cook   b: Feb. 11/1882

Mae Cook & J. Frank Cook
circa 1900

4.111) Frank Cook was an accountant for an insurance company in Piedmont, California. He married Mattie M. ___.
Child: 4.1111) John F. Cook (Jack)   b: 1919

4.112) Mae Cook married Arthur G. Willett. They lived in Berkeley, California.

--

100

4.12) Philomela Cook married John William Peart, son of Thomas and Marianne (Cribben) Peart, on Aug. 3/1837.

Children:

4.121) William Henry Peart   b: Dec. 5, 1837
     Married Ida Alice Hadley on Dec. 12/1875   and had **children:** Percy J. Peart, Arthur W. Peart, Gertrude Alice Peart, Roy Walter Peart, Elias Ray Peart, Ralph E. Peart.

4.122) John <u>James</u> Cook Peart   b: June 4/1840
     Married Victoria Maria Peart, daughter of Godfrey and Martha Peart.

4.123) Lucretia Ann Peart   b: Jan. 28/1842
     Married **1st)** Jim Steele, and **2nd)** Albert Phelps. At least 2 **children**: Stanley Steele [CR4.123] and Laura Steele.

4.124) Mary Ann <u>Lavinia</u> Peart   b: Oct. 29/1844
     Married Albert Horton. (Albert Horton was a deacon. Their only **daughter**, Hattie, died at age 15 in 1892.) [CR4.124]

4.125) Elias Cook Peart - See [CR4.125]   b: Nov. 9/1846

4.126) John <u>Marshall</u> Peart   b: Sept. 24/1852   d: 1940
     Married Maria Penny, daughter of Capt. Thomas and Frances Penny, on Dec. 24, 1873. They migrated to California. **Child:** Frank Aubrey Peart (1889-1971).

4.127) Edmund F. Peart   b: @ 1854
     Married Sally Green. Migrated to Colusa, California.

4.128) Emma B. Peart   b: @ 1847
     Married David Grant, son of Alexander and Ann Grant of Antigonish, on Nov. 22/1870.

4.129) Annie Peart   b: @ 1857
     Married George L. Beals at Salem, Mass.

--

4.13) Benjamin Cook was a farmer. He married Sarah Ann McKenzie @ 1845. She was a daughter of Edward and Elizabeth (Diggedon) McKenzie. She was a seamstress, and was born @ 1826. **Children:**

4.131) George Washington Cook   b: Dec. 17/1846   d: Mar. 26/1939

4.132) Jeremiah Cook   b: @ 1848   d: May 1/1873
                                         Eastport, Maine

4.133) Robert Cutler Cook   b: Sept. 1/1850

4.134) Sarah Jane Cook   b: @ 1853

4.135) Elias Mack Cook   b: @1857

4.136) Benjamin F. Cook   b: @ 1862

4.137) Amelia Edson Cook   b: @ 1860   d: @1892

4.138) Annie Cook   b: @ 1859

4.139) Susanna Cook   b: June 5/1868

4.13<u>10</u>) Jennie <u>Alice</u> Cook   b: @ 1873

4.131) George Cook married Emmeline Amelia Horton, b: 1850, d: 1939, daughter of Charles and Eliza (Henley) Horton, on June 26/1868. She was born Apr. 24/1851. **Children:**

4.1311) Georgina Cook	b: May 26/1869
4.1312) Sarah Ella Cook	b: May 13/1871
4.1313) Agnes Godfrey Cook	b: Apr. 3/1874
4.1314) Annie E. Cook	b: May 10/1875
4.1315) Matilda Jane Cook	b: Feb. 18/1881
4.1316) Mahala Corkella Cook (Haley)	b: April 9/1881
4.1317) George Purvis Cook	b: Apr. 4/1884
4.1318) William Buckley Cook	b: Aug. 30/1886
4.1319) Gertrude May Cook	b: July 11/1888
4.131 10) Charlotte Noble Cook	b: July 7/1892

4.1311) Georgina Cook married Jeremiah Pelerine from the Tracadie area. (CR4.1311)

4.1312) Ella Cook married **1st)** John Bradley, a waiter, born in Ireland, in 1901. They divorced. She married **2nd)** Arthur S. Ricker, from Boston. No children.

4.1313) Agnes Cook married Thomas Berton Porter (#7.321), Roachvale, son of James and Ann Porter, on Sept. 22/1891.
Children:

4.13131) Edith Porter	b: 1896 m: Vernon Delaney
4.13132) Laura Porter	b: 1897 m: Wilfred Dort
4.13133) William Porter	b: 1900 m: Maggie Spanks
4.13134) Owen Porter	b: 1904
4.13135) Myrtle Lillian Porter	b: Mar.11/1915 m: W. Horton

4.1314) Annie Cook married Daniel Gould, Cook's Cove, who became a barber and had a shop on Main Street, Guysborough.

The Dan Gould Family

Children:

4.13141) William R. Gould	b: Aug. 8/1892
4.13142) Harry R. Gould	b: Sept. 3/1896
4.13143) Charles Daniel Gould	b: Oct. 4/1911

4.1315) Matilda Cook married Patrick E. Farrell, widower, Lower Glencoe, on Jan. 25/1906. A daughter, Agnes married William Feltmate and had **children**: Maurice Sylvester Feltmate, Kaye (m: Venedam), Hilda (m: Gottchall), Loretta (m: Welsh), June (m: Rod MacDonald), Shirley (m: Bill MacGillivray), John Feltmate, Pearl (m: Melanson), Anne (m: Hawley) James Feltmate (d: infancy), Mary Isabelle Feltmate (d: infancy).

4.1316) Mahala Cook married James Roger Morash, an electrical engineer, son of James and Emma (Young) Morash of Lunenburg, NS, at Lynn, Mass. in 1903. They migrated to Oak Park, Illinois. They later divorced.

Children:

4.13161) Helen Louise Morash	b: Mar. 21/1909 Lynn	
4.13162) Jean Lorraine Morash	b: Mar. /1914 Illinois	d: Apr./1914
4.13163) James Roger Morash	b: Aug. 16/1916	d: 1993
	m: Beatrice "Betty" Kozel	

4.1317) George Purvis Cook married **1st**) Martha Ann Slate on Oct. 10/1904. He married **2nd**) Lila Belle (Slate) Gammon, a younger sister of his first wife. She died in November, 1970.

Children:

4.13171) Hazel Martha Cook	b: Nov. 10/1905 d: July 15/1918
4.13172) Flora Belle Cook	b: Aug. 31/1907 (m: George Hirtle)
4.13173) Lillian Rose Cook	b: July 13/1909 (m: Purvis George)
4.13174) Harold George Cook	b: Feb. 13/1912 (m: Ruth Whitman)
4.13175) Helen Anita Cook	b: Apr. 10/1914 (m: **1st)** Perry Sangster, **2nd)** Walter Jones)
4.13176) Lola Vera Cook	b: Aug. 23/1920 (m: Layton Gillie)

4.1318) William Cook married Susan Maria Spanks on Oct. 27/1920.

Children:

4.13181) Alice Belle Cook	b: Sept. 3/1921 (m: Ralph Burns)
4.13182) Marion Cook	b: (m: Judson Parks)

4.1319) Gertrude Cook migrated to Mass., USA. She married William B. Crane in 1907.

4.131 10) Charlotte (Lottie) Cook married **1st**) Percy J. Peart, son of William and Ida Peart, on Sept. 25/1906. They lived at Cook's Cove. Percy Peart d: in 1923. *(My grandparents, Homer and Gertie Lumsden, bought this property next, and it passed to my father, Percy Lumsden. It was where I grew up.)*

Children:
4.131 <u>10</u> 1) Nita Peart
(Married Sylvester Uloth)
4.131 <u>10</u> 2) Pearl Glecia Peart
(married Alex Grant, son of John and
Sarah (England) Grant.
4.131 <u>10</u> 3) Gertie Peart
4.131 <u>10</u> 4) Earl Peart

Lottie married **2nd)** Joseph Grant, in
1924.
Child:
4.131 <u>10</u> 5) Theresa Grant

***Opposite: Earl Peart holding Percy
Lumsden***

4.133) Robert C. Cook was born on Dec. 27, 1927. He was a carpenter. He
married **1st)** Hannah S. Smith (born Sambro, N.S., @ 1858), daughter of Isaac
and Mary L. Smith on July 8/1881.
Child:
4.1331) Mary Ann Cook   b: Nov. 20/1881
He married **2nd)** Dora Horton, on Nov. 20/1883. She was born on Jan. 15,
1860, died on May 18, 1930. She was brought up by Edward (#2.6) and
Eleanor (#1.52) Cook. They lived at Roachvale, N.S.
Children:

4.1332) Sophia Cook	b: @ 1886	No further info.
4.1333) Robert Benjamin Cook	b: May 6/1888	
4.1334) Cranswick Cook	b: June 24/1890	Unmarried
4.1335) James Sharp Cook	b: Dec. 6/1892	
4.1336) Edward Purvis Cook	b: Nov. 1/1894	d: unmarried 1945
4.1337) Amelia Jost Cook	b: Sept. 26/1896	No further info.
4.1338) Erma Felissa Cook	b: Nov. 22/1900	

4.1331) Mary Ann Cook married Wylie Gordon Peart, son of William S. and Mary (Peddie) Peart, on Aug. 8/1906, at Roachvale, N.S. They had children.

The family of Mary Ann and Wylie Peart

4.1333) Robert B. Cook married Sarah Frances Sigston on Dec. 1, 1917. She was born in England. Robert was a Piano Tuner. They lived on Pleasant Street, Dartmouth. Robert died at age 50 in Dartmouth.

4.1335) James Sharp Cook married Ida Elizabeth Williams on Sept. 23/1936.

4.1338) Erma Cook married Lloyd Dukeshire of Clementsvale, Ann. Co., NS, in 1925.

--

4.134) Sarah Jane Cook married James Carey, widower, from St. Francis Harbour, on Oct. 1/1894. He was a son of William and Bridget (Dunn) Carey.

--

4.135) Elias Cook was a farmer and carpenter. He married Eliza Elmira Rhynold (May 24, 1868 – Aug. 7, 1958), daughter of John and Margaret (Hayden) Rhynold from Little Dover, N.S., on July 13/1888. They lived at Roachvale.
Children:
4.1351) Violet May Cook   b: Apr. 29/1889   d: young
4.1352) Harriet Louisa Cook   b: Sept. 18/1890

4.1353) Mable Elizabeth Rosalin Cook   b: July 12/1892
4.1354) Ethel Victoria Cook   b: June 25/1895
4.1355) Esther Jane Cook (Essie)   b: Jan. 25/1896

There is a discrepancy in birthdates for Ethel and Esther - I believed them to be twins, born in 1895; however, on the Delayed Registration of Births, Essie's birthdate is given as Jan. 25, 1896. One or the other date is probably still in error, because there is only a 7 month time difference between the two births.

Elias Cook died in 1898, and some of the children were brought up by other families/relatives in Guysborough County. James and Esther Rhynold of Dover had **Esther** Cook, his niece, living with them at the time of both the 1901 and 1911 census. They also had Jennie Greencorn, widow, mother age 80. Godfrey and Ida Dort (Alice Dort's parents) had **Mabel** Cook living with them in 1911. She was listed as "adopted daughter".

Eliza married **2nd**) Joseph William Gosbee on Sept. 20/1898. They had a large family. On the 1901 census the household of William and Eliza Gosbee included daughters Violet, Harriet, Martha and Margaret, and Edward Greencorn, age 3, "border".

4.1352) Harriet (Hattie) Cook married **1st**) Wesley Ward Sangster from New Harbour. **Children:** Theresa (m: Manthorne), Victor, Marshall, Violetta (m: Harry Gosbee), Myrtle A. (m: Lamont V. Sangster).
She married **2nd**) John James Robertson, of Barney's River, Pictou County, on March 4, 1930. **Child:** Anna Mae (m: O'Connor).

4.1353) Mable Cook married Thomas Alfred Jones, widower, on May 19/1912. He was a son of Thomas and Annie (Strople) Jones. At the time of their marriage, he was 36 and she was 20.

4.1354) Ethel Cook married **1st**) John W. Shorten, Jr. on April 20, 1909. He was born at Halifax, the son of John and Alice (Walsh) Shorten. They lived in the Ogden area. At the time of their marriage, he was 31 years, 9 mos. old; she was 15 years, 10 mos. old. Ethel married **2nd**) ? Marshall. She died at age 89, @ 1984. There were more children from the second marriage.

4.1355) Essie Cook married Stephen Kennedy, a soldier stationed at Hazel Hill. He was born at Inverness, Cape Breton, son of Archibald and Sarah. They were married on Sept. 6, 1915, at Dover, where she grew up.

--

4.137) Amelia Cook married John C. Cook, shoemaker (#1.10 19), on Mar. 21/1878.

--

4.138) Annie Cook died in the County Home, Antigonish, aged 85, on March 12, 1944. Her son, Ernest Cook, was also an Inmate of the County Home, and he died on Feb. 2, 1927. Both are buried at Guysborough.

--

4.139) Susan Cook married Levi Myers, son of John and Charlotte Myers, on March 13/1895. She died at age 42, on Dec. 24/1910. This entire family had tuberculosis.
Children:

4.1391) Lottie Ann (Annie) Myers	b: Feb. 14/1899	d: Dec. 10/1915
4.1392) William B. Myers	b: Apr. 5/1896	d: Apr. 25/1918
4.1393) George David Myers	b: May 25/1910	d: Oct. 31/1910

--

4.1310) Alice Cook married David Steele Hendsbee, son of John and Abigail (Nolan) Hendsbee, from Half Island Cove, on Nov. 21/1895. He was born on June 11, 1861 and died on April 21, 1931. He was the Registrar of Deeds, Guysborough. They had **children:**
4.1310 1) David Steele Hendsbee - (Married Lena S. Hendsbee in 1919)
4.1310 2) Jennie A. Hendsbee - (She was a nurse. She married Henry
        Clayton Lethbridge of Stewiacke in 1927, at Halifax.)
4.1310 3) Wilfred Laurier Hendsbee - (Married Katherine McPherson in 1927.
        They lived in Port Hawkesbury.)
4.1310 4) Abbie Beryl Hendsbee - (b: 1905. Married Allan Maxwell Robertson
        of Sydney on June 20, 1927, at Antigonish.)
4.1310 5) Duncan Cameron Fraser Hendsbee (b: 1907)
4.1310 6) Douglas Adelbert Hendsbee (b: Dec. 10,1901)
4.1310 7) Gussie Hendsbee (b: Nov., 1900)
They also had several children who died at birth.

~

4.14) Elias William Cook married Mary Ellen Brodie, daughter of Charles Brodie from Crow Harbour, on Nov. 17/1849. She was born Apr. 17, 1830, d: 1903. **Child:**
4.141) Charles Edward Cook   b: Oct. 31/1850
Charles Cook was a farmer. He married Arvella M. (Ella) Jenkins (b: Jan. 20/1865), daughter of Elisha and Maria (Scott) Jenkins. (4.212) They lived at West Cook's Cove.
Children:

4.1411) Augusta Randall Cook   b: May 23/1891   d: Dec. 15/1918
      Married Murray Jones on Dec. 3/1918
4.1412) Amelia Pearson Cook   b: July 24/1893
4.1413) Charles <u>Clinton</u> Cook   b: May 24/1895
4.1414) Lillian M. Cook   b: June 4/1900
In 1928, this family moved to Stewiacke, N.S. (except for Gussie).   Charles died there in the early 1930's, and his son Clinton died in 1935, aged 40, unmarried.

--

4.15) Francis Cook was a farmer. He married Lavinia <u>Maria</u> Tobey on July 8/1854. She was a daughter of Joseph and Ruth Tobey, a granddaughter of Samuel and Elizabeth (Whitford) Toby, and a great-grandaughter of Nathaniel Tobey, who was the grantee of the land on the north side of Cook's Cove, and whom the small cove there was named Toby Cove.

Children:
4.151) Odessa Lavinia Jost Cook   b: Aug. 21/1857
4.152) Caroline Matilda Cook   b: Feb. 28/1859
4.153) Cordelia Edson Cook   b: Nov. 5/1860   d: 1946
4.154) Harriet Rebecca Cook   b: Mar. 9/1861   d: Apr. 4/1940
4.155) Arthur Morton Cook   b: Nov. 19/1862

    All the above children except Caroline were mentioned in their grandfather's will @ 1870, so she probably died young.
    Francis died July 1/1864, age 43, and Maria moved in with her in-laws. She married her brother-in-law, John James Hyde Cook, after he returned from the U.S.A. Then they migrated to California, and settled west of Cacheville (Yolo), where there were several more children born (See 4.11).

Lavinia <u>Maria</u> Toby   **Odessa Lavinia Jost Cook**

4.151) Odessa Cook married Charles D. Beach. They lived in San Francisco, then migrated to Washington. She was a widow in 1920, when she lived with her daughter's family in Portland, Oregon, then in 1930, she was living with her widower brother, J. Frank Cook and his son in Oakland, California.

Children:
4.1511) Clarence Dwight Beach   b: Feb. 11/1881   d: July 25/1957
      He married Josephine Crowley & had a daughter, Ruth L. Beach.

4.1512) Helen <u>Vida</u> Beach   b: Oct. 30/1884   d: Nov. 22/1968
      She married Charles M. Wilden (b: Dec. 7/1885, d: July 5/1960). They
      had a daughter, Helene Wilden.

--

4.153) Cordelia Edson Cook   married Francis George McLean on Dec. 8, 1887.   He was a son of Murdoch Hector McLean, (High Sheriff of Guysborough, NS, 1836-1862) and Elizabeth Mary Armstrong Cutler, daughter of Hon. Robert Molleson Cutler, M.L.C., of Guysborough.   Frank McLean emigrated to Lynn, Mass in 1880 and then settled at Grimes, Colusa County, California, as a general merchant.   He was the Postmaster of Grimes 1887-1906. [CR4.153] They had one **child**:

4.1531) Frances May McLean   b: 1904   d: 1979
      She married a Davies.

Harriet Rebecca Cook
1883

Harriet and George Hatcher
50th Anniversary, 1933

4.154) Harriet Rebecca Cook   married George Pierce Hatcher, son of William and Sarah Frances (Mullins) Hatcher, on Feb. 6, 1883 and had **children**: [CR4.154]

4.1541) Claude Clinton Hatcher   b: 1885
4.1542) Earl Kelsey Hatcher   b: Aug. 21/1886   d: Jan. 13/1975
4.1543) Lola V. Hatcher   b: 1893

4.1541) Clinton Hatcher married Calthia B. Ogden, and had **children**:
4.15411) Roma Alice Hatcher   b: 1908
4.15412) Daryl Clinton Hatcher   b: May 5/1909   d: Feb. 11/1985
4.15413) Pierce O. Hatcher   b: 1911
4.15414) Claude Clinton Hatcher, Jr.   b: 1916

4.1542) Earl Hatcher married Venus Virginia Bullivant, and had **children:**
4.15421) Thomas E. Hatcher   b: 1911   d: 2002
4.15422) Kelsey Wallace Hatcher   b: Dec. 8/1913   d: June 6/2006

4.1543) Lola V. Hatcher married Edgar Lyon Pockman.

--

4.155) Arthur Morton Cook married Edith Adel in 1900. They lived in Grafton township, Yolo County, California. Arthur died on June 28/1946.
Children:
4.1551) Francis Murice Cook   b: 1902
4.1552) Elizabeth Ray Cook   b: 1904
4.1553) Jack Hartley Cook   b: 1905
4.1554) Arthur M. Cook, Jr.   b: 1907
4.1555) Hattie Belle Cook   b: 1909

~

4.16) Moses Cook moved to the U.S.A. He married Martha Hadley (1825-1905) in July, 1852 at Bridgewater, Mass.
Children:
4.161) Clinton Hadley Cook   b: 1858
4.162) Mary Randall Cook   b: 1860   d: 1907
4.163) Walter Wyman Cook   b: 1865   d: 1955

4.161) Clinton Cook married Julia Esther Ferguson.
Children:
4.1611) Clinton Wesley Cook
4.1612) Grace Cook
4.1613) Robert Malcolm Cook

4.162) Mary Randall Cook married Charles Henry Bass (1851 - 1939), in 1887. They lived in Medford, Mass, then migrated to New York, where she died in 1907.
Children:
4.1621) Ernest O. Bass   b: May/1888
4.1622) Chauncey H. Bass   b: June/1890
4.1623) Gladys Bass   b: Jan./1892
4.1624) Lewis Kingsley Bass   b: June/1894
4.1625) Mildred Bass   b: Mar./1896
4.1626) Guy Russell Bass   b: Sept./1899

4.163) Walter W. Cook married Etta Mary Jacobs (1868 - 1950). They had a son, Leon W. Cook.

~

4.17) Zipporah M. Cook married John Alexander Steele, Esq., who was born in Scotland. He was a widower from Manchester, on Sept. 20/1853. His first wife, Lydia M. (Hart), died at age 37, on Jan. 16/1852, leaving 8 children.
Children from his second marriage with Zipporah:
4.171) Thomas Alonzo Steele	b: @ 1855
4.172) Edgar Allison Steele	b: @ 1856
4.173) Arthur Cook Steele	b: @ 1859
4.174) Gregor McKinnon Steele	b: @ 1861
4.175) John Steele	b: @ 1864

4.173) Arthur Steele was a farmer at Manchester in 1901. His mother, a widow at that time, lived with him.

4.174) Gregor Steele married Blanche Hall. They migrated to Worcester, Mass., where he worked as a Machinist. They had four daughters, Blanch I. Steele, Mildred Steele, Marion Steele and Grace W. Steele, and one son, Sherwood W. Steele.

~

4.19) Sarah Jane Cook married Hiram A. Edson on June 26, 1858, at North Bridgewater, Mass. She died in 1893 at Brockton, Mass.
Child:
4.191) Anna Cordelia Edson   b: Sept. 1/1859
          Married Dean Chandler Dunbar in 1879.
          Children: Guy Dunbar and S. Retta Dunbar.

~~

4.2) Moses Cook married Ann Foster (#1.93) on Jan. 26/1816. She was born @ 1794, and died in January, 1893, age 99. (CR4.2W)

Children:

4.21) Philomela E. Cook	b:Jan. 21/1817	d: May 10/1862
4.22) William Foster Cook	b: Feb. 11/1820	d: June 8/1820
4.23) Moses Cook	b: Sept. 19/1821	d: Feb. 17/1823
4.24) Eliza Cook	b: @ 1818	d: Feb. 13/1884
4.25) Moses James Cook	b: Dec. 1/1826	died young
4.26) Maria Jane Cook	b: @ 1835	
4.27) Mary Randall Cook	b: Oct. 19/1830	

4.21) Philo Cook married George Edmund Scott, son of Lemuel Scott on Feb. 11/1834.

Children:

4.211) Moses Cook Scott		b: Sept. 19/1835	
4.212) Frances Maria Scott		b: Nov. 12/1838	d: 1923
4.213) Arabella Wilson Scott		b: Jan. 7/1841	
4.214) Annie Eliza Scott		b: Jan. 7/1844	d: 1891
4.215) Carolyn Elizabeth Scott		b: May 10/1846	
4.216) Lemuel Joseph Scott		b: Nov. 28/1848	d: June 17/1866
4.217) Philomela Scott	twin	b: May 12/1851	
4.218) George Francis Scott	twin	b: May 12/1851	
4.219) Ida Madonna Scott		b: Jan. 16/1854	

4.211) Moses Cook Scott was the first Lighthouse Keeper in Guysborough, and a 40 year member of the Masonic Lodge, becoming Worshipful Master. He married Matilda Ehler in Dec., 1864. They had a family of ten **children**:

4.2111) Joseph P. Scott		b: Sept. 3/1868
4.2112) John Havelock. Scott		b: Dec. 9/1870
4.2113) George Edwin Scott		b: Dec. 25/1872
4.2114) Lois Amelia Scott		b: Feb. 7/1875
4.2115) Bessie M. Scott		b: May 28/1877
4.2116) Sanford M. Scott		b: Oct. 6/1879
4.2117) Hattie L. Scott		b: Dec. 11/1881
4.2118) Gertrude M. Scott	twin	b: Feb. 6/1885
4.2119) Roy Gordon Scott	twin	b: Feb. 6/1885
4.211 10) Clarence M. Scott		b: Dec. 15/1887

4.2111) Joseph Scott married Alma MacKenzie. They had twelve children: William, Bessie, Walter, Eva, John, Maggie, Jennie, Alvin, and four that died young - Hazel, Mabel, Clyde and Dudley. Joe and Alma both died and the younger children were brought up by relatives.

4.2112) John Havelock Scott was a Customs Officer in Sydney. He married Josie Hadley, daughter of Joseph W. and Isabella (Logan) Hadley, of Guysborough. No children.

4.2113) George Edwin Scott took over as Lighthouse Keeper from his father. He married Bessie J. Flemming of Wine Harbour. Two children: Helen and Eileen.

4.2114) Lois A. Scott married 1ˢᵗ) Lothrid Whitman, a 58 year old widower, 2ⁿᵈ) E. Ford Racey of the former NW Mounted Police. As members of the NWMP were not allowed to be married, he left his career and became an insurance salesman. No children.

4.2115) Bessie Scott married Alvin W. Sinnamon (b: Northern Ireland). No children.

4.2116) Sanford Scott married Frances Humphrey. Two children, Douglas and Sanford.

4.2117) Hattie Scott married William D. Smith. Three children, Hazel, Eva and Hilda.

4.2118) Gertrude Scott married Homer A. Lumsden. Three children, Mildred, Ruth, and Percy.

4.2119) Roy Scott migrated to western Canada. He married Rachael Warren (Rae) Chafe from Winnipeg, on Oct. 18, 1917. She was a daughter of James and Adelaide (Roberts) Chafe who had emigrated from Quidi Vidi, Newfoundland, to Manitoba. Roy and Rae had one daughter, Phyllis, who married a minister. Roy and Rae later lived in Windsor, Ontario.

4.211 10) Clarence Scott married Elsie May Buck (b: May 23, 1896 Manitoulin Island, Ontario), daughter of Henry Ormand and Martha Priscilla (Tracy) Buck, who migrated to Noyes Crossing, near Onoway, Alberta (north of Edmonton). They had one son, James (who was killed in a car accident in 1921) and one daughter, Patricia Gertrude. In 1923 they moved to Vancouver.

4.212) Frances Maria Scott married Elisha Jenkins (1829-1911), in 1862. They had **children:**

4.2121) Arvella M. Jenkins	b: 1864	
4.2122) Philo Georgina Jenkins	b: Sept. 16/1866	
4.2123) Sophia Jenkins	b: 1869	d: young

4.2121) Arvella Jenkins married Charles Cook (#4.141).

4.2122) Georgina Jenkins married Ernest Rupert DesBarres in 1893.
Children:
4.21221) Harold Rupert DesBarres   b: Jan. 31/1894
4.21222) Marie Letitia DesBarres   b: Oct. 19/1895
4.21223) Jean Aberdeen DesBarres   b: Aug. 13/1897
4.21224) Elsie Croft DesBarres   b: Oct. 2/1899
4.21225) Erna Hart DesBarres   b: July 9/1903
4.21226) George Mortimer DesBarres   b: Mar. 26/1906
4.21227) William Frederick Clyde DesBarres b: Aug. 25/1908

4.213) Arabella Scott married Charles B. Cunningham, a shoemaker at the time of their marriage, son of John and Susan Cunningham of Guysborough, in Sept., 1868. They moved to Roachvale, where they farmed.
Children:
4.2131) Laura B. Cunningham   b: 1869   m: David Graham/ Roachvale
4.2132) George F. Cunningham   b: 1873   d: 1902
4.2133) Ada May Cunningham   b: Sept. 17/1873   d: 1877

4.218) George Francis Scott married Sarah Bigelow Matthews (b: Oct. 25, 1864), daughter of John and Catherine Matthews of Canso, in 1882. They lived in Canso, where he was a commercial fisherman.
Children:
4.2181) Katherine Lillian Scott   b: Feb. 26/1887 m: Charles Needs
4.2182) Clara Hilda Scott   b: Oct./1888   m: Harold Goodwin

--

4.24) Eliza Cook never married.

--

4.26) Maria Cook married Charles William Bigsby (b: June 15/1822), a merchant, on Feb. 1, 1855, at Guysborough. He was a son of John and Rachel (Critchett) Bigsby They moved to Isaac's Harbour where he became the lighthouse keeper. He also worked as a carpenter.
Children:
4.261) James Hart Bigsby   b: Nov. 22/1859   d: Dec. 11/1860
4.262) Elizabeth Bigsby   b: @ 1863
4.263) Alva Bigsby   b: @ 1869
4.264) Annie Maria C. Bigsby   b: Dec. 3/1874   d: Mar. 22/1876

--

4.27) Mary Randall Cook was a school teacher @ 1850. She married James Sutherland on July 19/1853.

~

4.3) William <u>Francis</u> Cook, Esq. married Eliza Cunningham on May 5/1822. She was born Jan. 20/1802, and died Jan. 3/1850. Francis Cook was a prominent citizen of Guysborough County, holding various public offices. In later years, he moved to Canso, where he was involved in many business activities. (CR4.3)

Children:

4.31) Eliza Cook	b: Sept. 1/1823	d: Nov. 12/1895
4.32) Thomas Cutler Cook	b: Aug. 28/1828	d: Nov. 12/1898
4.33) Ruth Amelia Webb Cook	b: Aug. 11/1830	d: July 26/1831
4.34) Harriet Amelia Cook	b: Mar. 15/1833	d: July 18/1851
4.35) Francis Cranswick Cook	b: Nov. 12/1835	
4.36) John Cunningham Cook	b: Dec. 6/1837	drowned
4.37) Sophia Grace Cook	b: Jan. 19/1840	
4.38) James Randall Cook	b: Feb. 21/1843	

4.31) Eliza Cook married Jairus Hart (b: Mar. 31/1819, d: Oct. 25/1906), on Feb. 11/1846. They had no children. Jairus was a son of Tyrus and Martha (Ingraham) Hart, and was a partner in Young and Hart Co. of Halifax. He became a director of the Bank of Nova Scotia before becoming president in 1899.

In November 1989, their former home was designated as a City of Halifax heritage property.

Jairus and Eliza (Cook) Hart House
1340 Barrington Street, Halifax
*(Now used as Engineering
Mathematics Building
for Dalhousie University)*

--

4.32) Thomas Cutler Cook held various positions in the town of Canso. He was appointed a Notary Public on July 9/1862. In 1865 he was a school teacher. In 1871 he was the Enumerator of the Census. He was a merchant, and became Collector of Customs. He married Emma J. Bigelow on Jan. 5/1860. She was born @ 1839, and died Sept. 5/1899. She was the daughter of William Bigelow, the Collector of Customs at Canso.

Children:

4.321) Sarah Eliza Cook	b: Apr. 20/1862	d: 1949
4.322) Frank Bigelow Cook	b: May 6/1863	
4.323) Sophia Pamela Cook	b: Oct. 15/1865	d: Sept. 6/1868
4.324) Wm James Coleman Cook	b: July 15/1867	d: May 21/1925
		(CR4.324)
4.325) Emma Harriet Cook	b: Oct. 15/1869	d: Apr. 15/1916
4.326) George Cunningham Cook	b: May 10/1871	d: Nov.21/1928
4.327) Maria Norris Cook	b: Oct. 31/1873	
4.328) Lavinia Whitman Cook	b: Jan. 13/1876	
4.329) Edna Corinna Cook	b: Sept.22/1879	
4.32 10) Thomas Whitman Cook	b: Sept.10/1882	

4.321) Sarah Cook (Sadie) married Charles Ephraim Lohnes, a skipper from Lunenburg, on Nov. 11, 1879, at Halifax by Rev. J. B. Uniacke. He was given command of the schooner *Reliance*, owned by his father-in-law. (CR4.321)
Children:

4.3211) Blanche Esther Lohnes	b: Sept. 7/1888	d: Apr. 5/1974
4.3212) Frank Chester Lohnes	b: June 15/1881	
4.3213) Child died a baby	b: ?	

4.3211) Blanche Lohnes married Alexander Millar Davis on Nov. 30/1905. He was born in Wanstead, England, and came to Hazel Hill to work at the Commercial Cable Co. They had eight **children:** Ross, Olga (m: Neal), Francis, Pool, Alexander, Charles, Dora (m: Woodworth), Muriel (m: Sealey).

4.3212) Frank Lohnes married Elva Williams. **Children:** Nelson Lohnes, Frank Lohnes, Alice Lohnes.

--

4.322) Frank Cook migrated to Oakland, California, where he became a grocery merchant. He co-owned and operated a store there, with his brother, Will. He married Maud A. Thomas, youngest daughter of William and Susan Thomas of Canard, Cornwallis, on Oct. 20, 1888.
Children:

4.3221) Frank B. Cook, Jr.	b: Oct./1889
4.3222) Maud Cook	b: Dec./1898

4.3221) Frank B. Cook, Jr. became an engineer. He was a Lieutenant in the US Marines during WWI, taking part in the events at Chateau-Thierry, June 6, 1918. He received the D. S. C. for extraordinary heroism. After the war, he became a Civil Engineer for the State of California.

4.3222) Maud Cook married Marshall Evans.

--

4.324) William J.C. Cook (Will) migrated to California, and co-owned and operated a store with his brother Frank. He married Mary A. McKenzie. He died in 1925.[CR4.324]
Child:
4.3241) Edna May Cook   b: @1905
        Married Howard W. Cliff, a mechanic. They lived in Napa, California.
4.3242) Child who died an infant.

--

4.325) Emma Cook married Dr. DeBlois C. Harrington, a dentist from Philadelphia on Aug. 18, 1892.
Child:
4.3251) Frances Harrington

--

Sam Lord's Castle

4.326) George Cook was acting Paymaster on board the Niobe, a Canadian Navy Ship in Halifax Harbour when the Halifax Explosion occurred in 1917[CR4.326a]. He married Lillian Florence (Lilly) Hanson (b: 1876 Virginia, USA – d: 1945) in 1894.

Family tradition is that George and Lily owned and lived in Prince's Lodge, the Duke of Kent's estate on Bedford Basin.[CR4.326b] In later years he and Lilly bought a castle in Barbados that had belonged to the Pirate Sam Lord. Family legend has it that George was murdered in Barbados by being fed ground glass by the servants. [CR4.326]
Child:
4.3261) George Elliot Cook [CR4.3261]

--

4.327) Maria (Minnie or Min) Cook never married. She was well educated and became a governess.

--

4.329) Edna Cook married Ernest Chipman Harper on Sept. 28, 1903. She was one of the early women graduates of Acadia University. She taught school at Canso Academy, and @ 1908 was a teacher of English at the Provincial Normal School, Truro.
Child:
4.3291) Ernest Harper

~

4.35) Francis Cranswick Cook married **1st)** Sarah Alice Fuller from Lower Horton, N.S., on Oct. 14/1864. He was a merchant in the Port Mulgrave area @ 1870-1880.
Children:
4.351) Leila Alice Euphemia Cook	b: Jan. 8/1866	d: 1873
4.352) Francis Clement <u>Hartley</u> Cook	b: Mar. 12/1870	
4.353) Aubrey Fuller Cook	b: July 16/1876	
4.354) Estelle Amanda Cook	b: Feb. 15/1875	

He married **2nd)** Elizabeth Catherine Wylde on Aug. 21/1878.
Children:
4.355) Carrie Evelyne Louise Cook	b: July 19/1879
4.356) Genevieve Cook	b: July 13/1881

Some of this family migrated to California:
Hartley (who died in Oakland), and at least one sister. The parents moved to California also, and died there.

--

4.37) Sophia Grace Cook married William J. Coleman, Jr., on June 18/1867, at the home of Jairus Hart.
Children:
4.371) Eliza Hart Coleman	b: Aug.12/1868	d: 1895

    Married Frederick Hart. No further info.

4.372) Florence Louise Coleman	b: May 8/1871

--

4.38) James Randall Cook married Margaret Lowden Nichols, daughter of Robert and Mary (Williams) Nichols of St. James' River, Antigonish Co., on Jan. 13/1884. This family lived at Bayfield N.S. James died of "Lagrippe" in 1917.
Children:
4.381) Sophia Grace Cook	b: Aug. 14/1885
4.382) Mary Elizabeth Cook	b: Aug. 20/1887
4.383) Lillian Evelyn Cook	b: Nov. 9/1889
4.384) Francis Benjamin Randall Cook (Frank)	
	b: May 15/1892

4.381) Sophia Grace Cook married Francis B. MacKenzie, Post Master at Truro, N.S.
Children:

4.3811) Mary Catherine MacKenzie   b: Nov. 19/1903
4.3812) Evelyn Jean MacKenzie   b: Oct. 13/1910
4.3813) Margaret Lucy MacKenzie   b: May 5/1912
4.3814) Francis MacKenzie   b: July 11/1914

4.382) Mary Elizabeth Cook lived to be 96 years old. She married James B. Fraser.
Children:
4.3821) Isabelle Evelyn Fraser   b: Mar. /1911
4.3822) Mary Fraser   b: Oct. /1913   d: infancy
4.3823) Basil Fraser   b: June/1916
4.3824) Margaret Fraser   Married Joseph Cooke
4.3825) Mary Fraser   Married Harold Schultz
4.3826) H. Spurgeon Fraser
4.3827) Jairus Fraser

4.383) Lillian Evelyn Cook married John Bertram MacDonald, a roofing contractor.
Children:
4.3831) Bertram Randall MacDonald   b: Jan. 30/1915
4.3832) Gordon Henry MacDonald   b: Feb. 1/1916
4.3833) Jean Margaret MacDonald   b: Aug. 2/1917
4.3834) Clare Peace MacDonald   b: Feb. 25/1919

~

4.4) Mary Elizabeth Cook married James Randall, son of Elisha and Mary (Tuttle) Randall, of Little River (Tracadie), N.S., on Jan. 25/1818.
Children:
4.41) Elisha William Randall   b: Apr. 30/1819
4.42) Francis Cook Randall   b: @ 1825   d: Mar. 5/1833

4.41) Elisha Randall married Ruth Amelia Randall, daughter of Elisha Matthew and Mary (Cunningham) Randall, on Mar. 17/1858. **Children:**
4.411) Elizabeth Randall   b: Mar. 4/1859   m: George Hart
4.412) William Francis Randall   b: Nov. 27/1860   d: June 2/1861
4.413) Emma Mary Randall   b: Dec. 22/1862   m: Rozell Stevens
4.414) Sophia Grace Randall   b: Sept. 19/1865   m: Charles Gass

~

4.5) Sarah <u>Amelia</u> Cook married John Jost (b: 1797, d: July 12, 1883), on Sept. 5/1820. John was a shoemaker, the son of John Casper and Catherine Jost. John and his brother Chris established J. & C. Jost store in Guysborough. He later started a business of his own. John and Amelia built a home on Main Street in Guysborough, that is featured as a beautifully restored heritage home, in the book Early Homes & Families of N.S. (Atlantic Hearth: Mary Byers & Margaret McBurney).

Children:

4.51) Mary Elizabeth Jost	b: Nov. 28/1830	d: Dec. 28/1898
4.52) John Francis Jost	b: Aug. 20/1833	d: Feb. 18/1858
4.53) Catherine Maria Jost	b: Aug. 10/1835	d: Feb. 8/1919
4.54) Lavinia Davis Jost	b: Feb. 28/1838	d: Sept. 10/1872
4.55) James Randall Jost	b: July 29/1840	d: Oct. 23/1857
4.56) Henry Marshall Jost	b: Apr. 20/1843	d: Aug. 25./1929

4.51) Mary Elizabeth Jost never married. In later years she kept house for her brother Marsh.

--

4.52) John Francis Jost died at age 25, unmarried.

--

4.53) Catherine Maria (Kate) Jost married Rev. Thomas Gaetz, a Methodist Minister, on July 9, 1857. (He died Oct. 24/1860 in Newfoundland.) Although she is buried in Red Deer, Alberta, there is a memorial stone in the old Methodist Cemetery at Guysborough in her name.

Child:

4.531) John Jost Gaetz	b: June/1859	d: Dec. 24/1937

He was a farmer at Red Deer, Alberta (born in Newfoundland). The 1891 census of Red Deer shows him, his widowed mother, Henry and Mary Jost, and Thomas Ferguson, all living in the same house. He married Grace M. Elder. Thomas Ferguson was still living with this family in 1911.

--

4.54) Lavinia Davis Jost married Jonathon Hartley on Dec. 11/1861. She died before the 1881 census.

Children:

4.541) Lavinia Tyson Hartley		b: 1862	d: Apr. 8/1925
4.542) Henry Fenwick Hartley		b: 1865	
4.543) Kate Amelia Hartley	twin	b: May 27/1870	d: Feb. 23/1889
4.544) Lily Hartley	twin	b: May 27/1870	

4.541) Lavinia Tyson Hartley married Thomas Downie Kirk, a dry goods merchant, of Antigonish and had children: Hartley Kirk, Colin F. Kirk, Henry Kirk, and Douglas Kirk. Her father, Jonathan, lived with them in 1891, at Antigonish Harbour, Southside.

--

4.55) James Randall Jost died at age 17.

--

4.56) Marsh Jost never married. He was a merchant at Guysborough for some years.

~

4.6) Benjamin Cook never married.

~

4.7) James William Cook was a carpenter, and became the Postmaster of Belle Creek, P.E.I. [CR4.7] He married Sarah Ann Bears (1821-1908), daughter of David and Dorcas (Whitman) Bears[CR4.7W], on Jan. 5/1841.
Children:

4.71) Abraham Whitman Cook	b: Oct. 9/1841	
4.72) John Spearwater Cook	b: June 5/1843	d: June 26/1853
4.73) Isaac Cook	b: Jan. 16/1845	
4.74) Joseph Cook	b: Aug. 20/1846	d: Jan. 22/1850
4.75) Letitia Cook	b: Aug. 28/1848	
4.76) James Cook	b: May 14/1851	
4.77) Alfred Cook	b: Oct. 20/1854	
4.78) Charles Cook	b: Feb. 4/1857	
4.79) Francis Cook	b: July 11/1860	

4.71) Abraham Whitman Cook married Ellen MacDonald on Oct. 6/1864.
Children:

4.711) Francis Isaac Cook	b: Mar. 4/1865
4.712) Abraham Whitman Cook	b: Mar. 24/1867
4.713) Donald MacDonald Cook	b: June 11/1868
4.714) James William Cook	b: Jan. 5/1871
4.715) Angus Cook	b: Aug. 6/1872
4.716) Wellington Dixon Cook	b: Sept. 1/1874
4.717) Isabella Cook	b: Mar. 3/1876
4.718) Alfred Henry Cook	b: Jan. 6/1878
4.719) Joseph Cook	b: May 22/1879

--

4.73) Isaac Cook married Susanna Bears on Apr. 7/1870.
Children:

4.731) Benjamin Cook	b: Feb. 13/1871	
4.732) Daniel James Cook	b: Oct. 22/1872	d: Mar. 31/1873
4.733) David Albert Cook	b: Apr. 13/1874	d: Sept. 4/1876
4.734) Mary Elizabeth Cook	b: June 13/1876	
4.735) John Cook	b: June 26/1879	
4.736) David Cook	b: July 31/1881	
4.737) Olivia J. Cook	b: @ 1889	Married Christopher Donohue at Lynn, Mass., in 1909.

--

4.75) Letitia Cook married Donald McLeod on Feb. 4/1875, and had **children:**

4.751) James William McLeod	b: Jan. 22/1877
4.752) Angus McLeod	b: Dec. 2/1878
4.753) Christina McLeod	b: May 16/1880
4.754) Daniel/Donald McLeod	b: Mar. 16/1882
4.755) John Francis McLeod	b: Aug. 1/1885
4.756) Joseph Charles McLeod	b: ?
4.757) Sarah Ann McLeod	b: Oct. 19/1891

--

4.76) James Cook was a preserver of fish and meat at Carleton Point, P.E.I. He married Flora McQuarrie on Feb. 20/1875.
Children:

4.761) Sarah Ann Cook	b: Dec. 23/1875	d: Jan 20/1949
4.762) John Cook	b: Dec. 26/1877	
4.763) Margaret Ellen Cook	b: Nov. 18/1880	d: 1953
4.764) Mary Letitia Cook	b: Oct. 2/1882	
4.765) James Herbert Cook	b: Nov. 20/1884	

4.761) Ann Cook married Thomas Bears.
Children:

4.7611) George Bears	b:	
4.7612) Flora Ann Bears	b: Feb. 9/1901	Married Cyril Stanton Lewis.
4.7613) John Stewart Bears	b: Dec. 29/1902	
4.7614) Alfred Edward Bears	b: Sept. 13/1908	
4.7615) James Thomas Bears	b: Mar. 14/1905	
4.7616) Sarah Ellen Bears	b: Feb. 17/1911	
4.7617) Jeanette Bears	b: May 2/1914	
4.7618) Marion Esther Bears	b: Aug. 4/1915	
4.7619) Walter Leslie Bears	b: Sept. 19/1917	

--

4.77) Alfred Cook was a carpenter at Carleton Point, P.E.I. He married Hannah Campbell on Apr. 13/1881.
Child:
4.771) Charles Hector Cook   b: Mar. 15/1882
4.772) James William Cook   b: Dec. 26/1883

--

4.78) Charles Cook was a farmer at Bell Creek, P.E.I., and later became a carpenter. He married **1st)** Margaret Stewart, of Springton on Oct. 2, 1883, at Belfast. They immigrated to Massachusetts in 1888, living in the Boston area. After Margaret's death, he married again. **Children**:
4.781) James Cook   b: April/1885
4.782) Mary Cook   b: April/1887
4.783) William Wickliff Cook   b: Mar.17/1889
4.784) Albert Cook Cook   b: Dec.22/1892
4.785) Margaret Cook   b: Nov.21/1894
4.786) Sarah Ellen Cook   b: Sept. 29/1896
4.787) Charles Stewart Cook   b: May 9/1899 USA
4.788) Catherine Letitia Cook   b: Dec. 19/1900 USA

**William W. Cook Sr.,
Albert Angus Cook
and
Charles Stewart Cook,
in that order,
sons of
Charles and Margaret Stewart
Cook** [CR4.78]

4.783) William Wickliff Cook married Edith Mae Baker on March 17, 1915. They had 11 **children:** (some who died at birth).

4.7831) Mae Ellen Cook	b: May 1/1915
4.7832) Catherine Stewart Cook	b: May 20/1921
4.7833) William Wickliff, Cook, Jr.	b: 1922 d: 1944 WWII
4.7834) Charles Albert Cook	b: Nov. 15/1924
4.7835) Addie Frances Cook	b: Nov. 30/1925
4.7836) James Howard Cook twin	b: @1927
4.7837) John Howard Cook twin	b: @ 1927
4.7838) Ralph E. Cook	b: Feb./1930

--

4.79) Francis (Frank) Cook was a shoemaker at Bell Creek, P.E.I. He married Mary Belle MacKay from Scotsburn, N.S.
Children:

4.791) James William Cook	b: Aug. 19/1889
4.792) Martha Thompson Cook	b: Dec. 3/1894
4.793) Joseph Henry Cook twin	b: Feb. 15/1897
4.794) Isabella Cook twin	b: Feb. 15/1897
4.795) Francis Alfred Whitman Cook	b: Dec. 25/1899
4.796) Robert Thompson Cook	b: Apr. 7/1903
4.797) Letitia Cook	b: May 8/1905

--

4.791) James W. Cook was a mover of buildings, with capstan and horse. He married **1st)** Sarah Euphemia (Sadie) Ross, and **2nd)** Adeline Mabey (after 1945), daughter of George and Dorcas (Horton) Mabey. They had 9 **children,** including:

4.7911) Isabella Cook	b: May 3/1914	d: Mar. 17, 2007
4.7912) Mary Bell Cook	b: July 22, 1915	d: Feb. 20, 2002
4.7913) John Cook	(married Mary Bell)	
4.7914) Shirley Cook	(married Krug)	

--

4.792) Martha Thompson Cook married Charles Hancock. **Children:**

4.7921) Martha Hancock	b: Aug. 1/1915
4.7922) Fannie Gay Hancock	b: Aug. 26/1919

--

4.793) Joseph Henry Cook was a farmer and also like his brother James W., moved buildings with capstan and horse. (CR4.793) He married Elsie Adelia MacDonald (1903-1942). The lived in the Belle River area. They had 3 **children:**

4.7931) Daniel Archibald Cook - Became a Marine Engineer & farmer.
4.7932) Gladys Isabel Cook - Married John Charles MacLeod.
4.7933) Frances Cook

--

4.794) Isabella Cook married Murdoch Gillis; they had one **son,** Malcolm Gillis (1927-1988).

4.8) William Cameron Cook married Sarah Esther McAllister (#1. <u>10</u> 51), from Salmon River, on Jan. 25/1844, at Lynn., Mass. She was born Sept. 24/1824, and died Nov. 21/1922. At the time of the US 1900 census, she was the mother of 10 children, 8 of whom were living. Living with her were daughters Minnie E., age 34, and Esther Grader, age 32, and 2 Grader grandchildren.

Children:

4.81) Charles Albert Cook	b: Feb. 24/1845	
4.82) John Henry Cook	b: Nov. 11/1846	
4.83) Herbert W. Cook	b: Jan. 30/1849	
4.84) Joseph C. Cook	b: May/1851	
4.85) Barlow M. Cook	b: Aug. 9/1853	
4.86) Caroline E. Cook	b: Dec. 4/1855	
4.87) Maria Cook	b: Dec. 2/1858	
4.88) Sarah A. Cook	b: Apr. 2/1860	d: Nov. 2/1897
4.89) Emma A. Cook	b: June 15/1864	d: 1908
4.8 <u>10</u>) Esther Cook	b: Aug. 20/1866	d: Feb. 2/1920

4.81) Charles A. Cook never married.

--

4.82) John Henry Cook married **1st)** Annie Maria McDonald (b: 1857), daughter of John and Christiana McDonald, from Clam Harbour, on Sept. 27/1876.

Children:

4.821) Ethel Augusta Cook	b: July 6/1878	d: Nov./1980
4.822) Mabel Cook	b: Sept. 25/1884,	d: 1892 Lynn, Mass.
4.823) Clarence William Cook	b: Feb. 9/1888	d: July 13/1961
4.824) John Murray Cook	b: Aug. 21/1889	d: Aug. 22/1919

The Family of John Henry Cook

John Henry and Albert Cook

John Henry Cook married **2ⁿᵈ)** Sarah Jane (Stearns) Carr on Apr. 9/1901. She was born at Goshen, N.S. , the daughter of George and Esther (Malloy) Stearns. *George Stearns was a son of Dr. Benjamin Stearns of Mass., who was one of the early settlers at Antigonish, although he lived in various places throughout Nova Scotia. George Stearns married three times and had a number of children. Esther Stearns died of Typhoid Fever in 1886.* Sarah Jane Stearns Carr was the widow of George Carr of Ragged Head. She died of breast cancer on Nov. 4/1918 at Cook's Cove.
Child:
4.825) Albert Henry Cook   b: Apr. 18/1902   d: June 9/1979

--

4.821) Ethel Cook married John Obed <u>Parker</u> Sangster on Aug. 1/1903.

4.823) Clarence Cook became a Baptist minister. He married Gladys Eaton from Granville Ferry, N.S., on June 18, 1919. Clarence was a veteran of World War I. He was an airman, shot down, and landed in a potato field. He was captured and spent two years in a prison camp,. where he did ministry work among the soldiers. He was wounded in his breast and lung. He died of lung cancer at age 74. [CR4.823]
Child:
4.8231) Murray <u>Eaton</u> Cook   b: 1923   drowned, N.B.,1949[CR4.8231]

4.824) John Murray Cook married Gracy Gertrude Turner (Gertie) Burton from Arichat, Cape Breton, on Jan. 1/1919, in Pictou County. She was a daughter of Henry Arthur and Mary (Minnie) Burton. Her father was a Harness Maker. They were married only seven months when he died of heart failure, on August 23, 1919 at Antigonish. He was thirty years old. Gertie married Horace Leander Kinsman in 1922, at Wolfville.

4.825) Albert Cook married Amelia Peterson, daughter of Alexander and Laura Jane (Teed) Peterson from Cape Breton, on Oct. 20/1923. She was born Jan. 19/1903, and died Mar. 18/1985. They had four **children**: Mabel (d: infant), Esther (m: Earl Myers), Murray (m: **1ˢᵗ)** Blanche Taylor, **2ⁿᵈ)** Nancy McCarthy), Laura (m: Daniel Weir).

--

4.83) Herbert W. Cook migrated to Lynn, Mass. in 1870. He was a carpenter, and then became a real estate agent. He married Mary <u>Isabelle</u> Carson from Maine. According to the 1900 US census, she was the mother of two children, both of whom were living. They lived next door to his mother, Esther Cook, age 73. Isabelle died in December, 1911, and is buried in Pine Grove

Cemetery, Lynn. (CR4.83)   **Children**:
4.831) Cora B. Cook   b: 1882
4.832) Laura Cook   b: 1894

--

4.84) Joseph C. Cook migrated to Lynn, Mass. In 1870. He worked as a cutter in a shoe factory in 1910. By 1930, he was living in Flint, Michigan, and working as a janitor in an auto plant. He married **1st)** Frances M. Morgan, daughter of John and Elizabeth (Callahan) Morgan of Guysborough. She died in 1895 at Lynn, of Typho-catarrhal fever.
Children:
4.841) William Cook   b: Oct. 16/1877
4.842) Esther Cook   b: Mar. 28/1880 She married Austin F.
        Paine and had a son. She died before the 1910 US census.

Joseph C. Cook married **2nd)** Matilda L. (Spinney) Harding (b: 1866), a widow with children, on May 29, 1900, at Beverly, Mass. She was born in Central Argyle, Nova Scotia, to Simeon and Abbie Spinney.
Children:
4.843) Lloyd I. Cook   b: 1902 (divorced by 1930 census)
                                       (Lived at Waterford, Michigan)
4.844) Linden E. Cook   b: 1904 Married Emma L. ___. They had a
        son, Charles Cook (b: 1918). It was stated on the 1930 census that
        they were both married at age 17. They also lived in Flint, Michigan.
--
4.85) Barlow M. Cook was a plumber. He married Nellie Miriam Rhodes, daughter of Charles M. and Harriet A. (Downing) Rhodes, on Aug. 1, 1883, at Lynn, Mass. Barlow was an ice cream merchant in 1910. Nellie died on Mar. 9, 1900.
Children:
4.851) Hattie E. Cook   b: May 9/1884
4.852) Albert Barlow Cook   b: July 12/1887

4.851) Hattie E. Cook   married Albert Romdey, son of Albert and Deborah (Crowell) Roundy of Marblehead, on May 23, 1906. He was a milk team driver at Lynn. On the 1910 census, her brother Albert and father Barlow Cook lived with the family. **Child**:
4.8511) Albert Mercall Roundy   b: Feb. 9/1910
4.852)   Albert Cook was, at the time of his first marriage, an ice cream manufacturer. Later he became a Jitney driver. He married **1st)** Mattie M. Johnson on Apr. 19, 1906, at Lynn. They divorced and he married **2nd)** Alice Newhall, a music teacher, on Oct. 1, 1914, at Lynn. **Children**:
4.8521) Albert B. Cook
4.8522) Bromley Newhall Cook   b: Oct. 8/1916   d: Apr./1985
4.8523) Robert Cook

4.8522) Bromley Cook was a police officer (CR4.8522). He married Arlene A. Darsney.

--

4.86) Caroline Cook married Thomas Cook (#1.319). Children are listed under that number.

--

4.87) Maria (Minnie) Cook married Charles B. Dow, son of Porter and Laurinda (Reed) Dow, on June 18, 1903, at Lynn, Mass.

--

4.88) Sarah (Sadie) Cook never married.

--

4.89) Emma Cook married Frank G. Orcutt, son of Henry and Cynthia J. Orcutt of Maine, in 1885, at Lynn, Mass. She died in January, 1908.
Child:
4.891) Mildred O. Orcutt   b: Jan./1886
4.892) Emma Orcutt   b: & d: 1889

--

4.8 10) Esther Cook married Frank Grader. They had children:
Helen M. Grader (b: 1891 d: 1958, m: Hodgkins) and Esther L. Grader (b: 1895 d: 1969; m: Gorman).

~

4.9) Lucy Maria Cook married James Alexander Horton, son of Isaiah and Zipporah (Hyde) Horton, on March 4/1841. He was a Ship Carpenter. They moved to River John, Pictou County, then to Pugwash, before settling in Boston, Mass. Some of their children remained in Cumberland County. Lucy was a widow at the time of the 1880 US Census.
Children:
4.91) Caroline Elizabeth Horton   b: 1842   No further information.
4.92) Lucy Maria Horton   b: 1844
4.93) George Wentworth Horton   b: Apr. 5/1847   d: 1928
4.94) James A. Horton   b: 1849
4.95) Melissa L. Horton   b: 1851   d: 1851
4.96) Emma C. Horton   b: 1856
4.97) Charles M. Horton   b: 1861
4.92) Lucy Maria Horton married Judson Eaton in 1868 and had seven **children**: Eva Eaton, George R. Eaton, James L. Eaton, Annie Eaton, Asa B. Eaton, Morton Eaton, Minetta Eaton.

--

4.93) George Wentworth Horton was a carpenter. He married **1st)** Jane A. Kittrell, daughter of Charles L. & Sarah (Sylvester) Kittrell of Quincy, Mass., at

128

Hingham, Mass., on Apr. 5, 1873. Jane died in 1905. He married **2nd)** Annie P. (Eaton) Wieneau on Aug. 31, 1912. Later they migrated back to Canada and lived at Beckwith, Cumberland Co., NS. **Children**: Harry Horton, Ervin Horton, James Horton.

--

4.94) James A. Horton married Mary P. Washburn of Taunton, Mass., daughter of Albert W. and Clara Washburn, on Apr. 5, 1873. **Children**: Clara M. Horton, Mary W. Horton, James H. Horton.

--

4.96) Emma C. Horton married George W. Emerson, son of Moses and Lydia Emerson of Beverly. It was his 3rd marriage.

--

4.97) Charles M. Horton married Charlotte McKenzie on Jan. 19, 1881. She was also born in NS, a daughter of James C. and Harriet A. McKenzie. **Children**: Hattie L. Horton and Olive L. Horton.

~

4. 10) Caroline Cook married William Freeman, son of James and Hannah (Barss) Freeman of Brookfield, N.S. on Nov. 9/1841.
Children:

4. 10 1) Joseph Henry Freeman	b: 1843	d: Mar. 20/1915
4. 10 2) Henrietta Louisa Freeman	b: Nov. 8/1844	d: Nov. 30/1931
4. 10 3) Lucy Maria Freeman	b: Aug./1846	d: Dec. 3/1931
4. 10 4) Sylvanus Morton Freeman	b: Dec. 1849	d: Aug. 12/1909
4. 10 5) Manton Freeman	b: 1860	d: 1953

Caroline and William moved with some of their grown children and their families to Monticello, Minnesota. Caroline, William and Henrietta (Etta) are buried there. The remaining family moved to Lougheed, Alberta, in 1905/06, and from there branched out into Manitoba, B.C., Ontario and various states in the U.S.

4. 10 1) Joseph Freeman married Adelia Sophia McNayr, daughter of Israel and Elizabeth McNayr, on June 20, 1869. They migrated to Springfield, Annapolis County, where they farmed.
Children:

4. 10 11) Caroline Hulda Freeman	b: June 21/1870	m: Titus J. Ramey
4. 10 12) Hulbert Atwood Freeman	b: April 4/1873	m: Eva A. Littlefield
4. 10 13) Agnes L. Freeman	b: Dec 2/1877	m: Emery C. Durling
4. 10 14) Leslie C. Freeman	b: July 2/1880	m: Helen ?
4. 10 15) Lena Gertrude Freeman	b: June 22/1891	m: Shaw/Hamilton

4. <u>10</u> 2) Henrietta (Etta) Freeman married William Douglas Carder, son of Richard and Louisa Carder, on Nov. 12, 1874, at Brookfield, NS. They had four children. They migrated with her parents to Minnesota. William died in 1889. **Children:** Gertrude Carder (married Horace Wood), Clive Carder, Harry Carder, John Carder.

--

4. <u>10</u> 3) Lucy M. Freeman married Alexander McDonnell son of Angus and Margaret McDonnell, on June 15, 1869. They migrated to Minnesota, then North Dakota.
Children:

4. <u>10</u> 31) Clark Wilson McDonnell	b: May 19/1870	m: Emily Hoblit
4. <u>10</u> 32) Angus McDonnell	b: Mar. 31/1872	m: Laura Pettibone
4. <u>10</u> 33) Edna McDonnell	b: July 10/1874	d: Aug. 6/1874
4. <u>10</u> 34) Aubrey W. McDonnell	b: Mar. 3/1876	m: Bessie Johnson
4. <u>10</u> 35) Ella McDonnell	b: June/1886	m: Andrew B. Grieve
4. <u>10</u> 36) William Freeman McDonnell	b: July/1888	m: Mary M.Thorburn

--

4. <u>10</u> 4) Sylvanus Freeman married Nancy A. Burke, daughter of Benjamin and Elizabeth Burke, on July 26/1873. They migrated to Minnesota, then Alberta. **Children**:

4. <u>10</u> 41) Nina Freeman	b: June/1874	d:Feb./1881
4. <u>10</u> 42) Vance <u>LeRoy</u> Freeman	b: Dec. 2/1875	
4. <u>10</u> 43) Rupert Leon Freeman	b: June 16/1882	

--

4. <u>10</u> 5) Manton Freeman (CR4.<u>10</u> 5) married Nettie J. Sutherland. They lived in various places throughout the USA and Canada, settling in Pouce Coupe, BC. He is buried in Jasper, Alberta.

Manton Freeman

Children:
4. <u>10</u> 51) Edwin Ray Freeman   b: 1891   d: 1962
4. <u>10</u> 52) Hazel May Freeman   b: 1893   d:1954
4. <u>10</u> 53) Nettie Blanche Freeman   b: 1896   d: 1974
4. <u>10</u> 54) Bernice Elizabeth Freeman   b: 1901   d: 1974
4. <u>10</u> 55) Helen Vivian Freeman   b: 1906   d: 1971

~

4. <u>12</u>) Joseph Henry Cook moved with his mother, when she remarried, to Milton, Queens County, N.S., and was educated there. He married Sophie Freeman (b: May 23/1837, d: Oct. 22/1910), daughter of Samuel and Mercy (Knowles) Freeman. Joseph H. Cook became a prominent merchant, was named Justice of the Peace in 1861, holding the position for 52 years. He served as Colonel of the Militia in 1879 during the Fenian Raids. He was elected a Municipal Councillor for Queens County in 1861, and represented Queen's County in the Nova Scotia House of Assembly from 1882 to 1890 as a Liberal member.

Children:
4. <u>12</u> 1) Charles A. Cook   b: Apr. 10/1855   d: July 14/1919
4. <u>12</u> 2) Caroline Seymour Cook   b: @1867
4. <u>12</u> 3) Minnie K. Cook   b: Sept. 4/1857   d: Feb. 15/1935
4. <u>12</u> 4) Snow Parker Freeman Cook   b: Oct. 12/1861   d: Apr. 6/1934

--

4. <u>12</u> 1) Charles A. Cook married Dorinda Winnifred Churchill (Winnie), daughter of Albert and Mercy (Freeman) Churchill, on Dec. 9/1888. **Child:**
4. <u>12</u> 11) Shirley Seymour Cook   b: Oct. 7/1889   Married Masie Armstrong. They lived at Hamilton, Ontario, where he worked as an electrical engineer.

--

4. <u>12</u> 2) Caroline (Carrie) Cook married Charles H. Day, son of Rev. George E. Day of St. John. They had two children, one son, Charles H. Day, Jr., and a daughter, Dorothy Day.

--

4. <u>12</u> 3) Minnie K. Cook married Newton Clark Freeman, widower, on Aug. 12/1914. They had no children.

--

4. <u>12</u> 4) Snow Parker Freeman Cook never married. He became a doctor and opened a medical practice in Oxford, Cumberland County in 1886. In 1892 he sold his practice to continue his medical studies in Europe. He later settled in Gloucester, Mass., where he practiced specialized medicine. [CR4.12 4] He is buried at Milton, N.S.

This ends the section on Benjamin Cook

5) Elizabeth Cook married John Wheaton, son of Caleb and Mary (Owen) Wheaton, on May 15/1796.

This ends the section on Elizabeth Cook

7) James Cook married Bede (Beda/Biddy) Luddington, daughter of Titus and Miriam (Parker) Luddington, who had immigrated from New Haven, Connecticut.
Children:
7.1) Susannah Cook   b: July 4/1797
7.2) Lydia Cook   b: Oct. 8/1799
7.3) William Cook   b:
James Cook died, and his widow, Bede Cook, married John Conrad Demas, widower, on Aug. 8/1802. When he also died (1817), she married for the third time, to David O'Brien.

7.1) Susannah Cook - May have been the Susanna Cook who married Robert Whooten on December 31, 1811, but, if her birthdate is correct, she would have been only @ 14 years old. The names of the **children** of Robert and Susanna (Cook) Whooten were: John Demas Whooten (b: 1812), William Whooten (b: 1815), Godfrey Peart Whooten (b: 1817), Robert Henry Whooten (b: 1818) and Francis Cook Whooten (b: 1828).

--
7.2) Lydia Cook – No further information.

--
7.3) William Cook married **1st)** Margaret Whitman, on Jan. 4/1827.
Children:
7.31) Child   b: Oct. 19/1827
7.32) Hannah Cook   b: Sept. 5/1829   d: July 23/1914
                                    buried Dort's Cove
He married **2nd)** Bethia Godfrey[CR7.33] on March 21/1832. She was a daughter of Benjamin and Catherine (Bigsby) Godfrey.
Children:
7.33) Benjamin Godfrey Cook   b: Mar. 17/1836   d: Oct. 4/1905
7.34) Caroline Elizabeth Cook   b: Dec. 22/1834
7.35) William Cook   b:
After the death of William Cook, Bethia Godfrey Cook married Benjamin Gerry (10. 11) and had children: Elbridge Gerry, Maria Gerry, Donald Gerry, Freeman Gerry and John Gerry.

7.32) Hannah Cook married James Porter, widower, son of James and Elizabeth Porter, on July 16/1868. James Porter, Sr. was born in Scotland. James Porter had, by his first wife, children: William, Levi, Thomas, Margaret and Mary. (Thomas married Agnes Cook # 4.1313.)(Levi Porter married Margaret Myers, migrated to Country Harbour to work in the gold mines; they had 9 children including: Nora Porter, Henry Clinton Porter, Edith Mary Porter, Walter Porter, Effie Porter, Murdock Porter, Stella Porter, Ernest Porter, Stanley Porter – at least 4 of whom died young of TB.)

7.33) Benjamin Godfrey Cook was a sailmaker, who migrated to Gloucester, Mass. He married Catherine Haskins, daughter of John and Catherine Haskins of Liverpool, NS, on July 3, 1857, at Gloucester.
Children:
7.331) Almon B. Cook   b: Nov. 20/1859
7.332) Bethiah Jane (Jennie) Cook   b: 1860
7.333) Minnie (Mina) Cook   b: 1866   d: 1900 unmarried

7.331) Almon Cook was a merchant, and a member of the Masonic Lodge of Gloucester. He married Rose C. (Chase) Osier, daughter of John and Elizabeth Chase of Maine. He was a Clothing Dealer, she was a Dressmaker. She had children from her first marriage, they had none together.

This ends the section on James Cook.

10) Lydia Cook married **1ˢᵗ**) (Perhaps) Daniel Gerry (the record is transcribed *Domnick Gary*) at Marblehead, Mass. on Sept. 26, 1780. ^(CR10) They had a **son:** 10. 1) Daniel Gerry
She married **2ⁿᵈ**) John Collyer (Collier), also at Marblehead, Mass, on Dec. 4, 1787. (The record reads: Mrs. Lydia Gary). She was a widow on June 20/1809, when she gave her land to her son, John Collyer (Collier). The land was in the Bantry area, and had been given to Lydia from her brother, Benjamin Cook.
Children:
10. 2) Lydia Collier   b: 1788 Marblehead
10. 3) John Collier   b: 1791 Marblehead
10. 4) Elizabeth White Collier   b: 1794 Marblehead
10. 5) Ebenezer Collier   b: Mar. 1798   d: Nov. 30, 1847
and probably:
10. 6) Mary Ann Collier   b: 1799 Nova Scotia
On Nov. 23, 1809, Lydia Collier, widow, married **3ʳᵈ**) Titus Luddington, widower.

10. 1) Daniel Gerry received a gift of land from his uncle, Benjamin Cook, in 1805. He married Sarah Bigsby, also in 1805. This marriage was not successful, and Sarah's brother, John Bigsby, was called upon to support his sister both before and after her husband's death.
Children:

10.11) Benjamin Gerry	b: Apr. 12/1806
10.12) Catherine Gerry	b: Oct. 7/1808
10.13) Sarah Gerry	b: Nov. 2/1812
10.14) Lydia L. Gerry	b: Nov. 15/1814 d: Apr. 19/1878
10.15) daughter	b: ?

10. 11) Benjamin Gerry married Bethia (Godfrey) Cook, widow of William Cook (#7.3), and had **children:**
10. 111) Elbridge Gerry {see (CR10. 111)}(m: **1st)** Martha Jones, daughter of Thomas and Ann Jones of Cook's Cove, on Nov. 9, 1872, at Pictou, **2nd)** Janet Andrews)
10. 112) Daniel W. Gerry (b: 1852) married at Gloucester, Mary Wilkinson
10. 113) Freeman Cobs Gerry (b: 1854, d: 1920, Truro, m: **1st)** Esther Jones, sister to Martha Jones, on Apr. 27, 1880 and he m: **2nd)** Elizabeth George, daughter of James & Ann (Jamieson) George, on May 30, 1897)

--

10. 12) Catherine Gerry married Elias Cook (#1.14).

--

10. 13) Sarah Gerry was a school teacher @ 1839. She married Benjamin Godfrey, son of Benjamin and Catherine (Bigsby) Godfrey, on Nov. 25, 1843.
Children:
10. 131) Agnes Osborne Godfrey
10. 132) Esther Godfrey - never married.

10. 131) Agnes Osborne Godfrey married James Albert Peart. She died before the 1881 census. **Children**:
10. 1311) Harris Gordon Peart (never married) was a veteran of WWI
10. 1312) Albert Osborne Peart migrated to St. John, N.B.   He married Elizabeth Duroche and they had a son, Harry Peart.

--

10.14) Lydia L. Gerry married **1st)** Charles Thistle Harris, Jr., a mariner, at Beverly, Mass., in 1835. They had **children**:

10.141) Mary Jane Harris	b: Apr. 1/1840	
10.142) George W. Harris	b: 1840	d: 1841

She married **2nd)** Samuel Curtis, widower, son of Samuel Curtis of Boston, in 1853, at Lynn, Mass. He was an accountant. He d: of consumption in 1854.
10.141) Mary Jane (Jennie) Harris married Samuel N. Frothingham on May 9/1860. They had a son, George N. Frothingham, b: 1864

~

<u>10</u>. 2) Lydia Collier married Wintrop Cook (#1.4). See children under that number.

~

<u>10</u>. 4) Elizabeth White Collier married George Henry Hadley, son of Joseph and Eleanor (Abbot) Hadley, in 1815. They had 7 **children**:

<u>10</u>. 41) ? Child	b: 1818 No further info.
<u>10</u>. 42) Joseph Henry Hadley	b: 1819
<u>10</u>. 43) George Thomas Hadley	b: 1822 No futher info.
<u>10</u>. 44) John Collier Hadley	b: 1827 No further info.
<u>10</u>. 45) Ruth Elizabeth Hadley	b: 1830
<u>10</u>. 46) William Hadley	b: 1833
<u>10</u>. 47) James John Hadley	b: 1837

George Henry died and the family migrated to Gloucester, Mass. Elizabeth lived with her son Joseph's family until Oct./1880, when he died of a shock from injuries at age 60, and his 83 year old mother died the very next day.

--

<u>10</u>. 42) Joseph Henry Hadley became a Ship Carpenter, and later was a Superintendant of the Marine Railroad at Gloucester. He married Annabella Lucas, daughter of Thomas and Hannah (McKenzie) Lucas of Guysborough Intervale, at Gloucester. They had **children**:

<u>10</u>. 421) Georgianna Hadley	b: 1844
<u>10</u>. 422) William H. Hadley	b: 1845
<u>10</u>. 423) Jerusha Elizabeth Hadley	b: 1848
<u>10</u>. 424) John F. Hadley	b: 1850
<u>10</u>. 425) Joseph Franklin Hadley	b: Mar. 9/1859

<u>10</u>. 421) Georgianna Hadley married George W. Adams, a Fish Dealer, who was born in Virginia. They had **children**: Mabel P. Adams (m: Frank N. Hodgkins, merchant of Gloucester), Alice G. Adams (never married), Elizabeth Adams (m: Frank L. Stevens).

<u>10</u>. 422) William H. Hadley died of consumption at age 17.

<u>10</u>. 423) Lizzie Hadley married Francis E. Johnson, a fish merchant, of Brooklyn, NY. They had a **son**, F. H. Johnson (b: Sept./1880).

<u>10</u>. 424) John F. Hadley was a carpenter. He married Henrietta Buffum of Salem in 1875, at Gloucester. They had a **son**: William Buffum Hadley (b: 1880).

<u>10</u>. 425) J. Franklin Hadley became a physician in Waltham, Mass. He was a member of the Masonic Lodge. He married Mary A. Friend, daughter of

William and Anna (Waite) Friend at Gloucester. He died of Chronic pneumonia at age 35, in 1894. They had two **daughters**: Hortense V. Hadley (b: 1887), and Mildred Gertrude Hadley (b: 1892), who m: Elmer E. Sherwood and lived in Ridgewood, N.J.

--

<u>10</u>. 45) Ruth E. Hadley married Edmund Pyne in 1849, at Gloucester. They had **children**: Emma Pyne (d: age 24), Alfred Pyne (m: Ida Bogart), Florence Pyne, Alvin Pyne.

--

<u>10</u>. 46) William Hadley married Eliza J. Cunningham of Rockport, Maine. He was a Trader. They had **children**: Grace C. Hadley (m: George B. Walker), Edith L. Hadley, Mary L. (May) Hadley, Jennie Hadley (m: Henry M. Taylor).

--

<u>10</u>. 47) James John Hadley became a butcher. He married Amelia B. Lane at Gloucester in 1859. They had **children**: Carrie C. Hadley (married D. Frank Smith), Lena Hadley (d: young), Joseph H. Hadley (married Frances M. Hanley, daughter of Freeman and Amelia Hanley of Guysborough, NS).

~

<u>10</u>. 5) Ebenezer Collier was a cordwainer. He died in Marblehead from typhus fever age 49, on Nov. 30, 1847.

~

<u>10</u>. 6) Mary Ann Collier married Simon Walsh and had a son James Walsh (b: 1827).

This ends the section on Lydia Cook.

References

Most vital statistics and census' records are available online through various websites. I used Ancestry.com, Nova Scotia Historical Vital Statistics, FamilySearch.org, AmericanAncestors.org - (through N.E.H.G.S.), FindAGrave.com, Internment.net, and various other regional online sources. **Many individuals** have shared information with me.

(CR000) I wish I could take credit for writing this, however, I gleaned it from a Rootsweb Listserve off the Internet. There was no author/writer named.

(CR001) The earliest found records show Marblehead, Massachusetts as the residence for Elias Cook. Marblehead was settled as a fishing village in the first half of the 1600s. In 1629 a large amount of English Puritans with a charter and a mission to set up a Puritan commonwealth established a settlement on the Massachusetts Bay. Nearly 20,000 English immigrants arrived within the next decades (called the Great Migration). The village in 1650 was about 100 inhabitants; by 1680 it had grown to 600. By the 1670's Marblehead's original 44 householders had grown to just over 100.

The local society consisted of two groups, the men who managed the fishing industry and those who laboured at sea. Neither group closely followed the values and institutions of Puritan Massachusetts. Closer counterparts to Marblehead were the settlements of the Isle of Shoals (Maine), and other centers of the fishing industry. These were fishing camps for **West Country men** rather than experiments for devout Anglicans.

Our Elias Cook may have been a west country man. The West Country is an informal term for the area of south western England which encompassed Cornwall, Devon, Dorset and Somerset and the City of Bristol.

Elias Cook (1st) married a Pederick, which name has long been associated with the Cornwall and Devon area. Elias Cook (2nd) married a Haynes, and the Haynes name also stems from Devon. Elias Cook (3rd) married a Searle, and the Searle name was also found heavily in Devon. Cook offspring also married into families with names found in the West Country – Tucker (Cornwall/Devon), Collier (Devon), Cleaves (Devon), Hooper (Devon). As well, there are Cooks to be found in that area, including the name of Elias Cook. However, until proof is found, this remains just a possibility.

(CR002) History of Essex County, Massachusetts : with biographical sketches of many of its pioneers and prominent men, by D. Hamilton Hurd - Page 955 mentions Elias Cook, who came from Marblehead, and in 1734 had a grant of sixteen rods of land. * Sandy Bay used to be a part of Gloucester, then became Rockport.
History of Gloucester – John Babson, Page 74 – Elias Cook had a dwelling house in Sandy Bay in 1738.

(CR002a) The Essex Antiquarian, 1906, Vol. 10 : Pg. 48

(CR002b) The names of Heines/Haynes, Nickleson and Francis Grant are found in early documents of Marblehead.

(CR002c) Marblehead Reporter – 2010, Letter: **Lifting the Veil on Miriam Grose** by Robert A. Booth, *abridged* - Regarding the old gravestone of **Mrs. Miriam Grose**, he mentions that it is "unique to find a stone that doesn't have a death date." Maybe so, but I might put it differently. The gravestone epitaph says that she died at the age of 80 leaving 180 living children, grandchildren and great-grandchildren. Obviously, her family felt that, in light of this profusion of life, death came in second — besides, they all knew when she died. They were on to something, since Mr. Myjer is fascinated by her stone precisely because it has no death date — Mrs. Grose's numerous family are still calling attention to her, three centuries later!

There really is no mystery, though, about her date of death: She died in September 1717, per the records of the First Congregational Church of Marblehead, as listed on page 568 of Marblehead Vital Records, Vol. II, published by the late lamented Essex Institute in 1904, a volume that is available seven days a week at Abbot Public Library. Her age-at-death is also listed, as 80, taken from the gravestone record at "Old Burying Hill cemetery" (per the Vital Records book; "Burial Hill" seems to be a neologism, since the old-timers called it "Burying" Hill, just as Salem's graveyard was, and is, Burying Point).

Who was this **Mrs. Miriam Grose**? In 1654 or so, Miriam, aged 17 (I don't know her family surname), married **John Pedrick** (1625?-1686), a 29-year-old fisherman who had settled in Marblehead by 1648. John was probably from Devon or Cornwall in the West of England, where the name Petherick (Pedrick) was not uncommon. In fact, there was another John Pedrick (c.1638-c.1706) living in Marblehead in the 1600s.

Miriam and John had at least nine children, the eldest being Agnes, born 1655, and the youngest **Johannah**, born 1680! They all survived to adulthood, and all had children except for son Benjamin (evidently).

In the 1670s, the John Pedrick family (two sons, seven daughters) moved to Marblehead Neck (no yacht clubs then; plenty of fish yards though) and settled on eight acres. Miriam was 49 when her husband died in 1686 (probably he was buried on his homestead), and late in 1688 **she married Richard Grose**, likely a widower, aged about 45. Her eldest daughter, Agnes, married John Stacey c.1673 and had 11 children; her eldest son, John, married Mary Brown and had nine children, and others of her offspring were similarly prolific.

Miriam and Richard lived together for almost 23 years, until he died in September 1711, aged 68 (his gravestone is on the old hill). Six years later, Miriam died, too.

As to Mr. Myjer's question about her descendants, it is safe to say that nearly every "old family" in Marblehead traces back to Miriam.

(CR002d) Transaction date 6 Sept. 1704, recording date 19 Aug. 1707. Vol. 20, page 46.1.

(CR003)   Elizabeth (Hooper) Haines/Haynes was a grandaughter of Robert "King" Hooper, Esq., through his son John Hooper. "King" Hooper, as he was known, was not only one of the town's wealthiest men but one of the wealthiest in New England prior to the Revolution. His ships sailed to every port of Europe and the West Indies, and his name and fame as a merchant extended to all the mercantile centers of the world. He lived in princely style, frequently entertaining the highest dignitaries of the land. His uniform courtesy and kindness, and his benevolence to the poor, endeared him to all, especially the people of Marblehead. Fishermen gave him the nickname "King," not because of his wealth, but because of his honor and integrity in dealing with them. Contrary to the practice of some of the merchants, King Hooper was never known to cheat them. The Robert "King" Hooper Mansion, built in 1727, is a historic house at 8 Hooper Street in Marblehead, Massachusetts. It was added to the National Register of Historic Places in 1976.

Marblehead In The Year 1700, by Sidney Perley, Pages 42, 50, 51: Francis Haines/Haynes was a gunsmith as early as 1699 at Marblehead, and is mentioned as such in several land transactions there. By 1718 he had become a fisherman, and he sold land in Marblehead to John Conant for 160 lbs. It mentions him, and also wife Elizabeth on page 51.

(CR004) Francis Cook, son of Elias and Sarah Cook of Marblehead, was a cabinetmaker. He was not married. In January, 2010, Sothebys auctioned a chest attributed to **Francis Cook for $698,500.00 USD**. Details are as follows: LOT 505 - PROPERTY FROM A PRIVATE NEW ENGLAND FAMILY - THE IMPORTANT RANLETT-RUST FAMILY CHIPPENDALE FIGURED MAHOGANY BOMBÉ SLANT-FRONT DESK, PROBABLY BY FRANCIS COOK, MARBLEHEAD, MASSACHUSETTS CIRCA 1770 appears to retain its original surface, hardware, and key.

ATTRIBUTION TO FRANCIS COOK

Placing the desk in Marblehead is relatively straight forward. Identifying the specific cabinetmaker's shop is somewhat more difficult. Fortunately for scholars today, a higher percentage of Marblehead furniture is signed by the maker than the output of any other Massachusetts town.

This provides a significant lexicon of known makers' working characteristics. A detailed comparison of construction techniques and of the chalked numbering on drawers was made. A match was made to a chest-on-chest, signed by Francis Cook (1734-1772), now in the collection of The Marblehead Historical Society. Matching construction details include:
• center drops
• identical placement of the glue blocks supporting the rear and front feet
• drawer bottoms with grain direction perpendicular to the drawer fronts
• drawer bottoms attached to drawer backs with eleven or twelve small sprigs
• wide-spaced double bead to the top edge of the drawer sides
• identical style of dovetails with large dovetail at the top; relatively shallow angled pins; no dovetail at the bottom; an average 3/16 inch step from the top edge of the drawer front to the top edge of the sides.

Final proof that this rare form originated in Cook's shop is based on a comparison of the chalked numbers on the inside face of the back boards on the chest-on-chest and the numbers on the interior of this desk.

Information on Francis Cook is sparse. He was born in Gloucester, Massachusetts, August 10, 1734, **son of Elias and Sarah Cook**. By 1744 the family had moved to Marblehead. At age 27 he purchased a house from fellow joiner, William Ingalls, and then mortgaged the full purchase price to Marblehead wig maker, Joshua Kimball. There is no record of his having married. He died sometime before November 1772. His estate was valued at £126, a modest sum at the time. His house and land accounted for 87% of the total estate value. Joiner's tools, a bench and walnut and pine boards are included in the inventory. Like many cabinetmakers of the period, he had apparently led a quiet and modest life.

Although few products survive from his shop, Cook had an assured understanding of superior design. The curvature of the desk sides extends through the second drawer of the main case, eliminating the "pot-bellied" appearance of earlier work. He also understood the potential weak points of the bombe design. The bottom two drawers are prone to overloading, due to their size and the outward slope of the sides. Placement of dovetails in the conventional position might allow the side to be pushed outwards and prevent the drawer from opening. Cook compensated for this potential problem by reversing the direction of the rear dovetails. He also reinforced the bottom edge of each drawer side by adding an extra strip of wood which distributes the weight over a wider area and minimized wear to the lower drawer blade.

(CR004a) Sarah Cook probably married John McGuckin on July 5, 1753 at Marblehead. Her brother Elias named a child Sarah McGuckin Cook in 1757.

(CR005) Ambrose Cleaves was born in Beverly, Mass. to Ebenezer and Sarah (Stone) Cleaves. They had five children: Anna Cleaves (1743 -), Andrew Cleaves (1746 -), Edmund Cleaves (1748-1748), Molly Cleaves (1751 - 1811), Ambrose Cleaves (1754 – 1825).

Ambrose Cleaves was a partner in the Land Bank of 1740. The Land Bank scheme was aimed at a perennial problem - a shortage of money in circulation. The monetary system consisted of a patchwork scheme of bills of public credit, some serving as legal tender, some redeemable as taxes, some loaned at interest. The British government was opposed to the colonists printing paper money in whatever form, and told Gov. Jonathan Belcher Jonathan Belcher (colonial governor of Massachusetts, New Hampshire and, New Jersey).

In 1739, a group of members of the Massachusetts Assembly pushed through a plan to set up a Land Bank, using land as collateral instead of silver or gold, empowered to issue up to 150,000 pounds in bank notes, redeemable in currency or in specified commodities.

The Land Bank idea was popular in some parts of the state. Merchants along the eastern coast were less enthusiastic. A group of them came out with a rival plan for a Silver Bank.

In September 1740, despite the objections of the governor and the Council, the Land Bank began to issue 50,000 pounds of notes that had no legal authorization.

Governor Belcher fought back. He proclaimed that the Land Bank notes were worthless, he sacked office holders who accepted them, and he refused to grant licenses to businessmen who wanted to use them as currency. Public confidence waned, and soon Land Bank notes were being rejected right and left. The bank itself was eliminated by an act of Parliament after hardly a year in existence, but it was one of the main issues that primed Massachusetts for independence.

(CR006) *History of the County of Guysborough, by Harriet Cunningham Hart,* **Page 54**:

From frequent kindly intercourse with the Indians, the Messrs. Cook had made themselves familiar with the Micmac language and customs and had become their firm allies. A vessel belonging to Chedabucto was chased up the bay by a privateer and when near the harbor Mr. Cook, who was watching his neighbor's distressed condition, ran quickly from his house shouting some peculiar cry previously agreed upon in case of trouble, when so many Indians came rushing and whooping to their canoes upon the shore that the privateer turned and fled in dismay.

One day, while Mr. Jack Cook was out fishing, he was captured by the noted Paul Jones. The pirate compelled Mr. Cook to pilot him around the coast, and show him the way into certain harbors, using thumbscrews and other persuasive powers to affect his object. He was thus unwillingly employed for three weeks, and then set on shore. Some of his adventures came to the ears of a captain of a cutter upon the coast, and the poor man was seized and tried as an accomplice of the celebrated sea rover. His innocence was easily proved, however, by the unanimous testimony of his neighbors.

(CR1.1)   Elizabeth (Hopkins) (Godfrey) Tobey of Massachusetts and Nova Scotia: her identity and her children, by Lois Ware Thurston: American Genealogist, April 1991, p. 78-87.
Further notes: Benjamin Godfrey was a son of Moses and Deborah (Cooke) Godfrey, who was a daughter of Josiah Cook, Jr., of Eastham, Mass. and Deborah Hopkins, a descendant of the Mayflower Hopkins'.

(CR1.1a) Other children who were educated "Gratis" in 1826 in the Salmon River district were: Ann and Priscilla Whitman; Patty, George, Charles and Thomas Bigsby (who were children of John and Rachel (Critchett) Bigsby; their father died in 1826, just before the birth of his 10th child - see CR1.5); Benjamin and Bethia Godfrey (children of Benjamin and Catherine (Bigsby) Godfrey).

(CR1.1b) Thomas Hart was a son of Jairus and Frances (Godfrey) Hart. Frances Godfrey was Deborah Godfrey's sister.

(CR1.141W – On the 1870 Census for Cedar Falls Ward 3, Black Hawk, Iowa, Jane Kearsley is shown living next door to Daniel G. Cook and wife, and in the same household as William, Charles F. and Stephen N. Cook, all who worked in woolen mills, as did Daniel G. Cook. The Census gives her birthplace as Massachusetts. She probably was a Cook relative. William and Charles were also both born in Mass., but Stephen was born in Rhode Island.

(CR1.1411) Elias began a life of petty thievery as a child, when, in 1874, he and three other boys from 8-12 years old, were arrested for stealing "paper rage" (sic) from merchants in Cedar Falls, which they afterward sold to other parties. They all pleaded guilty to petty larceny and were each sentenced for five days imprisonment in the county jail. *(Cedar Falls Gazette: May 15, 1874)*
        Another incident of theft occurred in 1890, another in 1897, when he was given a sentence of three years. *(Waterloo Courier, Jan. 13, 1897)*
        In 1903, he was arrested again and charged with incendiarism, in burning the barn of T.B. Carpenter. *(The Glenwood, Iowa, Opion, Oct. 29, 1903)*. There are other articles in various newspapers, until 1904.
        His wife, Lucia, was granted a divorce in 1912 on the grounds of desertion.

1.142) Thanks to Weldon Corder via Sarah Sully for the photo of Duty and Sarah Paine.

CR1.1422 – Information from her death record at www.findagrave.com (Memorial #24573335) Details include: Sabrina W. Paine, daughter of Sarah Marie (Cook) and Duty Sayles Paine. Married Martin Luther Nichols, March 05, 1879, Black Hawk County, IA.
        Same source – Information on Martin Luther Nichols - Birth: Aug. 20,

1855, Cattaraugus County, New York, USA.   Death: Nov. 8, 1915, Orleans, Harlan County, Nebraska.

Martin L. Nichols, son of Sarah Sarepta (Woolley) and Luther Ford Nichols. Married Sabrina "Brina" Walling Paine, March 05, 1879, Cedar Falls, Black Hawk Co., IA. Adopted Grace Sabrina Nichols. Methodist Minister.

(CR1.1433) www.findagrave.com - Find A Grave (Memorial #17733084. Her husband – Memorial #17733075)

(CR1.16) There are records of a Godfrey Cook who migrated to Mass., USA., who may be #1.16). However, it is possibly #2.36), a son of John Cook. (The Milner middle name is not found in any of the records.)

This *George* Godfrey Cook married Catharine Poor, both of NS (he was born in Guysborough, she was born in Canso) on May 29, 1842, at Gloucester. Catharine died after a few years along with children Elisha Henry Cook b: Nov. 23, 1842, d: 1845, of scarlet fever. Another child by the same name was b: on June 10, 1845, d: Mar. 12, 1849. George Lander or Leander Cook b: Apr. 23, 1848, d: Mar. 24, 1849: Children of George Godfrey and Catherine Cook.   Another child, Charles Wellington Cook (b:@ 1850), apparently survived, as he is listed on various Census records (as Charles N. Cook).

A marriage of a Godfrey G. Cook took place at Lowell, Mass., when he married Sarah Burnham, on Jan. 2, 1856. 1860 census for Beverly shows George G., age 35, Sarah B., age 36, and son Charles W. age 10. George G. was a shoemaker, born NS. Sarah and Charles were both born at Mass. There is a confusing entry on the 1870 Census, which states that George G. 50, was born in Maine, Sarah B. 45, in New Hampshire and gives name of Charles as Charles P, age 20, Mariner.

(CR1.312)   Pictures and detailed genealogical information on this family branch was generously shared with me by **Joan Mackay**.

(CR1.316H) Leonard Choate was an inmate at the Massachusetts State Prison in 1880, as shown on the US Census for Concord, Mass. By 1900, he was a prisoner at the State Farm, Bridgewater Town, Plymouth, Mass. He was still there in 1910. He died between 1910-1920 (Emmeline was a widow on the 1920 census, but stated that she was a widow on the 1910 census).

In 1870 there is record of a court case between the Commonwealth of Massachusetts v. Leonard Choate for burning a building in the night time. The building was the Belleville Congregational Church which was rebuilt as the United Church of Christ in, Newburyport, MA. The history of the church states:

January 8, 1867 - the third Meeting-house was again totally destroyed by fire caused by arson. Between 1862 and 1866 numerous properties were hit by arson, including several other churches. In 1869, Leonard Choate was tried, convicted and sentenced to imprisonment for life for the arson .

The Petersburg Index, Thursday, March 23, 1871, Petersburg, Virginia: **"The Imp of Fire."** If there can be such a thing as an artist in the matter of incendiary fires, Massachusetts has that specimen of human depravity now securely caged in the four walls of her penitentiary, serving out a life term for arson. **Leonard Choate**, the "fire-bug" *par excellence*, was arraigned at Newburyport under fifteen indictments for arson. Of this number two were selected as test cases, and he was tried and found guilty on both. This man is said to be of respectable family, but the inclination to burn buildings, churches, dwellings, workshops, barns, etc., was with him a passion. That terrible but impalpable genius of destruction, whom imaginative and lively writers for the press denominate the "fire fiend" and "the imp of fire", was his familiar, and was always prompt at his bidding......All the home influences of Choate's early youth are said to have been good, and he himself is possessed of property to the value of $10,000. But he was, in the worst meaning of the term, a public enemy. Wherever he went a fire followed, to the consternation of the community, and nothing was sacred from his combustible touch.....

Petitions for a Pardon: Boston, April 19 - A petition was presented to the pardon committee of the executive council yesterday for the pardon from state's prison of **Leonard Choate**, where he is now serving a life sentence for arson. Drs. Hazelton and McLaughlin reported that they were of the opinion that Choate was laboring under a mania for setting fires. He was sentenced Feb. 13, 1871, and is now 59 years old. *The Herald And Torch Light, Thursday, April 26, 1894, Hagerstown, Maryland.*

(CR1.31 10) Grand Lodge of Masons Membership Cards give his name as Christopher Columbus Cook, and his date of death as 1926-5-29.

(CR1.31 1011) www.findagrave.com – Find A Grave (Memorial #46076673).
Inscription: Sgt. US Army
Burial: Waterside Cemetery, Marblehead, Essex County, Mass.

(CR1.4) A Louisa Cook married Henry Myers. Their son Stephen Myers' death record in 1925 names Henry Myers and Louisa Cook as his parents. George Myers was the father of George Stephen Myers, who married Leannis Hayes (1.4144). There were a large number of Myers families living in the Stormont/Isaac's Harbour area and it is difficult to establish relationships between them. The earliest Census, in 1817 had only one Myers in the area - a John Myers with a wife and four sons. By 1861, there are six Myers families: 3 John Myers', George Myers, Charles Myers, Henry Myers.

One John Myrs, with a family of 5, lived next door to Edmund Cook. The 1871 census shows a 60 year old John Meyers, who was born on Sable Island, with wife Mary and son David at Isaac's Harbour, next door to Stephen and Amy Meyers.

The 1881 census has 75 year old Polly Myers living with John and Amy Myers (parents of John H. Myers, who married Hattie Hayes).

A John Myers married Margaret Johnson, daughter of David Johnson in 1813, and had a son James.

There was a Henry Myers (b: @1837) who was a shoemaker in the Isaac's Harbour area.

The Fisherman's Harbour area had George Myers (b: @1835) who married Mary Hines and had a large family.

Charles Myers (b@1840) lived in the Country Harbour area. He married Sarah Jane Hudson and they had a large family.

For other Myers connections within the Cook extended family, see also: #1.4142, #1.4144, #1.4171, #1.4191, #1.4195, #1.4511, #7.32.

(CR1.411) The Robars of Sherbrooke (St. Mary's) and Wine Harbour, Guys. Co. were descendants of Abraham Robert/Robar, a French protestant who was among the founding families of Lunenburg in 1753. Like all of that group, Abraham, his wife Elizabeth Catharine and a young daughter lived in Halifax, in their case from their arrival in 1752 until the whole group was transported to Lunenburg in the spring of 1753.

John Fred Robar, Valentine Robar and siblings were the children of John Robar and Susan Ridman who were married in the Sherbrooke area (in the record Saint Mary's River) Nov. 13, 1816. In the 1838 census John Robur [sic] is listed with 2 boys and 1 girl under 6, 2 girls 6 to 14, 2 boys over 14, and his wife.

Valentine married Catherine McConnell on 14 Sept. 1841. Valentine's sister Caroline married William McAndrew 23 Dec. 1844, also at St. Mary's. *John Frederick's son was named William McAndrew Robar.* The census data supports a birth date for Valentine of ca. 1819, although his headstone (in the Barachois Cem.) would put his birth as ca 1810. Valentine seems to have lived most of his adult life in Wine Harbour and his house is marked in the A.F. Church map of the area, ca. 1876 .

The McConnells lived on the east side of Indian Harbour. There is a listing in the land grant maps for the area of a very small piece of land shared by Valentine Robar and Experience McConnell on the coast at Wine Harbour. In the 1871 census John was living (as a widower) with his son Valentine and family.

As for the parents of John Robar (who married Susan Ridman) there are two choices: two of Abraham and Elizabeth Catherine Robar's sons had children named John, both born in or around Lunenburg and both it would seem in 1791. George and Mary Margaret (Darree) Robar's son John was christened in Sept. 1791 so probably was born in that year, while Andrew and Barbara (Motz) Robar's son John was born and christened in July of 1791. One of the two Johns seems to have stayed in the Lunenburg area and married Catherine Dimon in 1814, while the other John moved to Guys. Co.

and married there. **Taken in part from the Robar Family Genealogy Forum as written by David Spencer.**

(CR1.413) Presbyterian Witness newspaper Sat. Dec. 2, 1871, Vol. XXIV, No. 48, p. 384: Cooke, Martha married Josiah Jordon on the 22nd. Daughter of Edward (sic) Cooke, of Guysborough. Married by Rev. J.C. Cochran in Trinity Church (Halifax).

(CR1.417) **History of the County of Guysborough, by Harriet Cunningham Hart**, Page 153 - Elias Cook....had been at Wine Harbor a short time before, and had brought back with him some specimens of gold bearing quartz. He began to study the rocks around him, in company with Allan McMillan, but no gold reqarded their search. Finally he dropped one of his specimens, which Mr. McMillan picked up. The report that they had found gold was soon in circulation, and a number of the inhabitants repaired to the favored spot, but all their investigation was without success. Joseph Hynes was not to be baffled without a more thorough prying into the secrets of the rocks, and in the afternoon his perseverance was reqarded and he found several sights on what has since been known as "the free claim".

(CR1.41731) Stellarton, N.S. -- (CP) -- Seven coal miners are believed to have been killed today in an explosion which sent hundreds of tons of rock and coal crashing down on their working place in the Allan shaft, where eighty-eight men perished in an explosion in 1918.

The men were trapped 1,500 feet underground while rescue workers were trying to fight their way through a barrier of fallen debris which clogged the passageway for 1,000 feet.

The mass of coal and stone blocked the way to safety for any possible survivors, though little hope was held that any still lived. Fearful fellow workers expressed belief all must have been buried alive.

All others of the 196 men who entered the pit today were accounted for, according to D. H. McLean, superintendent of the Acadia Coal Company, and Dominic Nearing, sub-district board member for the United Mine Workers. They were all on the surface except for rescue crews and about fifteen officials who had stayed below to supervise the work of digging for the trapped colliers.

The cause of the explosion was undetermined. The nearest workers, 1,500 feet away from the spot where the seven were working, said they heard only a dull, muffled thud followed by a whistling blast of air which swept one man off his feet and hurled him several yards.

The seven men trapped are: ROSS FLEMING. DICK CLARK. ALEXANDER J. BEATON. **ABRAHAM HENNESSEY.** EGNUT BORTNICK. JAMES A. McEACHERN. JOHN McEACHERN.

Wives and relatives of the missing men gathered anxiously around the pit mouth as soon as word of the explosion spread through the town. This afternoon hundreds milled about the colliery yard, waiting anxiously for word from below.

What news trickled up carried little hope. Crews equipped with masks for work in gas and some "bare-faced" miners had gone down, but they could find no trace of the buried men.

Found online at: http://www3.gendisasters.com/mining-explosions-accidents/12372/stellarton-ns-mine-explosion-apr-1935

(CR1.4174) On their marriage license, there is a "Private Note" attached by J.C McNaughton, Issuer of Marriage Licenses, which states : You will notice that in issuing the License to this man, he swore that Miss Silver was 21 years or over. The age given by her is 17. Her mother is dead. Her father is somewhere. She had a child about a year ago. They are both illiterate. I gave the License in good faith as he swore she was 21 or over. It is a case, I think, where "Better to marry than burn". Signed by J.C. McNaughton - Issuer of Marriage License.

There has been some uncertainty as to whether or not this was Foster Cook, son of Elias Foster Cook and Priscilla (McConnel) Cook, or another Foster Cook. The marriage license has several "untruths" : both their ages are wrong and, if neither could read nor write, then all the information contained on the license must have been given verbally, and could easily have been written down in error. The license gives Foster's mother's maiden name as Priscilla Cameron. That there could have been another Elias Cook, born in Isaac's Harbour, married to a Priscilla, with a son Foster - is almost impossible, and if so, in over 30 years of genealogical research, I have never come across one other reference to another family with these same names. I believe this to be Foster Cook, son of Elias Foster Cook and Priscilla McConnel Cook. Also, on his brother Edmund Cook's death certificate, in 1940, their parents names are written as Elias Cook and Priscilla McCormick, another error. His headstone, in Evergreen Cemetery, Crossroads Country Harbour, gives his birthdate as 1896, and I feel that is another error.

The date of birth from the official record is May 22, 1874. Discrepancies abound in census records for both Foster and his father, Elias - there is absolutely no consistancy in ages from one ten year period to another.

(CR1.4174a) Conversation between Iris Martin and Margaret Sinclair noted that Ollie was 6, Daisy was 8, and Margaret was 10 years old when they went to live with John and Elsie Hayne. Gladys, the oldest, went to live with, and work for Jim and Edith Mason.

(CR1.41751) Thanks to Betty Tambeau for the photo of Orris Cooke.

(CR1.418) A close look at the 1881 census shows that there was another child in this household - Evered (Everett?) *Cook?* born Oct. 1880. At that time, there were already children William (Marcus) and Hugh; Zuleika died in 1874 and Leander and Tremaine had not yet been born. A strong possibility is that Everett is a child of Ida May Robar, who was 15, and who lived with the family at that time. However, Evered is listed under Cook, Ida May is listed next, under Robar. I have found no further information on Everett Cook or Robar.

It seems strange to me that our family has never heard of a child named Evered or Everett, while baby Zuleika, who died and is buried in an overgrown grave somewhere in Stormont, was talked about and remembered.

Charles Cook fathered a child before his marriage to Betsy Findlay. He was named as the father of "Juanna" Bell Cook, illigitimate daughter of Elizabeth Fenton, born on Jan. 25, 1869 at Country Harbour, and who married John Adam Cook, and they did not have children. (CR1.48) She drowned in her well in 1912. Her name is spelled various ways – the death record calls her "Elvinora". The 1871 census shows her name as Ivanorabell. She was called Nora Bell. Her mother, Elizabeth Fenton, was a daughter of Jacob Fenton and was a sister of Stephen Fenton, who married Lucinda Cook.

(CR1.418w) William and Margaret (Addison) Findlay immigrated to Prince Edward Island, Canada from Cullen, Banffshire, Scotland, which is between Aberdeen and Inverness on Moray Firth coast, in 1867 with their children.

Their daughter, Elizabeth Macbeth Findlay (Betsy) married Charles Cooke. Charles and Betsy lived where Leander, and then Leo Cook lived. The original house burned down completely in the 1930's, destroying many photographs and historic documents of this Cooke family. After Charles and Betsy's marriage, her parents, the Findlays, moved to the west side of Country Harbour, with their son John. There was another daughter born, Jane Findlay, after they moved there, but she died in infancy.

Betsy's brother, **William Findlay**, stayed in Prince Edward Island, where he was a farmer and a photographer. He lived on Lot 40, near Morrell. He married Marcella, had 3 daughters, Margaret, Catherine and Lottie. Betsy also had a sister, Catherine.

Betsy's other brother, **John Lyman Findlay** (1860 – 1947) migrated to the U.S.A. and became a painter. He painted landscapes, murals on the interiors of churches, miniatures for ladies' lockets, scenes of the Boston area and Scotland, among other things. He had at least one exhibition of his work at the Boston Art Club, and in 1901 he was presented to the State House at Boston. The names of two of his paintings are: *Mountain Torrent* (a rock-strewn river with fall foliage), and *Unloading the Catch*. Portraits include: *David Remington* (1841-1917) painted in 1906, oil on canvas; *Joseph Jenkins* (1781-1851), in oil; *Thomas Pedrick* (1846-1920) oil on canvas, dated 1910.

Several of our family members have other paintings. John married twice; his second wife was Emma H., also a painter, and in the later years, a dressmaker. They lived on Boylston Street in Boston, in an area populated by other artists. They had no children.

Unloading the Catch

From *The Boston Globe*, Feb. 22, 1987: In reply to a query about the artist **John Findlay**, Norma Mosby of the fine arts department of the Boston Public Library says you apparently are referring to John Lyman Findlay, who was born in Cullen, Banffshire, Scotland, on November 17, 1861. Findlay, it appears, emigrated as a youth to Canada, then came to Boston, where he began his art career doing crayon portraits. He graduated to oils and later studied in London and Paris. At one point he was asked to return to his native Scotland to do scenes descriptive of Scottish history. Back in Boston, he became noted for his large portraits and for miniatures done on ivory. At least two of his portraits hang in the Masonic Temple at 186 Tremont Street in downtown Boston. One is a full- length picture of George Washington in Masonic regalia; the other is of a former Grand Master, Leon M. Abbott. Findlay died in Boston on September 13, 1947.

(CR1.4181) Schooner John A. Beckerman – Manifest, 1919 from Sherbrooke to New York:

Harris Mason, Mate	Harold A. Cooke, A.B.
David J. Shiers, Cook	Bruce Langley, A.B.
Onslow Clyburn, A.B.	**Marcus W. Cooke**, Master

(CR1.4183 From: *The Pictonion Colliers* by James M. Cameron: 1906 - Excavation of the Allan Shaft continued. Two men died in a long fall when a staging broke, H.A. Cooke and A. Perris(Paris?). A third man, Alfred Skinner, was injured. Alexander Cameron was killed when overrun by a hopper in the Vale yard, and James Stewart died after being struck by a rake in the Albion.
From: The Eastern Chronicle, New Glasgow, N.S.
Tuesday morning, 5 December 1905 The Allan Shafts - While timbering in No. 1 shaft yesterday morning, a plank on which two men were standing broke under their weight and they fell about twelve (feet?) to the bottom and each had a broken leg. Their names were **Hugh Cook** and Alfred Skinner. They were taken to Aberdeen Hospital and we learn that in the case of the latter the fracture of the bone is so bad that the leg will have to be amputated below the knee.
Friday, 8 December 1905 - Hugh Cooke, one of the men injured in the Allan shaft as stated in these columns in Monday's issue, was yesterday morning very low and it was not expected that he would recover. At first it was

thought that his injury was only a broken leg; but later he became violently insane and on examination it was found that he was struck on the head and the skull fractured. An operation was performed on his head and the injury was found so serious that his life was despaired of. We could not learn at the hour of going to press how the unfortunate man was.

Friday, 8 December 1905 - The young man, Cook, who was so severely injured in the Allan Shaft on Monday, belongs to Issac's Harbor. His mother came on yesterday.

Tuesday, 12 December 1905 - Verdict of Jury: The following is the Verdict of Jury - in case of Hugh A. Cooke injured at Allen Shaft, from which injury he died: That said Hugh A. Cooke came to his death at Aberdeen Hospital, on the eight day of December, 1905, from injuries received on the fourth day of said month, by the falling of a scaffold in the Allen Shaft, at Lourdes. The jury are of the opinion that the part of the material used in the construction of said scaffold was unfit for the purposes for which it was used.

(CR1.4199) Thanks to Carole (Cooke) Perkons for the photo of Errington, Edison and Bruce Cooke.

(CR1.41 10) Discrepancy in the marriage date of Sarah Cook and Henry Robar: From daughter Ida May's birth record, it states the parents were married in Jan., 1862. On son Charles' birth record, it states the parents were married at St. Mary's River in 1860.

(CR1.422) The first of our Hayes line was Gamaliel Hayes, who was one of the first settlers of Stormont - probably a U.E.L. He married Elizabeth Miller and had one son - Jonathan.

Jonathan Hayes married Rebecca Cook. Becky Cook was a daughter of Wintrop and Lydia Cook and had a brother, Edmund Cook. Jonathan and Becky had seven children, but most may have died young. In her later years, Becky Cook became blind. I have not been able to find further information about any of them except: **Edmund Hayes, Ann Hayes, William F. Hayes and Joseph Hayes**.

Ann Hayes married Samuel Cooke (a son of Edmund and Elizabeth Cook), who was the grandfather of Edison and Errington Cooke. They were first cousins. Edison had fifteen children, and Errington, who moved to Antigonish County, had five children.

Edmund Hayes married Louisa Cook (a daughter of Edmund and Elizabeth Cook and also a sister of Charles Cook). They were first cousins - Edmund Cook was a brother of Becky Cook.

Edmund and Louisa Hayes had 7 children: Mary Ann, Harriet Jane, Priscilla, Leannis, Sarah Elizabeth, Marshall, and Jessie Lois (or Louise).

Joseph Hayes married Lydia Cook (a daughter of Edmund and Elizabeth Cook) and they had four children: Alfred, Leonard, Eugenia, and Minnie. Thus, 3 children of Jonathan Hayes - Edmund, Ann and Joseph -

married 3 children of Edmund and Elizabeth Cooke – Samuel, Louisa and Lydia. It gets more confusing: A grandchild of Edmund and Elizabeth - Mark Cook (son of Charles) - married a daughter of Louisa Cook and Edmund Hayes - Sarah Elizabeth Hayes - his second cousin....or is that first cousin once removed???

William F. Hayes was a seaman (the 1901 census stated he was a cook onboard a schooner). He lived in the family home at Hayes' Hill with his parents. He was considered the head of household on the 1891 census, with mother Becky and nephew Alfred living with him.

(CR1.4414) Martha Arabella was born @ 1860, according to the marriage record . The record states that she is a daughter of Elias and Elizabeth Cook of Stormont. Her father's occupation was a labourer. They were married in the Anglican church at Stormont. The witnesses were Stephen Fenton and L. Fenton.

I feel strongly that this is a mistake in the record. There was no "Elias and Elizabeth Cook" family of Stormont. There was "Elias and Priscilla Cook" who lived at Stormont for a time. There was "Edmund and Elizabeth Cook" who lived at Stormont, but their daughter Martha Arabella Cook was born in 1837, thus probably too old to be the mother of these children. There was also "Samuel and Elizabeth Cook", but they lived at Fisherman's Harbour, not Stormont.

I believe this person to be 1.4414) Martha Arabella Fenton, daughter of Elizabeth Cook who married Joseph Charles Fenton from Fisherman's Harbour. When Elizabeth died, the children were raised by other people. Martha Arabella Fenton was born in 1860. On the 1881 census she is listed in the family of Charles and Betsy Cook of Isaac's Harbour, along with a 5 month old daughter, Elizabeth Fenton.

Her son William Mason gives the name of Martha Fenton as mother's name on his Delayed Registration of Birth, father's occupation as Sea Captain and Farmer, however, he gives his father's birthplace as Belfast, Ireland, which is, of course, wrong.

The Delayed Registration of Birth of Charles Francis Mason gives Martha Arabell Cook as his mother, and W.F. Mason, carpenter, as his father.

On son Ira Mason's death record, it shows Martha Fenton as mother's name; information was given by Ira's son Robert Mason.

(CR1.442W) Ambrose Cook's wife was named Sarah on death record, daughter of George and Elizabeth Taylor.

(CR1.443) Another son of John, Sr. and Mary Walsh was William Walsh, who married Esther Hallet (daughter of Guy Hallett). They were the parents of George Johnston Walsh, the author of ***Broadhorns***.

(CR1.4441) Thanks to Glenda (Sutherland) Cameron for this photo.

(CR1.4451) He was the son of Lucinda Cook and Caron/Kayson Walsh. Caron or Kayson was a son of John and Mary Walsh of the Forks of St. Mary (Glenelg), and was a brother-in-law of Desire Cook (Lucinda's sister), who married John Walsh, Jr. He is called Caron on census records. He is called Kayson on his marriage record - he married Elizabeth Dryden of Halifax in 1872.

(CR1.4457) There are discrepancies in his names and date of birth. From the Birth Register, his name and date of birth are given as James Charles Howard Fenton, born Jan. 5/1877. From his death certificate, his name is given as James Harold, date of birth Jan. 11/1870.

(CR1.448) Marcus Keizer had brothers Nathaniel and John Henry (who also married into the Cook family). Their mother was Ann (nicknamed Nancy) Johnson, who was born at Indian Harbour, Halifax County. Mark Kaiser's father, John, was born at Peggy's Cove. He died aged 88 years and 8 months at Port Bickerton in July, 1911.

(CR1.4482) Campbell Johnston was a son of Benjamin and Eliza (Pringle) Johnston. Benjamin was born at Middle Country Harbour in July, 1852. Eliza Pringle was born in Scotland. Campbell died in 1937.

(CR1.46) Because Guysborough County is nearest to Sable Island, most of the early life-saving station workers were hired from the Stormont area. Children were born there; there are records of Hallets, Fentons, Hodgsons born on Sable Island in the very early 1800's. Edward Hodgson was a superintendant of Sable Island at one time.

(CR1.47W) Charlotte Eve Beiswanger and Sarah Ann Beiswanger were daughters of Adam and Sarah (Pierce) Beiswanger. Adam was born in Germany. Sarah Pierce was born in South Carolina. Eve died at the home of her son, Elisha Cook, in Lockeport, Shelburne County, NS, aged 98 on Aug. 28, 1921.

(CR1.4712) Prince Edward Island Public Archives and Records Office - Online database of baptisms for this family names the father as Earnest/Ernest Cook and the mother as Margaret/Maggie/Mary M. McLean. They were all baptised at St. Margaret's Catholic Church.

(CR1.4827) Thanks to Iris and Henry Martin for the photo of Gordon Cook.

(CR1.4831) The City of Monticello belonged to the Yarmouth Steamship Co. She was an iron paddle steamer, with a wooden superstructure. She was built by Harlan & Hollingsworth, Delaware, and was first called the City of Norfolk. She was purchased by the Bay of Fundy Steamship Co., was rebuilt in 1889 and her name changed. She ran between St. John and Digby for several years and was a fast sailer. She was 232 feet long, 32 feet wide and 10.9 feet deep, registering 478 tons. She had four bulkheads and a vertical beam engine. She was insured for $25,000.

Tragedy struck the *City of Monticello* on November 10, 1900. The ship foundered in the Bay of Fundy four miles west of Chegoggin Point in Yarmouth County. Of the forty people on board, only four were saved, and Wilson Cook, Quartermaster, age 29, was one of them. He had replaced his uncle, Elisha Cook, for this trip.

(CR1.488) Photo shared by Carole (Cooke) Perkons.

(CR1.49) Records from the early days of the township of Stormont show that Francis Cook was a son of Wintrop Cook. The 1842 financial papers of the Overseers of the Poor listed the amount of money each taxpayer had paid on his account. Francis Cook's amount of five pounds and 4 shillings was paid on his behalf by "Wintrup" Cook. Later, Francis paid the balance of 5 pounds, 9 shillings by sending "articles" (probably flour or other basic goods, that were, in turn, given out to the needy of the community). In this very early method of taxation, which was based on the value of what you owned in livestock, fishing vessels or other boats, wagons, real estate, etc., the men of the community were given a choice of either paying cash or working "on the roads" for a time equal to the amount they owed. On the same financial account, it shows that John Cook, Edmund Cook, Jonathan Hays, among others, also worked off their amounts owing by working on the roads. "Wintrup" Cook, Jr., John Cook, "Wintrup" Cook, Sr., Jasper Grover, James Johnson, Edward Hodgson, and others, paid in cash.

(CR1.4912) Daniel F. Johnson : Volume 76 Number 2177: Date - January 16 1890, Newspaper - The Times

The schr. "Kezia", Capt. Rhude, arrived Tuesday afternoon, 20 days from St. Jago, Cuba via Lunenburg and reported the loss of two of her crew. The vessel was in the recent heavy weather and during the gale at 2 a.m. on Friday last the crew on the house engaged in furling the mainsail. The vessel gave a heavy lurch, which caused the bitt to which the main sheet block was fast to tear out. The crew who were on the house were struck by the boom, which was adrift, two of them being knocked overboard and the other two between the house and rail. Owing to the heavy wind and sea, nothing could be done to rescue the two men who were lost. Their names are **Abner LANGLEY**, Isaac's Harbor, N.S., mate and Hugh McIsaac, Lunenburg, C.B., able seaman.

(CR1.495) **Burtts Corner Church of Christ History** (Taken from: Reuben Butchart – The Disciples of Christ in Canada Since 1830 (1949):On August 10, 1901, Bro. H. E. Cooke was installed as minister. In 1905 a parsonage was erected. During Bro. Cooke's early years especially, the church prospered and increased in membership and Christian influence. The burning of the mill of Bro. Ed. Burtt set the community back for some years, owing to removals. W. H. Harding contributed an important meeting, and that of John H. Wells, in August, 1925, resulted in fifty-two additions. A thousand persons lined the banks of the Keswick to witness the baptisms. A vigorous Bible School acted as a feeder and there was some co-operation with the Foreign Christian Missionary Society. Christian Endeavor flourished in its season. Ministers or evangelists of the congregation have been Henry Stewart, W. H. Harding, George Garraty, T. B. Blenus, H. E. Cooke (32 years), Barry McLean, John Carr and C. E. Armstrong. After Bro. Boke's long pastorate had ended in 1932, Barry McLean was called and served until 1936; followed by John Carr, of Greenmount, P.E.I., who acted until 1939.

The remarkable service of Bro. H. E. Cooke deserves recognition. Born at Halifax in 1856, he was at sea for twenty-nine years, and at the age of nineteen had a captain's rank. In winters he studied for some time at Prince of Wales College, Charlottetown, and later at Johnson Bible College. His religious leadership was first given energetically to a congregation of Baptists, where he made such a success that he was gratefully remembered. In speaking of this to the writer he said, in nautical language: "They needed it: it was low tide with them." He began his work as pastor at Kempt, Queen's County, N.S. in 1889; served at Westport seven years, at Summerside, P.E.I. for three years; at Southville two years; at Burtt's Corners thirty-two years. In the early eighties an English Secularist, Charles Watt, tried to work havoc amongst the churches. (Secularism denied belief in God or a future life.) In Halifax he was brought to a halt by H. E. Cooke who challenged him to meet an unnamed opponent. On the appearance of Clark Braden, Watt fled without giving battle. (Clark Braden was from the U.S.A. and specialized in defending Christianity, on many occasions, some of them in Canada.) Bro. Cooke died in September 1941.

(CR1.5) A Genealogy of the Descendants of Joseph Bixby (Bigsby)....by Willard Goldthwaite Bixby has no mention of Eleanor Bigsby, but I feel strongly that she was a daughter of Daniel Bigsby and was a sister of John, Catherine and Sarah. There was only one Bigsby family living in the area. Daniel Bigsby married Catherine Grace at Halifax in 1769. Son John was born @1770, daughter Catherine @1778, daughter Sarah @1781, and Eleanor @1782. *(See Bigsby family connections in this book: #1.28, #1.14, #4.26, #7.3, #10.1, #10.13.)*

(CR1.61) The Olive Tree Genealogy - **A list of vessels and their crews Lost from the Port of Gloucester, Massachusetts 1852:**
This proved a still more disastrous year for the fishing business; thirteen vessels and thirty-two lives being lost. Five of these vessels were lost on Georges, and eight in the Bay of St. Lawrence as follows;

Schooner GOLDEN FLEECE, lost on Georges, in March, nine men: Sylvester Rust, Master; Samuel Rust, brother of the master; **Edmund Cook**, James S. Norwood, Henry Robinson, Samuel Jackman,George Blaisdell, Samuel Atwood,and one man unknown. Owned by W. H. Steele and Daniel Gaffney. Valued at $4,000; insuredfor $3,500.

(CR1.65) *The Bath Independent, Saturday, Nov. 25, 1911, Bath, Maine*: VETERAN COMMANDER.
Captain Samuel Cook of Bath Celebrated His Birthday Thursday.

Captain Samuel Cook of this city is one of the old time commanders who gave up life on the sea some years ago but who is still interested in the lives of the men who go down to the sea in ships and almost every pleasant day he can be seen along the water front or on our business streets ready for a good story or to exchange a bit of news with those he meets.

It was down on Indian Point, in Georgetown, that Captain Cook first saw the light of day, just 82 years ago last Thursday. His father was Captain Edmund Cook and his mother Elizabeth Hooton Cook. The captain as a boy resided on the home place gradually developing a desire to go to sea. When he was 12 years old the family moved to Five Islands and the next year he shipped on a fisherman, named Frances Ann, which sailed out of Southport and was commanded by Captain Samuel Pierce. They went to the Grand Banks and Captain Cook remained with the craft for two years. Then he went ot Gloucester, and shipped for the Georges where he sailed for a year or more.

In 1872, he took command of the sailing yacht Brenda which was built by Charles B. Harrington of Bath and owned by James L. Little of Boston. He remained in her for nine years and then took the sloop Active owned by Harry Dutton of the firm of Houghton & Dutton of Boston. Leaving her he commanded a sailing yacht for Charles Kenney who owned a large livery and sales stable in Boston and finally was engaged by Gen. Charles H. Taylor of the Boston Globe to command the steam yacht Ocean Gem. This craft had been built in Noank, Conn., some years before and Captain Cook went to New York and brought her to Boston. Then Gen. Taylor decided to have some changes made in her and Captain Cook brought her to Bath. "You see that derrick" said Captain Cook pointing to the derrick near the old Moulton machine shop "well that is one I used back in 1887 or 1888 to lower a boiler on board the Ocean Gem. We spent $11,800 on that craft here at that time."

For a number of years he sailed for Gen. Taylor visiting all parts of the world, even going down among the South Sea Islands. "He was a white man to work for", said Captain Cook to the Independent as he spoke of Gen. Taylor.

After leaving the Ocean Gem when Gen. Taylor sold her he came back home and with the exception of one year during which he was second pilot on the steamer Sagadahoc he has remained on shore ever since.

Captain Cook has had a number of interesting experiences while on the sea but was never ship wrecked but once. That was when he was a young man sailing on fishermen. The craft he was on was the Jane which was commanded by Capt. Joseph Harford. She ran ashore on Monhegan and although the craft was a complete loss the crew all escaped and landed on the island.

Captain Cook is still a bright and able man, his sight and hearing are excellent and he eats his three meals a day and sleeps well.

He has five sons and daughters as follows, his wife having died some years ago: Mrs. Duranda Blaisdell, Bath; Mrs. Albertine Oliver of Georgetown; Mrs. Martha Lewis of Bath; Edward E. Cook of Bath and Charles Cook of Bath. All of his children have reached the age of 50.

The many friends of the genial old commander hope that he may be spared these many years to help cheer them up as he always does when he drops in for a neighborly call.

(CR1.10 1) Mass. Vital Records Vol 504, Page 475 1841-1910:
Death record of Moses Cook gives name of his parents as Edward Cook and Eleanor "Ambers".

(CR1.10 32) From *Life With The Irish - Salmon River District*, by Ann Wallace, Page 60: The first locally owned sawmill was probably owned by Charles Kenny. It would have been a vertical saw, water-powered. Most of the later mills used the water wheel as well, except for the steam mill operated on the Dan Kenny property, now owned by Lloyd Doyle.

(CR1. 10 47) Website Out of Gloucester - http://www.downtosea.com/1876-1900/morning.htm: Sch. *Morning Star,* 59,92, built on Essex 1859, lost on Georges in February gale 1879. Owned by Joseph O. Procter, Jr. Valued with outfits at $1895, insured for $1721.
Crew list:
John B. Spanks, master, widow and three children
David B. Gorman, widow and two children
William W. Shelton, widow and two children
Antone Aveney, of Manchester, six children
David Jones, widow and two children
F. H. Stimpson
John Black
James Roberts
Charles Ibey
Michael Muldoon

(CR2.2) Vital Records of Liverpool, N.S., Page 322

(CR2.22a) **Nova Scotia petitions 1769-1799 ~ Cape Breton Island petitions 1787-1843:**
1816 - Lindloff, Hans - Petition to Fitzherbert: Petitioner, age 35, a native of

Sweden, has resided "fer" years in Cape Breton. He has a wife and eight children. He asks a lot at St. Peter's Bay, being a peninsula in the entrance and east side of River Tilia. Note: granted.

(CR2.23) LIST OF PROTESTANTS IN ISLE MADAME, 1852

This list was among the papers of the Rev James Allen Shaw, the first Rector of St Johns. It is dated about the time of his retirement in 1851. It represemts a census of all non-Catholics on Isle Madame, almost 20 years before the the first official nominal census in 1871. In most cases it also gives the maiden names of the wives.

List of Protestants in Isle Madame, January 1852:

Cook	Francis	Fisherman	32
"	Ellen Luce??		30
"	John		10
"	Amelia		8
"	Elisha		1

It is interesting to note some of the other names on the list include Guysborough County names such as George, Greencorn, Hart, Cutler.
Further Documentation on this family found in:
St. John's Anglican Church, Arichat, **Burial Records**:

Godfrey Cook - Abode - Glasgow's Point - April 2, 1852 - 70 years
Francis Cook - Madame Island - June 18, 1868 - 50 years
Marriages:
Francis Cook & Helen Snow - March 3, 1846
Baptisms:
Amelia Theresa Cook - St. Peter's Passage - Sept 5, 1846 – Parents Edmond & Ellen Cook - Fisherman
Elisha William Cook - Janvrin's Island - July 6, 1851 - Edmond & Ellen Cook - Fisherman
James Godfrey Cook - Madame Island - Dec 15, 1854, born Mar 9, 1854 - Francis & Ellen Catherine Cook - Fisherman
Levi Cook - Madame Island - Oct 14, 1859 - born Oct 20, 1857 - Francis & Ellen Catherine Cook - Fisherman
Ellen Cooke - Madame Island - July 4, 1865 - born Apr 3, 1865 - Francis & Ellen Catherine Cook - Fisherman
There are discrepancies in the ages on the List of Protestants which was supposedly written in 1852, and the other Vital records. I have mainly used the dates given in the Vital records.

(CR2.235) Down Guysborough Way by John A. Morrison, Dec. 15, 1944.

(CR4.0) John Cameron, a lieutenant in the King's Orange Raiders, was born at Fort William, Scotland, and died on Grand Manan Island, New Brunswick, on May 21, 1844 (tombstone).

The Cameron genealogy gives the birthdate of Caroline Elizabeth Cook as August 3, 1819 and lists her parents as **Charles** and Lucy Cook (Cameron). Documentation for the name of Charles was taken from death certificate of Caroline.
Notes taken from Freeman Family History and shared by Eileen Cooke.

(CR4.123) ***Cedar Rapids Times, Thursday, March 31, 1887***
A Bank-Robber Foiled: Halifax, N.S., March 28 - Stanley Steel, of Manchester, N.S., entered the Antigonish agency of the Merchants Bank of Halifax Saturday noon and shot twice at a clerk named W.S. Currie, inflicting slight wounds. Four men who heard the firing rushed into the bank and found a murderous struggle going on. When Steel was overpowered he said he was driven to rob the bank for want of money.
This family had migrated to Salem, Mass. between 1871 and 1880.
Laura married E. Gerry Emmons in 1896. In 1891 Stanley was a prisoner at Dorchester Penitentiary, where he was listed as being a tailor. In 1891 he was in Kingston Penitentiary.

(CR4.124) Newspaper: Messenger and Visitor, Saint John, N.B.   January 27, 1892:   d. Cook's Cove, Guysboro Co., N.S., 11th inst., Hattie HORTON only d/o Deacon Albert HORTON and Lavinia HORTON, age 15.

(CR4.125) **Colusa County Biographies:**   ELIAS C. PEART - Along the legitimate lines of business Mr. Peart has won creditable success and is today the leading merchant of Colusa. He was born at Cook Cove, Guysboro County, Nova Scotia, on the 9th of November, 1848, and is a son of John William and Philo Ann (Cook) Peart. On the paternal side his ancestry can be traced back to Godfrey Peart, who died on the 9th of November, 1868, at the age of seventy-nine years. Godfrey Peart, the grandfather, married Mary Ann Lavinia Cribbin, whose death occurred May 10, 1869, when she had reached the age of seventy-seven years. John W. Peart, the father of our subject, was born in Guysboro, Nova Scotia, on the 23rd of May, 1817, and died August 29, 1886, at the age of sixty-nine years. He was a farmer and trader. His wife was born at Guysboro, in 1812, and died in Colusa, California, June 16, 1895, at the age of eighty-three years. She was a daughter of Elias C. and Anne (Horton) Cook, the former born December 16, 1788, the latter April 23, 1794. The grandfather died August 28, 1870, at the age of eighty-two years, and his wife passed away December 11, 1894, when more than one hundred years of age.

Elias Cook Peart attended the public schools during the winter season and throughout the remainer of the year assisted in the work of the home farm, taking a man's place from the age of thirteen years. In 1868 he emigrated to California, by way of the water route from New York and across the Isthmus of Panama. He arrived in San Francisco the day before the great earthquake. In November of the same year he secured employment in a small store at Knight's Landing, where he remained until the spring of 1869, when he went to Grand Island, Colusa County, and since that time he has been a resident of the county which he regards as the most favorable spot in all the land. In this opinion he certainly cannot be far wrong, for nature has made this a very desirable location with its rich farming country well watered by good streams.

When Mr. Peart arrived in California he had a cash capital of only thirty dollars, nor did he depend upon influential friends to aid him. He enjoyed good health, was enterprising and possessed of resolute will and he stood upon his own merits. His first employer was Barney Roseberry, now of Woodland, California, and on leaving his service he entered the employ of H. H. Goodhue, formerly of Grand Island, but now deceased. After clerking for two or three years, Mr. Peart established a mercantile store at Leesville and entered upon a prosperous career at that place, but a disastrous fire swept his business entirely away. After paying all his debts in full he had only a linen duster besides the necessary clothing. With determined spirit, however, he established a business in Colusa on borrowed capital, but found the expense attached to an incorporated town too great for one of his limited circumstances. Accordingly he returned to Leesville where he erected a store building and dwelling, but in about two years he sold his business and real estate to Dr. J. H. Clark, for his health was failing him through overwork.

Hoping to be benefited thereby, Mr. Peart went on a sea voyage to New York and thence along the coast to Nova Scotia. He crossed the Bay of Fundy several times, but the experience was not a pleasant one and he says he has no wish to make the trip again. After returning to California he assumed the management of a general mercantile store at Grimes, California, owned by the Grangers' Corporation Company. In about a year he purchased the enterprise and successfully conducted it in connection with branch stores in Arbuckle and Colusa. He also at one time identified with the store in Maxwell, but has recently disposed of much of the mercantile business, although he is still conducting the leading establishment in his line in Colusa. He has at the same time given some attention to farming and grain dealing. The word discouragement seems to find no place in his business vocabulary, and by continued effort and by closely following the golden rule he has won a very handsome competence of which he well deserves.

Mr. Peart was united in marriage December 11, 1872, to Miss Clara H. Graham, a daughter of Edwin R. and Asenath L. (Stanton) Graham. Unto Mr. and Mrs. Peart have been born the following children: Emma C., Cora G. and Eulah M.

Mr. Peart gives his political support to the Democracy, but is not a bitter partisan, much preferring to deposit his ballot for a good Republican than a man of his own party who is not worthy of the public trust. He has always declined to accept public office himself, except that he has served as postmaster. He has established the post office at Leesville and filled the position there until he resigned. He also established the post office at Grimes,

Colusa County, and there filled the position until he handed in his resignation. He is now, by appointment of the state, a director in agricultural district No. 44, which district he organized. Socially he is connected with the Order of Friends, and his wife and children are members of the Christian Church. Through a long period Mr. Peart has been identified with the development of Colusa County, and his name therefore is inseparably interwoven with its history. The wonderful upbuilding of the golden state is due to such men; men of enterprise, sagacity, sound judgment and rare discrimination, whose methods are practical and whose plans are comprehensive and far-reaching.

Transcribed by Gerald Iaquinta: Source: "A Volume of Memoirs and Genealogy of Representative Citizens of Northern California", Pages 264-266. Chicago Standard Genealogical Publishing Co. 1901.

(CR4.1311) This family lived in the Merland area. Her death certificate shows name as Mary Pelrine, daughter of George Cook/Emmeline Horton, Guysboro. Husband's name - Michael Pelrine, Date of Birth - Feb. 4, 1869
1901 Census gives wife's name as Mary Pelrine (36), Husband Jeremiah (55), children: James P., Margaret S., Mary J.
1911 Census gives wife's name as Catherine Pelrine (48), Husband Jeremiah (67), children: James, Margaret, and Mary Jane.

(CR4.153) **Burke's landed gentry of Great Britain:** By Peter Beauclerk Dewar, Pages 935-936.
They are buried at Grand Island Cemetery, Colusa Co., CA along with their daughter, Frances McLean Davies, who had been in the Senior Class of 1927 at the University of California, Berkeley, and became a teacher.

(CR4.154) Photos and information on the Cook/Hatcher family were generously shared by Nancy McCullough.

Information on the Hatcher family from Census records, headstone inscriptions: Internment.net -
http://www.interment.net/data/us/ca/riverside/rivnat/h/riverside_h09.htm
Earl K. Hatcher, Venus Hatcher, George P. Hatcher, Hattie R. Hatcher are all buried in Mary's Cemetery, Yolo, Yolo County, CA
FindAGrave.com: #50787114
Daryl Clinton Hatcher was a Master Chief, US Navy, as per his obituary.

HISTORY OF Yolo County CALIFORNIA - Biographical Sketches of The Leading Men and Women of the County Who Have Been Identified With Its Growth and Development From the Early Days to the Present:
HISTORY BY TOM GREGORY AND OTHER WELL KNOWN WRITERS ILLUSTRATED COMPLETE IN ONE VOLUME HISTORIC RECORD COMPANY LOS ANGELES, CALIFORNIA [1913] -
Page 714 - HISTORY OF YOLO COUNTY (abridged) On this Yolo county

farm George P. Hatcher was born Feb. 3, 1863. A near-by school afforded him his primary education, which later was supplemented by attendance at a business college. Upon starting out for himself he embarked in the grocery business at Woodland, but at the expiration of two years he retired from that enterprise and removed to Yolo. For about three years he carried on a general mercantile establishment in that place. In 1893 he purchased the thirty acres which he now owns and occupies and on which he has erected a neat house and substantial outbuildings. Since then he has carried on this small tract, besides renting and cultivating other farm lands in the locality. The place is attractive, with its neat buildings, its beautiful trees and its air of thrift and comfort. The marriage of Mr. Hatcher was solemnized at Yolo February 6, 1883, and united him with **Miss Hattie E. Cook, a native of Nova Scotia, but a resident of Yolo county from early girlhood.** They are the parents of two sons and a daughter. The former, Clinton and Earl, are partners in farming operations and own a tract of three hundred and twenty acres near Plainfield, Yolo county. Both are married, the older brother having three children : Roma, Darrell and Pierce, while Earl is the father of one son, Thomas. The youngest member of the parental circle is Miss Lola, a popular young lady in the home neighborhood and an active worker, with her parents, in the Methodist Episcopal Church of Yolo. Ever since he began to devote his attention to agricultural pursuits Mr. Hatcher has made a specialty of the dairy business. Years of efforts and study have enabled him to build up a fine herd of registered Jersey cattle. Some of the pure-bred calves are sold to others and some are retained for the home dairy. Mrs. Hatcher attained an enviable local reputation as a butter-maker and for a long period sold butter to private customers in Woodland, but the work was so arduous and exhausting that a change has been made and the cream is now sold to the Yolo creamery. As a judge of Jersey cattle Mr. Hatcher is regarded as an expert and his opinion concerning this favorite type of dairy stock is regarded with deference by others similarly interested....

(CR4.2W) The Daily Telegraph, January 19, 893, Saint John, New Brunswick: d. Cook's Cove, Guysboro, N.S., Annie COOK relict of Moses COOK, age 95 years. *Note: Discrepancy in newspaper article and headstone inscription.*

(CR4.3) **COOK, WILLIAM FRANCIS**, merchant, shipbuilder, and office-holder; b. 4 Feb. 1796 at or near Guysborough, N.S., third child of Benjamin Cook and Philomela Hull; m. first, on 5 May 1822, Eliza Cunningham (d. 1850), and they had eight children; m. secondly, in the mid 1850s, Caroline Brown, and they had one child; d. 8 April 1862 at Canso, N.S.

Apparently Francis Cook was apprenticed to Thomas Cutler, a Guysborough merchant, in whose service he was brought up and in whose firm he eventually became a partner. In 1816, likely through Cutler's influence, he was made clerk of license by the Court of Sessions; he also served as gauger, as hog reeve, and as an inspector and culler of dry and pickled fish. In 1822 Cook left R. M. Cutler and Company and established his own business in Guysborough. He dealt in general merchandise, and he likely purchased the fish he shipped to Halifax whence it was reshipped by larger firms to the West Indies. He may even have shipped directly to the West Indies himself. He also owned seines and engaged directly in the fishery. Between 1836 and 1849 his shipyards launched a number of brigs, schooners, and barques.

Francis Cook served as a vestryman in Christ Church (Church of England), Guysborough, from April 1822 to March 1823. However in 1823 he was listed as a teacher in the newly formed Methodist Sunday School, and in 1830 he and his wife were among the seven original founding families of the "Society of People called Methodists" in Guysborough. In 1837 Cook was appointed justice of the peace, in 1838 judge of common pleas, and in 1840 assistant judge of the Inferior Court and Sessions of the Peace. He served as a trustee of Guysborough Academy in 1848 and was an officer of the local temperance society, being president in the 1848–49 term.

For many years his business flourished and by 1842 Cook paid the fourth highest assessment in Guysborough County. In the late 1840s, however, Cook had serious financial difficulties, being unable to repay loans chiefly from Halifax merchants. With outstanding mortgages of about £1,000, his business was placed in the hands of assignees early in 1850 and in 1851 his Guysborough operation was sold by the sheriff for debts. In 1850, following his wife's death, Cook moved to Canso where he re-established as a merchant. In May the Court of Sessions appointed him the weigher of flour and meal for Canso and in 1853 he became a commissioner for giving relief to insolvent debtors and for taking affidavits to hold to bail. By the late 1850s he was again in the fishery, maintaining a boat and employing four men. He also had the small subsistence farm that most Nova Scotians, regardless of their station, found convenient, if not necessary.

A relatively minor figure in a community decreasing in importance, Francis Cook is nevertheless interesting as a typical middleman in the Nova Scotia fishery. The business of shipping fish was a risky one, and it made or destroyed the fortunes of hundreds of Nova Scotian entrepreneurs.

Taken from : Dictionary of Canadian Biography Online

History of the County of Guysborough, by Harriet Cunningham Hart, Page 35:

Francis Cook, Esq., died at Canso, April 6, 1862. Any mention of his life properly belongs to Guysboro, where he lived until towards his declining years. There, he was actively engaged in business, employing many men in ship building, and in home and foreign trade. From his shipyard between 1836 and 1849 were launched the brigs *Manchester, Guysborough, Eliza, Francis and Active* - the schooners *Speculator, Harriet, and G.O. Bigelow* - the barque *Medora*, of three hundred and fifty tons, and the barque *Atlantic* of five hundred and twenty tons. He was a magistrate for many years, took a deep interest in the Temperance cause, the Sunday School, indeed in all religious and public affairs. His removal from Guysboro was universally regretted. He married Eliza, eldest daughter of John Cunningham, of Antigonish, who was a member for the County of Sydney in 1808 and 1815. Mr. and Mrs Cook's names were enrolled among the seven members who comprised the Methodist Church at its organization in Guysboro.

(CR4.321) Down Guysborough Way, by John A. Morrison, Dec. 14, 1844.

(CR4.324) **Find A Grave Memorial # 54527971**
Burial: Monticello Cemetery , Spanish Flat (Napa County) CA. An infant Cook baby is buried beside him.

The Oakland Tribune, Friday, May 22, 1925: CAPITALIST OF NAPA IS FOUND SHOT IN HEAD - Napa, May 22 - The body of **William C. Cook**, 55, wealthy resident of Monticello, Napa county, was found in a shed in the rear of his home today with a bullet wound in his head. A revolver was near the body. He had been in ill heath and is survived by a widow, a daughter and a brother, Frank Cook of Oakland.

(CR4.326) Death Register - Barbados, West Indies: Died 21 November 1928
George Cunningham Cook, Male Age 55 years
Occupation: Steamship Superintendant
Cause of Death: Hemorrhage of the lungs
Informant: Dr. F.W. Greaves, M.B., Ch. B.
Registered: 24 November 1928
Abode at death: Long Bay Castle, St. Philip
Monumental Inscription:
St. Philips Parish Churchyard
St. Philips Parish, Barbados, West Indies
plot/lot info - next to Lord family tomb
Comdr. Geo. C. Cook, R.C.N.
Born Canso, N.S. 1871
Died 1928
By Their Deeds Ye Shall Know Them

*Note - Sam Lord's Castle was gutted by fire, Oct., 2010

(CR4.326a) Worn out by wartime service and recommisioned as a depot ship in September 1915, *Niobe* provided accommodation, training, and office space for the Royal Canadian Navy. Following the collision between the SS *Imo* and the SS *Mont Blanc*, *Niobe* sent a boat to offer assistance to the *Mont Blanc*, which had come to rest about a kilometre away. The explosion killed all of the boat's crew, and inflicted considerable damage on *Niobe* as well, killing or seriously injuring a number of people on board.

(CR4.326b) A declaration on a passenger manifest dated 1922, where George Cunningham Cook travelled from Barbados to Canada, gives his former Canadian address as: Kent Park, Princes Lodge, Hfx. Co., N.S. *Today, Kent Park is a residential subdivision on the shore of Bedford Basin.*

(CR4.3261) Will filed 28 Nov 1928 by Cottle Catford & Co., granted 7 December 1928:
George Cunningham Cook of Lord's Castle, St. Philip, Barbados, West Indies
My only son - George Elliot Cook to get my naval sword - my solid gold watch with monogram and my Cook family gold finger ring
$500.00
Wife: Lily Florence Hanson Cook - sole Executrix
Will written: 20 April 1928
Witnesses: E. Maxwell Shilstone, solicitor - E.R.C. Boyce

(CR4.7) The Daily Telegraph, February 14, 1884, Saint John New Brunswick: d. Belle Creek, P.E.I., 22nd ult., James William COOKE, Postmaster, 72nd year, native of Guysboro, N.S.

Other information on the Prince Edward Island Cooks was generously shared by Harvey Bishop.

(CR4.7W) July 30 1887 - Saint John Globe: On 17th inst., one of the most remarkable gatherings occurred at the home of Henry A. BEARS, Murray River, P.E.I. The mother,Mrs. Dorcas BEARS, the eldest d/o late Abraham WHITMAN of Canso, N.S., now aged 87 1/2 years, still enjoying all her faculties, was favored with the gathering of all her family of 13 children, who met for the first time to greet her as an unbroken family, except the father, who died some 14 years ago, aged 77 years. On Monday morn. an artist was secured and a picture of the family group was taken. The names and ages of the family are as follows: The mother, Dorcas BEARS, aged 87 years 6 mos.; James W. BEARS, 67 years 8 mos.; Sarah A. COOK, 66 years 3 mos.; Dorcas L. GRANT, 61 years 9 mos.; Abraham W. BEARS, 63 years; Mercy C. HORTON, 61 years 8 mos.; Isaac A. BEARS, 59 years 9mos.; David A. BEARS, 57 years 3 mos.; Rebecca E. COOK, 55 years 6mos.; Hannah E. CUDDY, 54 years; John F. BEARS, 51years 8 mos.; Henrietta J. BREHANT, 48 years 10 mos.; Henry A. BEARS, 45 years 6mos.; George W. BEARS, 43 years 6 mos. Making a total of 826 years,10 mos. The grandchildren are now 65 living and 28 dead; the great grandchildren are 73 living and 4 dead. There was present at the gathering a brother and sister of the father.

(CR4.78) Thanks to Kami Cook Barrera for this photo.

(CR4.823) **COOK, Rev. Clarence W.** - CANNING, retired Baptist minister, died at his home in Canning on Thursday. He was 73. A native of

Guysborough County, Mr. Cook graduated from Acadia University with the degree of Bachelor of Arts in 1916. He served overseas during World War I, first in the Canadian Army, and later as a lieutenant in the Royal Air Force. Following the was, Mr. Cook served for 3 years as pastor of the United Baptist Church in Parrsboro. He resigned in 1922 to continue his theological studies at Newton Theological Seminary in Mass., from which he received the degree of Bachelor of Divinity in 1924. For the next 36 years he served the Baptist churches at Milton, Canning, Kingston, Berwick, and Chester Basin; Summerside, and Quebec City. He retired in 1960 and purchased a home in Canning. He was a member of the Markland Masonic Lodge, Kingston; a past grand master and past district general Chaplain. A member of the Canadian Legion, he was made chaplain of the Canning branch. He was also honorary pastor of the Canning Baptist Church. Mr. Cook is survived by his widow, the former Gladys Eaton of Granville Centre. His only son, Murray, predeceased him in 1949. Also surviving are a sister Mrs. Parker Sangster, and a half-brother, Albert Cook, both of Guysborough. The funeral was held Sunday afternoon at Canning Baptist Church by Lic. Vincent Rushton, assisted by Padre H. C. Grimmer, Camp Hill Chaplain. Interment was in Willowbank Cemetery, Wolfville. *Halifax Herald published his obit on Saturday, 13 July 1961*

COOK (EATON), Gladys - 80, widow of the late Rev. Clarence Cook, of Canning died Saturday at the Blanchard Fraser Memorial Hospital, Kentville. Born in Granville Centre, she was the daughter of the late Burton and Henrietta (Troop) Eaton. She is survived by four sisters, Estella Eaton, Nan Eaton, and Vera (Mrs.Ronald Longley), all of Canning; Leta (Mrs. Robie McNince), Stoney Creek,Ont.; one grandchild. She was predeceased by one son, Murray, three brothers, Arnold, Judson, and Burton, and one sister Ethel. The body is at the W. C. Hiltz Funeral Home, Kentville. Funeral service will be held Tuesday at 3 p.m. in the Baptist Church, Canning, with Rev. Ronald McCormick officiating. Burial will be in Willowbank cemetery, Wolfville. *Halifax Herald published her obit on Monday, 15 March 1971*

(CR4.8231) Murray Eaton Cook was the only son of C.W. Cook, Baptist minister in Berwick, Nova Scotia. He graduated in Arts from Acadia University in 1943. He served as a pilot in the R.C.A.F. overseas. He returned from duty to Canada in 1946 and enrolled in the forestry course at U.N.B. He graduated in May 1949. In 1947 he married Alice Avery. They were married in Juniper, NB by Rev. William C. Amey, United Church minister. In 1948 they had a daughter named Jayne. Murray took a job as a forestry engineer with Price Brothers of Chicoutimi, Quebec. In November 1949 Murray and a co-worker set out in aluminum boat to check out the amount of pulp in the Shipshaw River. When they didn't return at their scheduled time the company sent out a search party to look for them. On November 12, Murray's body was recovered, it was believed that the men had drowned on Wednesday, November 9.

Murray's funeral service took place in Nova Scotia at Berwick United Baptist Church, the service was conducted by Rev. Austin D. MacPherson.

Jayne Cook married Wayne Silsby; they have three children.

The information on Murray Eaton Cook was taken from the book: "Knowlesville II The Corey Story" by Judson M. Corey. First Edition April 2003, National Library of Canada Cataloguing in Publication. ISBN 0-9692176-1-7. The details were sent to me by Craig Avery.

(CR4.83) www.findagrave.com:
Find A Grave Memorial # 33399722
Birth: 1853, Death: Dec., 1911, USA
58 years old,wife of Herbert William Cook.
Burial: Pine Grove Cemetery, Lynn, Essex County
Massachusetts, USA
Plot: Plot-A,Lot-473,Grave-475

Find A Grave Memorial # 33399742
Birth: 1849, Death: Aug., 1925, USA
76 years old,husband of late Mary Isablle Cook.
Burial: Pine Grove Cemetery, Lynn, Essex County
Massachusetts, USA
Plot: Plot-A,Lot-473,Grave-476

(CR4.8522) *The Lowell Sun, Tuesday, Oct. 17, 1950*: Grid Experience Helps Lynn Cop - His gridiron exploits of other years today paid off for Police Sergeant **Bromley Cook**, who dropped a former convict with a flying tackle near the scene of jewerly store break.

Cook's captive was identified by police as Vaughn Stewart, 30. Officers said he had serviced a five-year term in state prison.

Police alleged that Stewart smashed a side window and entered the store to rifle display cases. Cook and a detail of officers raced to the scene in response to a burglar alarm and arrived as Stewart allegedly leaped out the window.

Cook took up the chase and brought Stewart down with a flying tackle. Stewart was booked on a charge of breaking and entering in the nighttime and larceny.

(CR4.10 5) "Dad" Freeman lived near the highway in a nice cabin facing east. The land was cleared between his cabin and the highway and it had a nice porch where he could sit and watch any passers by. On the porch he had a most interesting chair made out of woven willows and I believe moose horns. It was very comfortable. I used to sit there with him and we had great talks.

The Poetry of Manton E. "Dad" Freeman:

INDEPENDENCE
by M. E. Freeman

My home is near Pouce Coupe,
Not many miles from town;
And I don't care a whoopee
If they call me Jones or Brown.
I have bread & praties plenty,
And a good roof o'er my head.
My age is over twenty
Just how much I've never said.
I can work when I feel like it
There is no boss over me
And if I want to hike it
There are none to care a D.
The rich may have their autos
The devil a bit I care
I have my own two trotters
That can take me anywhere.
Let the roads be dry or muddy
I don't have to put on chains
And I do not have to study
If the sun shines or it rains.
I can just get up and travel
At any time I like
And I only scratch the gravel
As I toddle down the pike.
Tho' some may like the city
The country life for me
Where I do not ask for pity
Or live on charity.
There are some might call me crazy
I do not care a bit
But am I tired or lazy?
Use your own name for it.
They may send me to the 'Sylum
Or put me in the pen
If I should chance to rile 'em
I do not care, by hen.
Should I like a glass of toddy
With nobody there to see,
Well -- I care for nobody,
And nobody cares for me.

On the Banks of Canyon Creek
by Manton Eastbourne Freeman

It is just a log shack on the hillside
But it's mine, and a place to call home
Where I'm not a burden to others
As I linger along all alone.
It is years since my dear one departed
I must finish my life's journey alone
And tho' I may go on broken hearted
No sorrows of mine can atone.
For the hardships that we suffered together
In the years that are long past and gone
Through stormy or sunshiny weather
As we struggled along for a home.
She sleeps on a hill in the sunshine
Resting free from all sorrow and care
Her soul is at home with her Saviour
I am praying that I'll meet her there.
I am lonely tonight for my children
They are scattered afar from my home
They all have their joys and their sorrows
Will they think of me when I am gone?
On this earth I may never more meet them
Their laughter may ne'er cheer me more,
But I pray God someday I may greet them
Safe at home on the Evergreen shore.
And when with this life I have finished
And God calls me home to my rest
May their joys never more be diminished
He knoweth their need and will bless.

History Is Where You Stand. Part 14: Pouce Coupe, Rolla and other South Peace Communities, By Glen Wade, 2001 -
We don't know a lot about "Dad" Freeman or just exactly where his homestead was – somewhere near the old road from Hythe to Pouce Coupe but on the other side of Canyon Creek. According to an early teacher in the area, Charlie Ovans, Mr. Freeman was "a very old man" in 1933 or 1934 when he acted as the janitor in the long-gone High Ridge School.   Mr. Freeman was a bit of a poet and some of the poems he wrote while living near Pouce have been sent home by a great-grandson, Charles Hart.

The photo of Manton Freeman was shared by his granddaughter, Jean (Robertson) Lundy.

(CR4.12 4) Snow Parker Freeman Cook , Gloucester, Mass.; University of Pennsylvania School of Medicine, Philadelphia, 1886; member of the New England Ophthalmological Society; aged 71; on the staff of the Addison Gilbert Hospital, where he died, April 6, 1921, of ulcerative colitis and cerebral hemorrhage.

Membership in the Massachusetts Masonic Lodge gives his death date as Apr. 6/1934, his birthdate as Oct. 12/1861,and also gives us the information that he was an eye specialist.

(CR7.33) – Death record of Benjamin Godfrey Cook, Sailmaker, born Guysborough, NS, d: Oct. 4, 1905:   Written BETHIA Godfrey in Mother's name.

(CR10)   Perhaps this is Daniel Gerry, a child of Thomas and Elizabeth (Greenleaf) Gerry, who were immigrants from Devonshire, England. Thomas Gerry became a prosperous Marblehad merchant. They had many children, including two Daniels who died before this Daniel. **Elbridge Gerry**, one of the signers of the Declaration of Independence, was a brother. There were three Samuels; the first two died young, two Elizabeths; the first died young.
   Although this is not proof that this is, indeed, Daniel, perhaps a more careful look at the original marriage document at Marblehead, Mass. will prove this to be true.   Daniel/Domneck Gerry's son, Daniel, had a son, Benjamin Gerry, who had a son, **Elbridge Gerry**. The Gerry surname has always had variations in spelling, ranging from Gary, Geary, Garry, etc.   In Marblehead during that time frame, there were no other families of Gerrys except for descendants of Thomas and Elizabeth.

(CR10. 111) The following was found in the Tewksbury Almshouse Inmate Case Histories, Vol. 31, 2/1879 to 10/1879, Tewksbury, MA., case 57861, and shared on the NS Roots Listserve by the late Shirley Rathbun:

168

Gerry, Elbridge, 36, came there from Gloucester Sept. 15, 1879. 36, born in Nova Scotia, came to Mass. 9 years ago and sailed out of Gloucester 2 years. In Pictou past 7 years. Left there 3 weeks ago and went to Denver, Col., then to Gloucester Sept. 13. Parents, Benjamin and Bethia, father born in Marblehead about 1800. Don't know when he left there. Paternal grandfather, Daniel Gerry, born Marblehead. Both sailors and man of wars men. Don't know about history. Mother born in New Canada, N. S. Wife, Martha, in Pictou. No settlement. Discharged Sept. 26, 1879.

UNDETERMINED COOK CONNECTIONS

There is record of a William Cook, son of Moses Cook, who migrated to Beverly, Massachusetts and married Mary E. Kilham who was born in New Hampshire. William was a cordwainer, and was born in Manchester, NS. She was a widow in 1904. There were children, including:
1) William H. Cook, born Canso, married Mary A. Peeples in 1885, and they had children.
2) Ella Elizabeth Cook b: 1849 Beverly, Mass.
3) Annie J. Cook b: 1862 Beverly, Mass.
4) Charles Edward b: 1865 Beverly, Mass.
5) Elisha F. Cook who married Hannah Early and had children.
6) Mary Alice Cook b: 1860 Beverly, Mass. - her birth record states her father in William 2nd.
There are several Moses Cooks who this William could be the son of, and without further documentation, I cannot accurately place him within any set family group.

--

A Godfrey Cook died on Feb. 7/1874 of Consumption, age 34 at Gloucester. Single. Born Guysborough, no parents names stated. (Born 1840)

~

(CR-DNA) **From FamilyTreeDNA.com:** One way to think about haplogroups is as major branches on the family tree of Homo Sapiens. These haplogroup branches characterize the early migrations of population groups. As a result, haplogroups are usually associated with a geographic region. If haplogroups are the branches of the tree then the haplotypes represent the leaves of the tree. All of the haplotypes that belong to a particular haplogroup are leaves on the same branch. Both mtDNA and Y-DNA tests provide haplogroup information, but remember that the haplogroups nomenclature are different for each.

A Y-DNA haplogroup is defined as all of the male descendants of the single person who first showed a particular SNP mutation. A SNP mutation identifies a group who share a common ancestor far back in time, since SNPs rarely mutate. Each member of a particular haplogroup has the same SNP mutation.

Each major haplogroups, or clades, can have subgroups, or subclades. Subgroups have a numeric name which follows the haplogroup name. For example, haplogroup E has two subgroups called E1 and E2. There is also a subgroup E* which belongs to haplogroup E but not either of the defined subgroups. Subclades can also have subgroups, which are noted with lower-case characters, such as E1a or E1b.

The Y Chromosome Consortium (YCC) developed a naming system for the Y-DNA haplogroups designed to easily accommodate expansion as new groups are discovered. The YCC has defined 20 major haplogroups, called A through T, which represent the major divisions of human diversity based on SNPs on the Y-chromosome.

ADAM: 'Y-Chromosome Adam' All Y-chromosome lineages lead to a single male, whom researchers named 'Y-Chromosome Adam'. While he was not the only male living at the time, no other lineages remain today.

Haplogroup G: Europe (20,000 years ago) The first branch of F, G traveled from the Middle East into both Europe and South Asia. The European lineages spread along the Mediterranean and eventually inland across Europe.

Haplogroup F: Levant (45,000 years ago) People followed herds through a stretch of savannah in their second migration out of Africa. Haplogroup F was born during or after this migration and is the parent of most non-African branches.

From Wikipedia: Haplogroup G has an overall low frequency in most populations but is widely distributed within many ethnic groups of the Old World in Europe, northern and western Asia, northern Africa, the Middle East, India, Sri Lanka and Malaysia. The oldest skeleton confirmed by ancient DNA testing as carrying haplogroup G was found at the Neolithic cemetery of

Derenburg Meerenstieg II, north central Germany. The only other ancient DNA skeletons with haplogroup G were found in present-day Bavaria, southern Germany, and date to the early Middle Ages.

General Information gleaned from various group discussions on the internet:
The highest frequency of Haplogroup G is among the Ossetians, who are considered the descendants of the Alans and Sarmatians. The Alans accompanied the Visigoths and the Vandals into Iberia and Gaul, settling in Brittany. Centuries later, some of their descendants joined the Normans in the invasion of England. The Sarmatians served in the Roman Army in Lancashire and along Hadrian's Wall.

A recent paper by I. Nasidze et al, entitled "Genetic Evidence Concerning The Origins of North and South Ossetians", has identified of levels of G in Northern Ossetia ranging from 21 to 75 percent, depending on the region. Since the Ossetians are considered to be the descendants of the Alans, the G haplogroup may be construed as a possible marker of Alanic or Sarmatian ancestry when it is found among Border Reiver descendants.

Facebook Discussion on Haplogroup G: The Romans hired the Sarmatians and Ossetians to patrol what is now called the borders, which is along Hadrians Wall, to keep the Picts and others from attacking them from the north. When Rome pulled out of England, the Sarmatians and Ossetians mainly stayed there and surely injected haplotype G into the population, as is now found in the border reiver descendants and ultimately spread around the British Isle's population.

171

Walsh Family Notes:
Descendants of John and Mary Walsh

John Walsh, Sr. was born in Ireland @1797. He was a carpenter. His wife was Mary "Millman", which originated as Mehlman and is called Mailman today. John and Mary Walsh lived in the what was called the "Forks of St. Mary's", which is the Glenelg area today. The Presbyterian Witness newspaper noted the death of Mary Walsh in 1891:

> d. St. Mary's, Guysboro Co., N.S., 13th ult., Mary WALSH widow of John WALSH and second d/o late John MILLMAN, left five daughters and four sons, 40 grandchildren and 20 great-grandchildren.

Children:
1) Margaret Walsh   b: 1832
2) James Walsh   b: 1838
3) John Walsh   b: 1840
4) Catharine Walsh   b: 1846
5) Caron/Keyson Walsh   b: 1848
6) William Walsh   b: 1855
7) Sarah Walsh   b: 1859
8) Mary Walsh   b: 1863
9) Daughter   b: ?

1) Margaret Walsh married Johan Levy (John Levi) Hain (Hayne), a Ship Carpenter who was born in Upper LaHave, NS. His father was born in Germany. They had children: William Hayne, Levi Hayne (m: Emma Fenton), Fred Hayne, James Hayne (m: Eva McDonald {see #1.4721 and #1.4841}, Mary Hayne, Aubrey Louis Hayne, Robert Hayne, Josephine H. Hayne, John (m: Elizabeth Cameron), Mary Eleanor Hayne, Sarah Hayne (d: age 3 from an accidental fall). *Johan Levy Hain was born to **Johan George** and Louisa (Sartie) Haines in Lunenburg County in 1828. **His** parents were George Frederick (b: Berschweiler, Germany) and Anna Maria (Hebb) Haines. Elizabeth Haine (who m: Samuel Cook, Fisherman's Harbour), was a sister to John Levi Hain. The Haines of Whitehead River and Little Dover probably also stem from the same family from Lunenburg County.*

2) James Walsh married Catharine McDonald in 1871, at St. Joseph's. They had children: Mary Walsh, Catharine A. Walsh, Margaret Walsh, Eleanor Walsh, Collin F. Walsh.

3) John Walsh married Desire Cook and had children: Henry Walsh, Margaret Walsh, Rosannah Walsh, David T. Walsh, John S. Walsh, Melissa J. Walsh.

4) Catharine Walsh married Donald/Daniel Mason, a farmer, son of John and

Lydia Mason of Country Harbour, at St. Joseph's Church in 1873. Catharine was a widow by 1891. They had children: Ellen/Ella May Mason, Mary Emily Mason, Lydia Jane Mason (b: 1879), John Nelson Mason, Daniel Lawlor Mason, James Charles Mason (b: 1884).

Ella M. Mason married Horace W. Stevens at Wakefield, Mass.

Mary Mason married Edward Rudolph, a fisherman of Liscomb. They had at least two sons: Donald E. Rudolph and William Eben Rudolph.

Lydia J. married John Grace. She died in Cleveland, Ohio, on Dec. 23/1943.

John Nelson Mason was a miner in Stellarton. He married and had at least one son, Bernard Mason.

Daniel Lawlor Mason was a miner, a grocer, a piano merchant at various times in his life. He married twice; first to Sophia McAllister, daughter of John and Jane McAllister of Ogden. She died in 1918. They had children: Lois Pearl Walsh, MIldred Walsh, Leonard Walsh (d: age 16 of TB), Stanley Walsh. He married secondly Josephine Long, daughter of Patrick and Minnie (Burns) Long of New Glasgow.

James Charles Mason was a lumberman. He married Sadie Belle McDonald of Marydale (*Their son, Lenny Mason, is a well-known NS folk singer*).

5) Caron/Kayson Walsh - He is called Caron on census records. He is called Kayson on his marriage record - he married Elizabeth Dryden of Halifax in 1872.

6) William Walsh married Esther Hallet, daughter of Guy and Eliza Jane (Hodgson) Hallet, at Melrose in 1877. William was a Ship Carpenter, then a miner. They had children: John Allan Walsh, Bessie May Walsh, Leonard Walsh, George Johnston Walsh, Frank Keith Walsh, a son born 1901.

Mason Family Notes

Of the fifteen children of William Mason and Mary Ann (Rogers) Mason, three of them married Cooks:

1) John Mason, born 1790, married Lydia Cook, daughter of John and Elizabeth (Callahan) Cook of Bantry/Salmon River area.
See 1. 10 2) for more information.

2) George Mason, born 1799, married Lydia Cook, daughter of Wintrop and Lydia (Collier) Cook of Stormont/Country Harbour.
See 1.45) for more information.

3) Joseph Morris Mason, born 1805, married Mary Ann Cook (parents not known at this time. They had **children**: William Mason (who married Lavinia Sponagle), Susan Mason (m: **1st**: David Clinch, **2nd**: John Hines), Mary Ann Mason, Elizabeth Mason; perhaps more. (*According to Lillian V. Salsman in her book Homeland Country Harbour, she mentions a shoe connection between Country Harbour and Lynn, Mass., USA:* **Elizabeth Mason** *of Cross Roads, Country Hrb, daughter of* **Joseph Mason and Mary Ann Cook**, *married John Creighton. They lived in Lynn, where he had the Creighton shoe business. These shoes were popular in NS. Merchant vessels brought the Creighton and Grover shoes right into Country Harbour where ships were met by the dories of local merchants.*)

INDEX OF NAMES

	107,134,137,139,140,142,146,147,150,158
Elisha	16,21,22,68,73,96,143,152,157,169
Eliza	66,74,97,112,114,115
Elizabeth	14,15,24,27,35,46,54,78,94,96,110,150,151,174
Ella	16,65,75,78,169
Ellen	96,157
Emery	17
Emily	68,71,72
Emma	25,26,28,57,116,117,125,128
Emmeline	24,28,143
Emmit	49,50
Erma	104,105
Ernest	24,66,67,107,152
Errington	50,51,150
Estelle	118
Esther	30,106125,126,127,128
Ethel	106,125,126
Eunice	54,56
Eva	69,70,71
Eve	72,152
Everett	147,148
Ewart	25
Flora	103
Florence	42,49,86,164
Florida	29
Forrest	30
Foster	38,41,147
Frances	124
Francis	14,25,27,34,35,74,85,94,96,99,108,110,115,118,121, 124,139,140,153,157,161,162
Frank	47,48,69,74,78,85,100,108,116,117,118,124,163
Fraser	75
Fred	28,29,79
Frederick	17
Freeman	94,95,96
Garfield	100
Genevieve	118
George	17,18,66,67,71,78,79,85,94,96,98,101,102,116,117, 143,163,164
Georgina	102
Gertrude	41,102,103
Gideon	15,16,18,21,68,70,77,79
Gladys	41,57,124,147,165

Godfrey	15,16,21,94,95,97,143,157,169
Gordon	69,70,152
Grace	69,85,110
Greta	70
Guyon	68,69
Hannah	132,133
Hans	95,96
Harold	30,44,45,67,103,149
Harriet	24,77,105,106,108,109,115
Harry	30,66,69
Hartley	118
Hattie	28,106,110,127,161
Hazel	103
Helen	103
Henrietta	25,26
Henry	21,22,66,94,95,97
Herbert	125,126,166
Hilda	56
Horace	85
Howard	31,74,76,153,154
Hugh	42,43,45,46,57,147,149,150
Ida	69
Ina	41
Irene	47,48
Irving	48
Isaac	121
Isabella	98,121,124
Jack	100,110
James	15,24,27,34,35,42,43,48,57,65,66,69,96,99,104,105, 115,118,121,122,123,124,132,157,164
Jayne	165,166
Jennie	18,25,26,133
Jeremiah	101
Jessie	25,26
Joan	32
Joanna	14,
John	14,15,21,33,34,35,41,49,56,64,65,66,68,73,77,85,86, 92,94,96,97,98,99,100,107,108,115,121,122,124,125, 126,143,148,153,157,174
Joseph	24,31,32,35,77,79,99,119,121,124,125,127,131
Josiah	94,142

Josie	31
Joyce	50,51
Julia	78
Kenneth	48
Laura	126,127
Laurella	49,50,54,
Laurilla	42
Lavinia	116,
Lawrence	46,47,95,
Leander	43,46,49,148
Leila	118
Lelia	24,25
Lemuel	78
Lena	30
Leo	46,47,148
Leon	111
Leonard	25
Letitia	121,124
Levi	96,157
Lida	75
Lillian	25,26,30,57,103,108,118,119
Linden	127
Lindsay	65
Lloyd	127
Lois	56
Lola	103
Lora	21
Loring	85
Lorne	57,86
Lottie	85,103
Louisa	35,36,38,39,40,62,64,68,73,97,144,151
Louise	41
Lucia	142
Lucinda	54,56,148,152
Lucretia	64,65
Lucy	68,72,78,85,99,128,158
Lydia	15,23,33,35,38,53,64,66,85,86,87,132,133,150,151, 174
Mabel	125,126
Mable	106
Mae	100,124
Maggie	69,

Mahala	102,103
Marcus	38,43,44,147,149,151
Mardon	69,70
Margaret	41,65,66,67,122,123,147
Maria	22,35,38,100,112,116,125
Maria	49,85,86,114,117
Marion	29,103
Martha	35,36,49,79,96,124,146,151
Mary	15,16,17,18,19,21,23,27,28,35,41,56,67,77,78,79,92, 94,99,104,104,110,112,115,118,119,122,123,124,166, 169,174
Mason	85
Matilda	102
Maud	116,117
May	78
Mildred	39
Mina	133
Minnie	30,69,96,128,131,133
Miriam	14
Moses	83,85,99,100,110,112,156,161,169
Murray	126,165,166
Nathaniel	94,95,96
Nora Bell	148
Odessa	75,108
Olive	41,67,147
Olivia	49,74,76,122
Orris	42,50,147
Paul	67
Pearl	29
Philomela	99,101,112,158
Phyllis	70
Price	75
Priscilla	41,54,62,147
Ralph	124
Rebecca	25,33,35,52,54,150
Rhoda	78
Rita	50
Robert	21,77,78,85,104,105,110,124,127
Roland	42,71
Russell	39,41,42,50
Ruth	85,88,115

Samuel	14,15,16,17,33,35,49,53,54,77,78,79,150,151,155, 172
Sarah	14,17,18,19,21,24,26,35,64,66,68,71,77,85,86,92, 94,95,99,100,101,102,105,111,116,120,123,125,128, 139,140,142,143,150,164
Sarah McGuckin	15
Seelye	29
Shadrack	68
Shirley	124,131
Snow	131,168
Sophia	54,56,58,104,115,116,118
Stephen	15,16,24,28,64,65,67,142
Susan	16, 21, 24,28,29,107
Susanna(h)	85,91,101,132
Thomas	16,17,24,25,29,30,74,75,79,115,116,128
Tremaine	43,47,62,148
Truman	75
Tyrus	38,39,41
Victoria	86
Vincent	70
Viola	17
Violet	76,105
Wallace	71
Walter	75,110,111
Warren	21,39
Wellington	121
Wentworth	99
Wilbur	31
William	14,16,18,21,22,23,24,27,28,30,39,56,57,66,68,69,71, 74,75,77,78,85,91,94,97,99,100,102,103,112,116,117, 123,124,125,127,132,134,142,161,163,169
Wilson	66,70,71,153
Winfield	79
Winnie	48
Winnifred	43,46
Wintrop	15,33,34,35,66,135,150,153,174
Zelma	41,48
Zipporah	100,111
Zuleika	43,45,147,148

INDEX OF NAMES (OTHER THAN COOK)

Blair	37
Blaisdell	79,155,156
Blakeley	38
Blanch	14
Blatchford	78
Bogart	136
Boon	27
Booth	138
Bortnick	146
Bourne	30
Brackett	28,91
Braden	154
Bradley	102
Bray	61
Brehant	164
Brennan	43
Brodie	107
Brown	138,161
Brownell	81
Bryant	81
Brydle	52,53
Buck	42,113
Buckley	92
Buffum	135
Bullivant	110
Burke	58,65,130
Burnham	143
Burns	23,103,173
Burton	69,126
Burtt	154
Butt	86
Callahan	85,127,174
Cameron	94,97,99,149,151,157,158,172
Campbell	79,123
Cann	71
Canning	63,64
Card	79
Carder	130
Carey	105
Carleton	27,30
Carpenter	18,142
Carr	126
Carroll	51
Carson	126

Cummings	68,82,83
Cunningham	114,115,119,136,161,162
Currie	158
Curtis	134
Cutler	109,157,161
Darsney	128
Darrach	36
Darree	145
Davidson	35,36,37,41,42,44,49,53,74
Davies	109,160
Davis	48,82,116
Day	78,131
Deal	44
Decatur	17
Deere	18
Delaney	102
Demas	24
DesBarres	114
Dewar	160
DeWolfe	48
Diggedon	101
Dimon	145
Dixon	93
Dod	14
Dolliver	35
Donohue	122
Donovan	46,48
Dort	102,106
Douthwright	63
Dow	128
Dowley	16
Downing	127
Doyle	88,156
Druce	95
Dryden	152,173
Dugay	36
Dukeshire	105
Dunbar	111
Dunn	105
Dunphy	89
Durkee	89
Durling	44,129
Duroche	134
Dutton	155

Gillie	103
Gillis	124
Glanville	92,93
Glencross	87
Godfrey	15,94,99,132,134,142,168
Goodwin	114
Gorman	89,90,91,128,156
Gosbee	97,106
Gottchall	103
Gould	102,103
Grace	51,154,173
Grader	128
Graham	114,159
Grant	26,27,43,80,81,86,87,90,101,104,138,164
Gratto	77
Green	101
Greencorn	96,106,157
Greenleaf	168
Gregory	160
Grieve	130
Grimstone	27
Grose	138
Grover	153
Hadley	37,79,94,101,110,113,135
Haine(s)	54,139
Hale	30,83
Hall	78,111
Hallett	33,34,53,55,64,69,74,151,152,173
Hamilton	129
Hancock	124
Hanley	136
Hann	73
Hanson	117,164
Harding	154
Hardy	20
Harford	155
Harnish	56
Harpell	57,59,60,61
Harper	117
Harrigan	59
Harrington	117,155
Harris	57,91,95,134
Hart	16,57,81,111,115,118,119,141,142,146,157,162,168
Hartley	120

Harty	80,84,86
Harvey	47,86
Haskins	133
Haskoll	15
Hastings	22
Hatcher	109,110,160,161
Hattie	58,63
Hawley	103
Hayden	105
Hayes	33,35,36,37,38,44,49,52,53,145,150,151,153
Hayne	33,67,68,71,172
Haynes	14,137,138,139
Hearn	95
Hebb	172
Helin	61
Henderson	83
Hendsbee	58,107
Hennessey	41,146
Henry	84
Herrick	17,78,91
Hills	29
Hines	49,69,145,174
Hingley	41
Hirtle	103
Hoblit	130
Hodgkins	128,135
Hodgson	70,72,74,89,152,153,173
Hoeg	57
Hogan	63,92
Holland	65
Holley	62,70
Hooper	14,137,138
Hooten	77,155
Hopkins	15,94,142
Horley	68
Horton	23,54,59,77,85,88,99,101,102,104,124,128,129,
	158,164
Howard	78
Hudson	62,70,145
Hughes	83
Hull	55,99,161
Humphrey	113
Hurd	137
Hurley	61
Huskins	65

Husted	21
Hutcheson	80,81,82,83,84
Hutchings	29
Hyde	99,128
Hynds/Hynes	61,146
Iaquinta	160
Ibey	156
Ingalls	140
Ingraham	115
Innocent	26
Jacobs	111
Jack	70
Jackman	155
Jackson	55,70
Jadis	35
Jamieson	134
Jarvis	54,57
Jenkins	107,113,114
Johns	20
Johns(t)on(e)	56,57,58,60,61,62,69,127,130,135,145,152,153
Jollimore	47
Jones	20,27,65,91,103,106,108,134,156
Jordan	36,37,39,63,146
Jost	120,121
Joy	37
Kaiser/Keizer	56,58,59,60,61,62,152
Kearsley	142
Keeler	76
Kelly	27
Kenaston	22
Kendall	78
Kennedy	49,88,89,106
Kenn(e)y	55,88,89,155,156
Kennie	83
Kilham/Killam	65,169
Kimball	140
Kinsman	126
Kirby	45,67
Kirk	120
Kittrell	128
Knowles	131
Kozel	103

MacMillan	75
MacPherson	57,61
Mailman	70,172
Major	16
Malloy	38,126
Manthorne	106
Martell	95,96
Mars	35
Marshall	106
Martin	46,48,70,147,152
Mason	33,37,39,40,48,54,55,56,57,58,61,62,63,64,77,87,88,147,149,151,172,173,174
Matthews	48,114
McAllister	89,91,92,125,173
McAndrew	145
McBain	70
McCarthy	126
McConnell	38,145,147
McCormick	147,165
McCoy	69
McCullough	160
McDonald	24,37,53,58,60,63,67,69,89,125,172,173
McDonnell	130
McDougall	57,84
McEachern	146
McGibbon	30
McGillivary	41
McGinnis	76
McGukin	140
McInnes	57
McIntosh	41
McIntyre	85
McIsaac	91,153
McKay	90,143
McKenna	37
McKenny	28
McKenzie	27,78,79,101,117,129,135
McLean	67,92,109,146,152
McLeod	122
McMillan	37,70,146
McNaughton	147
McNayr	129
McNeil	68,90
McNince	165
McPherson	88,92,107

McQuarrie	122
Melanson	103
Merchant	91
Middleton	78
Miller	76,150
Mitchell	31
Montminy	31
Moore	72
Morash	103
Morgan	127
Morris	82
Morrison	81,157,163
Morrow	20
Morse	17
Mosby	149
Mosher	61
Motz	145
Muldoon	156
Mullins	109
Munn	25
Murphy	64,92
Musgrave	68
Myers	37,39,49,53,54,62,107,126,133,144,145
Neal	116
Needs	114
Newhall	127
Nichols	19,90,118,142,143
Nickleson	138
Nickerson	68,71
Nieforth	84
Nixon	84
Nolan	107
Norrish	20
Norwood	155
Noyes	28
Oates	79
O'Connor	88,89,106
O'Bryan	81
Ogden	109
O'Gorman	89,90
O'Grady	64
O'Hara	61,81
Oliver	156

O'Neil(l)	88,89
Orcutt	128
Osier	133
Owen	132
Pace	39
Paine	19,20,21,22,127,142,143
Panton	98
Parker	132
Parks	103
Parris/Peris	149
Pashby	18
Peart	24,84,101,103,104,105,134,158
Peddie	105
Pederick/Pedrick	137,138
Peebles	80
Peitzsche	50
Pelerine/Pelrine	102,160
Pender	36
Penny	101
Pense	22
Pentz	82
Perkins	49
Perkons	150,153
Perley	30,139
Perry	68
Persjy	62
Peterson	126
Pettibone	130
Pettingill	29
Pickett	39
Pierce	29,81,152,155
Pitman	71,92
Pockman	110
Poor	28,143
Porter	102,133
Pousland	16
Pressey	30
Pride	36,69
Pringle	62,152
Procter	156
Purcell	90
Pyne	136

Quinlan	72
Racey	113
Ralph	36
Ramey	129
Randall	84,119
Rankin	63
Rathbun	168
Rawlings	72
Redden	95
Reed	128
Rhodes	127
Rhude	76,153
Rhynold	105,106
Richardson	75
Ricker	102
Ridman	145
Riley	39
Rishworth	63
Robar	35,36,38,51,52,145,148,150
Roberts	74,113,156
Robertson	42,63,106,107,168
Robinson	155
Robison	28
Rogers	26,61,87,88,89,91,174
Rose	28
Ross	68,75,124
Roundy	127
Rowe	47,79
Rowell	16
Rudolph	60,173
Rule	21
Russel	23
Russell	24
Rust	154
Ryder	23
Saddler	79
Safford	29
Salsman	174
Sands	16
Sangster	81,103,106,126
Sarty	54,172
Saunders	51,52

Sayles	19
Sayward	79
Scantlebury	26
Schultz	119
Scott	21,57,80,107,112,113,114
Scudder	94
Seaboyer	72
Sealey	116
Searle	14,137
Seddon	47
Seelye	29
Sharam	26
Shaw	129,157
Shea	92
Sheehan	98
Shelton	156
Sherman	20
Sherwood	136
Shiers	37,53,149
Shorten	106
Shupe	73
Sigston	105
Silsby	166
Silver	41,60,62,70,75
Sinclair	75,147
Sinnamon	113
Siteman	56
Skinner	149
Slate	103
Smith	19,26,37,38,67,68,70,104,113,136
Snow	96,157
Snowman	79
Snyder	20
Spanks	24,28,77,102,103,156
Spencer	146
Spinney	127
Sponagle	174
Stacey	138
Stanton	159
Stearns	27,29,126
Steele	101,111,155,158
Stephens	84
Stevens	41,51,119,135,173
Stewart	49,66,82,123,149
Stickney	31

Stillman	17,106
Stimpson	156
Stone	140
Sullivan	89,95
Sully	142
Sutherland	56,62,130,151
Suttis	62
Swain	68
Sylvester	128
Taker	71
Tambeau	147
Tart	20
Taylor	15,54,59,61,87,88,90,93,95,126,136,151,155
Taynour	14
Teed	126
Thomas	68,116
Thompson	26
Thorburn	130
Thurston	142
Tobey	15,94,108,142
Tompkins	22
Totten	79
Townsend	65
Tracy	113
Troop	17,165
Tucker	14,137
Tuttle	119
Uloth	104
Uniacke	35,116
Urquhart	95,96
Venedam	103
Vespia	37
Vinnard	22
Vogt	96
Waite	136
Waitt	16
Walker	136
Wallace	156
Walls	65
Walsh/Welsh	54,55,63,64,88,89,103,106,136,151,152,172,173
Wamboldt	53

Ward	50
Washburn	28,129
Watt	154
Weeks	46
Weir	126
Wells	154
Wheaton	132
Wheeler	21
White	88,89,90
Whitford	108
Whitman	23,24,46,55,81,103,113,121,132,142,164
Whooten	77,132,155
Wieneau	129
Wilden	109
Wilkinson	134
Willett	100
Williams	59,79,105,116,118
Wilson	60
Witham	78,86
Wood	23,37,68,130
Woodworth	116
Woolley	143
Worth	88
Wright	69
Wylde	118
Young	65,103
Yvon	95
Zwicker	48